Soci:
and Li
in the Victorian Novel

Social Identity and Literary Form in the Victorian Novel

Race, Class, Gender and the Uses of Genre

JILL FRANKS

McFarland & Company, Inc., Publishers

Jefferson, North Carolina

All illustrations in this book are in the public domain, retrieved from Wikimedia.

ISBN (print) 978-1-4766-8726-1
ISBN (ebook) 978-1-4766-4686-2

LIBRARY OF CONGRESS AND BRITISH LIBRARY
CATALOGUING DATA ARE AVAILABLE

Library of Congress Control Number 2022030600

On the cover: Queen Victoria, circa 1880 (Library of Congress)

Printed in the United States of America

McFarland & Company, Inc., Publishers
Box 611, Jefferson, North Carolina 28640
www.mcfarlandpub.com

To Susie L. Steinbach
for understanding the Victorians

Table of Contents

XI. *The Odd Women* (1893)

Preface

During the Covid-19 pandemic, university courses moved out of the classroom and onto the Internet. Adapting my pedagogy to the new milieu, I began writing lectures in a formal style and posting them as written essays to the online learning platform. For my pedagogy, the public health crisis had a silver lining: instead of teaching from notes and heavily marked-up novels, I began presenting carefully crafted lectures on Zoom, which—I readily admit—required far more preparation than the outlines from which I had previously taught. Writing lectures increased my level of engagement with the books, making me a better teacher and scholar.

The test of all pedagogical innovations is their effect on student performance. The outcomes after three semesters were positive. Students referred to my lectures in their discussions and essays in ways that indicated they had absorbed the material. They were thankful for having the two modes of delivery, written and oral; students could read the published lecture-essays before and after the presentation of them in class and also be present while I delivered the material orally in a synchronous learning format that gave the opportunity for questions and discussion immediately afterwards. In the Zoom classroom meetings, I lectured in real time (as opposed to pre-recorded lectures). This method was helpful because I could see students' reactions as I spoke—I did require students to attend class with their cameras turned on. Instead of reading my written lectures aloud, as one reads papers at a conference, I used them as guidelines for speaking. The lectures provided more in-depth analyses than my previous use of outlines had done, and students responded well to the formal, organized presentation of concepts. As a result of these outcomes, I decided to continue writing and posting lectures upon our return to on-ground teaching. A practice that requires more time and effort also

1

produces more pleasing results, and I am happy to deepen my engagement with the material, giving students my best effort.

After three semesters, I had compiled a substantial set of lectures, which a friend suggested I share with other scholars of Victorian literature as an aid to their own teaching and learning. I decided to produce a textbook. To prepare the lectures for publication, I needed a unifying title. The course is called *Victorian Imagination,* which is too broad for a book title. So I looked for terms that would apply to most of the lectures. For at least the past four decades, university literature classes have emphasized issues of race, class, and gender—paradigms explained further in the Introduction. To my subtitle, I added a fourth term, *genre,* which is an important aspect of literary study. *Genre* is a category of literature characterized by similarities in form, style, and subject matter. Genre criticism is the oldest form of literary analysis; Aristotle's *Poetics* laid out conventions of the genres in 335 BC. As a popular approach to literary criticism, it continued strong through the New Criticism and structuralist movements of the early and mid-twentieth century but faded with the theoretical turn to poststructuralism. In the 1980s, the combination of feminist, Marxist, psychoanalytical, New Historicist, deconstructionist, and cultural studies criticism edged out genre studies as popular ways to consider the meanings of texts.

Nonetheless, genre criticism remains a fruitful way to deepen one's understanding of a literary text. Especially in Victorian literature, so rich in genre variety, attention to genre conventions can cast our interpretation of texts in a new light. Genre selection has political dimensions, one of which is that writers of nondominant groups, such as women and people of color, may choose a genre for its ability to provide a space for advocacy or protection. Women often chose romance or realism, especially in the Victorian era, to comply with societal expectations for women's intellectual work. Alternatively, women may choose fantasy, as in the case of Mary Shelley's *Frankenstein* (1818) and Virginia Woolf's *Orlando* (1928), in order to interrogate patriarchal assumptions under cover of the nonrealist genre. Genre criticism helps place a text within the culture and history of its time, and it reduces the risk of presentism that poststructuralist approaches sometimes incur. (I address this problem at some length in Chapter VI, in a lecture called "Anti-Semitism, Casual Racism, and Pedagogy.")

Satire, social realism, and the Bildungsroman are genres favored by Victorian writers. Allegory, metafiction, and the novel of ideas also raise interesting questions, both political and aesthetic, in the selected novels. In *Vanity Fair,* I explore the metafictional aspects of the narrative style that hide the fundamental *aporia* around the narrator's moral code. In *A Tale of Two Cities,* Dickens's frequent use of allegorical names for characters and places replicates the practice of French revolutionaries and facilitates his own tendency to sentimentalize about moral properties. In a lecture on *The Odd Women*, I argue that Gissing's novel of ideas suffers from the weight of ideological representation. In this genre, the challenge for the author is to balance realism with ideology in order to create relatable characters who present the ideas sympathetically.

Besides the addition of *genre* to the familiar race/class/gender studies grouping, I need to explain the omission of the word *empire* in my title. Certainly, empire is a tremendously important subject in Victorian literary studies, and one that I address in the lectures. References to empire expand the geographical range of a Victorian novel; empire intersects with race/class/gender discrimination as a structure of oppression; and imperialist ideology illustrates the Victorian belief in what Kipling called the "white man's burden" or "bringing light to the heathens." But including the term *empire* in the title itself would create problems of economy and style. I didn't want to extend my title so much that it resembled a table of contents. I hope that professors searching for a Victorian literature textbook will read on past the title to discover my chapters on empire and imperialism, specifically those about the novels *Jane Eyre, Wide Sargasso Sea, Vanity Fair, Great Expectations,* and *Jack Maggs.*

The Victorian era was characterized by rapid economic growth, and Britain held the status of being the richest country in the world until the Long Depression of 1873–79. The British Empire was the largest in history. It expanded during Queen Victoria's reign to cover roughly a quarter of the world's land area and a quarter of its population, inspiring the colorful saying that "the sun never sets on the British empire." Race, class, and gender give rise to intersecting systems of social inequality, and imperialism intersects with them to oppress colonized peoples and deny their reality. With colonies and territories on every continent, British administrators interacted with a range of different populations, including black-, brown-, red-, yellow-, and white-skinned peoples, whom Victorians believed were "racially" distinct.* Fundamental to Victorians' justification for the British Empire was their belief in white Britons' racial superiority to all other peoples.

The nineteenth century saw progressive reform in many areas—

---

* In this book, I use the word "race" advisedly, since the concept of race as a scientifically identifiable entity has been rejected by academicians, though it is still widely used in non-academic discourse. I use the word "race" when denoting what Victorians were saying and thinking, but I try to use other descriptors, such as "populations" or "peoples" when referring to the social construct of race as we understand it today. Two texts that analyze the history of race and consider alternative ways in which to fruitfully conceptualize identities are *Race in the Making*, by Lawrence Hirschfeld (MIT Press, 1998) and *Racism, Not Race: Answers to Frequently Asked Questions*, by Joseph Graves and Alan Goodman (Columbia UP, 2021).

abolishing slavery, extending the franchise, improving public health, growing the middle class—but racial equality was not one of them. Belief in
white peoples' superiority to other peoples (especially Black) dominated
British thinking, despite the abolitionist victories of the early century—the
Slave Trade Act of 1807 and the Slavery Abolition Act of 1833. If anything,
the Victorians' enthusiasm for extending scientific inquiry into all fields of
knowledge only increased their attachment to the ideology of racial superiority. Scientific racism—the belief that racial differences are biologically
determined—thrived in Victoria's time and incorporated such notions as
racial degeneration (the idea that whites improved by working hard to adapt
to cold, northern climates, while Blacks degenerated due to the ease of living in the warm south), *polygenism* (the belief that the "races" derive from
different species), *racial prognathism* (the belief that Blacks are more closely
related to apes—as "proven" by similar skull shapes), and *social evolution* (a
misapplication to humans of Darwinian evolutionary theory).

Scientific racism culminates at the end of the nineteenth century
in *eugenics*—the belief that humans should practice controlled breeding
to ensure the dominance of the "optimal human race" in the interest of
improving civilization. In the twentieth century, the Nazis used eugenics
to justify the extermination or sterilization of Jews, Romani people, homo-
sexuals, and the mentally ill, as well as epileptic, alcoholic, and depressive
persons, to further the goal of the Third Reich—which was to dominate
world population with members of the "superior Aryan race." Not until
the world learned of the Holocaust did the tide begin to turn, albeit slowly,
against biological theories of racial difference.

Today, scientists reject biological race theory and argue that race is
a social construct. Racial categories lack a scientific basis. In fact, genetic
variations are greater within the groups formerly conceptualized as races
than they are across racial boundaries (Hirschfeld 3–4). Instead, race is
both a psychological and a sociological concept, reflecting ways in which
humans perceive and evaluate difference on an individual and collective
basis. Humans create races because of their need to conceptualize the
world as composed of distinct types, what Hirschfeld calls "human kinds."
These classifications are not merely descriptive; they also interpret and
evaluate differences (13). When we say that race is a social construct, we
mean that racialized terms and concepts are used to categorize and evaluate the social worth of various groups of people. In 1899, Joseph Conrad
deftly described the combined racist and imperialist views of most Europeans when he wrote, "The conquest of the earth, which mostly means the
taking it away from those who have a different complexion or slightly flat-
ter noses than ourselves, is not a pretty thing when you look into it too
much" (3). This book will look into the Victorians' conquest of the earth,

the patriarchy's conquest of women and the poor, and the many ways in which Victorian writers (and their neo–Victorian descendants) accepted, satirized, or exposed the social prejudices of their day.

In addition to issues of empire, race, class, gender, and genre, I also apply psychoanalytic concepts in my interpretations of literature. Victorian novels provide a mine of material for psychoanalytic reading, especially given the sexual repressions associated with the era. For example, *Dr. Jekyll and Mr. Hyde* is a classic example of unhealthy repression of the instincts which has the catastrophic effect of splitting the psyche. I am interested in ways in which novels' narrators both reveal and repress their own psychic drives. The chatty narrator of *Vanity Fair*, for instance, pretends that Becky Sharp is a kind of Everywoman whom we condemn at our peril, but his aporetic impasses regarding essential events of the novel tell a different story. In *Great Expectations*, the question of Pip's guilt arises when he describes a childhood of abuse and privation that infect him with a guilt complex long *before* his guilt-worthy actions of snubbing Joe and Biddy.

Finally, I am interested in the relatively recent phenomenon of neo–Victorian novels. The term *neo–Victorianism* describes a trend in contemporary fiction of turning to classic Victorian novels for inspiration and critique. Neo–Victorianists may be motivated by nostalgia, by the wish to parody the classics, or by the desire to explore Victorian social structures through a race/class/gender-studies critical lens. Often, the writer retells the original story from the point of view of a character who, for reasons of their class, race, or gender, was peripheral to the main action, and almost certainly was stereotyped in the original version. I've selected *Wide Sargasso Sea, Jack Maggs*, and *Mary Reilly* as neo–Victorian novels that revise and comment on *Jane Eyre, Great Expectations*, and *Dr. Jekyll and Mr. Hyde*, respectively. In each case, the neo–Victorian version provides psychoanalytical and cultural insights suggested by, but largely ignored in, the original novel. As such, the subgenre of neo–Victorian is a helpful tool for teaching the Victorian novel in our time. The "updated" characters may be more relatable to students, but this is not the main asset. The principal benefit has to do with opening up the novel to its inherent polyvocality. The discourses of subalterns, women, and minorities of every description are interesting to today's students, who are regularly exposed to debates about social justice. These other discourses respond ("talk back") to the middle-class, racist consciousness of most Victorian writers, producing new ways to appreciate the original novel and the social structures of the Victorian period.

The book chapters are arranged in the chronological order of the novels' publication dates. This arrangement assists the reader to see shifts in the Zeitgeist over the course of the Victorian era and highlights the ways in which the popularity of genres changes with time. The book thus moves from the gothic extravagances of *Wuthering Heights* to the strong social realism that marks the middle Victorian era, as, for instance, in Dickens's historical novel *A Tale of Two Cities*, Eliot's psychological-realist *Middlemarch*, and Thackeray's satirical-realist *Vanity Fair*. The Bildungsroman is solidly represented by Dickens's *Great Expectations*, the pastoral by Hardy's *Far from the Madding Crowd*, and the industrial novel by Gaskell's *North and South*. In the 1890s, we find the late Victorian cosmic irony of Hardy's *Tess of the D'Urbervilles*, the *fin-de-siècle* decadence of the Stevenson novella *Dr. Jekyll and Mr. Hyde*, and the New Woman question in *The Odd Women*. In two cases, I've chosen two texts by the same author instead of one. I double up on Charles Dickens because he is the most popular of Victorian novelists and also because the novels represent different genres. I've chosen two Hardy novels because of their different genres and also because, being seventeen years apart, *Far from the Madding Crowd* and *Tess of the D'Urbervilles* illustrate the phenomenon of the shifting Zeitgeist in the *fin de siècle*.

Other than the three neo–Victorian works, the texts are classic literary novels. What this category excludes is the "genre fiction" so popular in the Victorian era, notably the detective novel and novels of sensation, such as Wilkie Collins's *The Woman in White* (1859) and Mary Elizabeth Braddon's *Lady Audley's Secret* (1862). The popularity of sensation novels reflected Victorians' interest in scandal and horror, especially bigamy, adultery, and deception of a sexual nature. Due to the constraints of time and space, *Dr. Jekyll and Mr. Hyde* will have to suffice as a representation of psychosexual horror in Victorian times. Victorian genre fiction has generated much critical study during the last couple of decades, producing such titles as *From Wollstonecraft to Stoker: Essays on Gothic and Victorian Sensation Fiction* (Marilyn Brock, 2009) and *Late Victorian Crime Fiction in the Shadows of Sherlock* (Clare Clarke, 2014). My subject is different: this is a textbook for students of the Victorian literary novel rather than genre fiction such as sensation and detective novels.

The format of my book chapters is somewhat unusual, being a series of lectures for undergraduates rather than academic essays. The differences in these two types of academic writing are several. *First*, the rhetorical aim of an academic essay or scholarly monograph is to expand the known parameters of a given topic for the use of professional scholars, whereas my rhetorical aim in these lectures is to teach the novels, while also introducing undergraduate students to concepts in literary history and criticism, as this may be their first encounter with the texts. *Second*, scholarly monographs are characterized by extensive research on narrowly honed points of inquiry, whereas my lectures are characterized by general professional knowledge gained over three decades of teaching literature, as well as research for my prior publications on such subjects as D.H. Lawrence, Charles Darwin, Margaret Mead, and several British and Irish women writers. Although I consulted critical literature while preparing these lectures, such secondary-source research is not my primary method. Instead, I perform close readings of the novels using a variety of approaches and looking for textual evidence to prove my arguments. I prioritize my own interpretation, just as I request undergraduate students to prioritize theirs. *Third*, my purpose in publishing the lectures—both online (during the time of teaching the class) and for posterity in this book—is pedagogical; I am modeling the argumentation method used in literary criticism so that students have examples in hand when they write their own essays. A Works Cited list is included at the end of each lecture—instead of at the end of the book—to remind students of its importance in academic writing. In the teaching of writing, I put clarity of expression and support of argument (with quotations) as the two primary objectives.

Because of the unique circumstances that generated this book, the length of the lectures varies. When Covid-19 struck and educators turned to Zoom course delivery, my first concern about length had to do with class time. I divided the class period of seventy-five minutes into roughly equal parts, so lectures lasted about thirty-five minutes. When the book proposal for the present work was accepted by the publisher, I began writing longer lectures with the new, additional audience in mind. My imagined audience gradually shifted to include readers of the proposed book in addition to the students I was currently teaching. During class periods, lecture would be followed by discussion—I've included additional discussion questions in Appendix A for use by students, teachers, book clubs, and other readers. This book is intended as a critical supplement to the Victorian literary novels that are standard curriculum in a high school or undergraduate course in Victorian or British Literature. The lectures are written in an accessible prose that can be enjoyed by nonacademic readers as well as academics.

Each lecture starts with a question meant to elicit interesting discussion in the classroom and to direct one's search into the text for possible answers. When the lecture is the first in a series of lectures on the same novel, I follow the question with a brief plot synopsis. Then I present an analysis that answers the question through close reading of the novel to find textual evidence that supports my answer. Although I do consult secondary sources, I try to keep them to a minimum because I use the lectures to model the method that I'd like students to use when writing their own essays. In undergraduate classes, I don't require students to use secondary sources, that is, published literary criticism about the novel. My pedagogical reason for this choice is that I want to encourage students to construct meaningful questions, answer them with their own arguments, and trust their own interpretations. Reading secondary material before making an argument sometimes precludes the student's ability to make an original argument. In my lectures I do, however, introduce and apply theoretical concepts. Upper-division seminars or graduate classes are a good setting for students to engage with theory and criticism, including extensive readings in secondary source material. For an introductory Victorian literature class, I teach skills of close-reading textual analysis first, and theory as a second priority. For a supplemental text that grounds the course in historical facts and cultural interpretations, I assign readings in Susie L. Steinbach's *Understanding the Victorians: Politics, Culture and Society in Nineteenth-Century Britain*, published by Routledge. This cultural history textbook has proven valuable to my classes because of its astute historical perspectives and sensitive cultural analysis, especially around questions of class, gender, race, and empire. I cite *Understanding the Victorians* in many of my lectures.

In addition to the audience of teachers and students that I've just described, I envision another type of reader: the lovers of Victorian literature who wish to extend their knowledge by reading critical material—I'll call them Victoriaphiles. I know they exist in great numbers. The proliferation of feature films; of BBC, Masterpiece Theatre, Apple TV, and Netflix adaptations; of neo–Victorian novels; and frequent reissues of the classics: all these point to the ongoing appeal of Victorian literature, even one hundred and twenty years after Victoria Regina's death. Victorian novels retain their appeal because their themes and symbols are well constructed, their characterizations in-depth, and their plots often complex, yet rewarding to follow. Furthermore, the social rules governing the characters' lives are clear; though constraining, this social structure lends certainty to characters' roles and provides boundaries that they transgress at the risk of stigma and ostracism. Such rules and consequences provoke today's reader to question our own social mores in comparison to those of the Victorians. What have we lost, what gained, by changing much of our social framework? As our social framework changes, does our moral code shift as well? Are we living in a more or less ethical era than the Victorians? For enrolled students and lifelong scholars alike, this book offers a clear-voiced, jargon-free introduction to the period through close readings of its most famous works.

Works Cited

Conrad, Joseph. *Heart of Darkness*. Penguin, 1989.
Hirschfeld, Lawrence. *Race in the Making: Cognition, Culture, and the Child's Construction of Human Kinds*. MIT Press, 1998.

Introduction—
The Victorian Age
Progress and Paradox

Queen Victoria's reign changed what royalty meant to British people. As republican sentiments rose and fell in the eighteenth and nineteenth centuries, often in response to what was happening across the English Channel, the British monarchy shifted from being a political to a symbolic power, from a site of extravagant and illicit behavior to a model of morality and civic engagement. The royal family, consisting of mother, nine children, and one uxorious husband, became a role model for the middle- and working-class families of England and a public relations icon of family values. What was good for the Queen was good for all. Virginia Woolf made fun of an era which made women feel like mere vessels for the making of British citizens: "The average woman … married at nineteen and had fifteen or eighteen children by the time she was thirty…. The British Empire came into existence" (*Orlando* 229). The royal family's level of civic engagement was as remarkable as their domesticity. Victoria supported 150 charitable institutions, and the Prince Consort, Albert, was dedicated to enriching English culture; he developed museums, established the Great Exhibition of the Works of Industry of All Nations of 1851 (aka the Crystal Palace Exhibition), and was president of the Society for the Extinction of the Slave Trade. The Queen maintained a full schedule of civic, diplomatic, and imperial visits, including ceremonial oversight of the British Raj, of which she became Empress in 1876.

The Victorian era (1837–1901) is marked by rapid industrialization of Britain's economy, passion for social reform, expanding empire, world dominance of markets and finance, and codification of gender and class identities. English literature gains its world preeminence partly by

9

belonging to this most prominent nation. The novel was Victorian literature's most successful literary form. This book addresses the most popular
literary novels of the era.

Before introducing the novels, I'll briefly describe some of the
above-mentioned markers of the era—the reforming attitude and projects,
expanding empire and its racial justification, class stratification, and cod-
ified gender roles.

Reform and the Spirit of Melioration. *Meliorism* is the belief that the
world can be improved by human effort. As a group, Victorians were some
of the most philanthropic people in world history. *Noblesse oblige* became
not only the duty of the nobility, but also of the middle class, whose members assisted the poor, sobered up the intemperate, and rehabilitated
prostitutes. The spirit of melioration sparked major political reforms
that gradually transformed leadership and distributed power among the
classes. The Reform Acts of 1832, 1867, and 1884 extended the franchise to
middle- and working-class citizens. Before 1832, only aristocrats and gentry had the right to vote. Persistent political work incrementally won the
vote for men with property qualifications (at the value of £10 per year) in
1832, for urban working men in 1867, and for rural working men in 1884.
Women didn't gain the vote until 1918, though with an age qualification of
thirty years old. In 1928, women could start voting from age twenty-one.

As we see in novels by Charles Dickens and Elizabeth Gaskell,
industrializing England created atrocious social and labor conditions,
which were meliorated by passionate reformers. A series of Factory Acts
improved the conditions of children and women's labor by reducing working shifts to ten hours a day and outlawing the employment of children
under the age of ten. Prostitution was attacked rather than meliorated
by the Contagious Diseases Act, which enabled policemen to incarcerate
prostitutes who tested positive for venereal disease. Philanthropy was a
leading religious and cultural value that Victorians held dear, but charity
came with conditions. To be considered one of the "deserving poor" wor-
thy of charity, a person needed to prove themselves virtuous (by attending
church), temperate (by refraining from drink), and clean (cleanliness was
next to godliness).

Empire. The British Empire was the largest in history, covering a
quarter of the earth's landmass. The era from 1815 to 1914 is known as the
Pax Britannica (British Peace) due to the relative peacefulness of the empire
between the end of the Napoleonic Wars and the beginning of World War
I. There are, however, notable exceptions to this characterization: the
Crimean War (1853–56), the Indian Rebellion (1857), the massacre at Khar-
toum (1885), and the Boer War (1899–1902). In fact, violence was pervasive
and formed a part of imperial governance. Britain increased its power in

Asia, Africa, and South America through its control of financial markets, enforcement of protective tariffs, and use of extralegal police forces to protect British interests. Bringing Christian light to the dark races of the world was one way that Britain justified its control of colonies in Asia, Africa, Australia, New Zealand, Canada, the Caribbean, and the Pacific Islands. Rudyard Kipling described the duty of the British to colonize and Christianize other peoples as "the white man's burden." Queen Victoria believed that imperial expansion was justified by the duty to protect the weak and the vulnerable: "It is not in our custom to annexe [*sic*] countries unless we are obliged and forced to do so."* Such obligation derives from a deeply ingrained sense of British national and racial superiority.

Race. Victorians justified imperial expansion by the proclaimed superiority of white European peoples over all other types. Earlier in the century, Britons had a much better record of striving for social justice, demonstrating their concern for the protection of basic human rights by abolishing slavery within Britain's dominion. The Slavery Abolition Act (1833) anticipated similar legislation of the United States by thirty-two years and France by fifteen (Napoleon re-established the legality of slavery in 1802, thereby reversing France's 1794 abolition law). But scientific developments after 1860 changed people's ideas of the nature of race and justified Britons' sense of superiority on biological principles. Eventually, Darwin's theory of natural selection was interpreted to mean that humans were another of the species which he had described as evolving according to the law of the jungle—the survival of the fittest. By this theory, white nations were wealthier than Black and colored nations because whites were genetically superior. Some believed that the "races" had origins in different species and that Black and brown races were degenerating over time. *Eugenics*, a term coined by Darwin's cousin Sir Francis Galton, was a plan to rid the world of undesirables. The meliorating urge that had produced great social reforms in the nineteenth century also produced hubristic misappropriations of science for egregious social and religious projects such as eradicating Black and brown races and Christianizing the heathens.

Class stratification. Britain is a stratified class society, meaning that classes are strictly defined, and their borders are socially policed. It is difficult to overstate the importance that class distinctions acquired in British society beginning in the late eighteenth and early nineteenth centuries. As Susie Steinbach writes, "This is not to say that pre–Victorian Britain was devoid of social hierarchy or wealth disparities—far from it—but that an understanding of social difference as organized specifically by something

---

* Elizabeth Longford, *Victoria R.I.* Weidenfeld and Nicolson, 1964. 411.

called 'class' was a feature of the industrializing nineteenth century" (114). Members of all classes believed that there was something essentially and morally different between rich and poor folk. The most obvious marker of class is income, but education level and employment type are also key indices of class. The category of "shabby genteel," for instance, indicates a family living below the average income for their class but possessing good manners, substantial education, and ancestors who had land or wealth qualifying them for the gentry. Curates and parsons generally enjoy a higher status in their communities than those who might earn a higher income, especially if that income is earned in trade. To be "in trade" is a mark of inferiority because engaging in commerce is thought to taint one's character. In contrast, the professions, the military, and estate management are considered nobler ways to earn a living than commerce. Dealing in filthy lucre blackens the soul. People will snub or "cut" others on the basis of such distinctions. Class-based judgments and inflexible class boundaries are a major source of tragedy and satire in Victorian novels, especially for women on the marriage market. In *Vanity Fair*, Becky Sharp is cut, first by the high society ladies at the Marquis de Steyne's party, and later by the middle-class denizens of Bath and Cheltenham, where her reputation has been impugned. In *North and South*, otherwise generous Margaret Hale refuses to meet a family who makes its living by building and selling carriages.

Victorians made progress in educating and improving the lives of the working and middle class. The size of the middle class greatly increased as mass production made it possible to buy goods more cheaply and provided white-collar jobs for tens of thousands of people who formerly did manual labor. Increased leisure and literacy, combined with the doctrine of self-improvement, made the Victorians great consumers of literature and other forms of entertainment. The types of culture one enjoyed reflected one's rank in the social hierarchy. Upper-middle-class people read edifying novels and philosophy and went to theater performances in the West End and to opera and ballet at the Royal Opera House in Covent Garden. Lower-middle-class people consumed penny dreadfuls and attended vaudeville theater and circus performances. Working-class people enjoyed pub life, where they might sing around the piano or play darts. In all communities, from central London to rural Ireland, the pub was the hub of working-class social life, providing a center for networks of communication that enabled the community members to share gossip as well as take care of one another.

Many working-class and poor people had neither the time nor the money to attend events and venues that charged an admission fee, such as the theater, sports events, museums, music halls, art galleries, Vauxhall

Gardens, or the Crystal Palace Exhibit (admission one shilling). The poor would take or make their entertainment wherever they could find access— street theater, revivalist preaching, church hymn singing. The Salvation Army provided free entertainments, appealing to the poor by adapting popular leisure activities to its missionary uses: "Religious words were sung to music-hall tunes; circus posters and theater announcements were copied so closely that observers often failed to distinguish them; preachers imitated the idiom of street vendors; and congregations were encouraged to shout out responses to the preacher, much as they might in the music halls" (Walker 2).

Gender roles. Victorian England constructed the strictest divisions between males and females that have existed in Western history since ancient Greece. Virginia Woolf wrote, "The sexes drew further and further apart. No open conversation was tolerated. Evasions and concealments were sedulously practiced on both sides" (*Orlando* 229). The ideology or doctrine of separate spheres dominated the Victorian construction of gender roles. Men and women belonged to separate domains, and they were not to cross over into the other's territory. Men's sphere was public. They were in charge of earning money, engaging in politics, and representing the family's socioeconomic status to the outside world. Women's sphere was domestic. They were in charge of child-rearing, housekeeping, social visiting, charity, maintaining the virtue of their husband and children, and representing the family's moral and religious status in the community. The woman, especially if she is middle class, is expected to be the Angel in the House. Coventry Patmore's eponymous 1854 poem idealizes women's role in the home and sets exceptionally high standards of virtue and devotion for mothers and wives. Patmore describes the self-sacrifice of an ideal wife:

> Man must be pleased; but him to please
> Is woman's pleasure; down the gulf
> Of his condoled necessities
> She casts her best, she flings herself.

This masochistic "Angel in the House" loves best when most scorned:

> Dearly devoted to his arms,
> She loves with love that cannot tire;
> And when, ah woe, she loves alone,
> Through passionate duty love springs higher.
> [Canto IX. Book 1. The Sahara]

Middle-class women were not expected to work outside the home. Ideally, they would remain unemployed in their father's homes until marriage. Economic reality meant, however, that many of these homes could not afford to support their unemployed daughters. The only acceptable employment for these women was teaching or piece work—sewing jobs done at home for pay. Women could either teach in schools or be governesses at upper-middle-class or gentry estates. Governessing was a challenging job because of its nebulous status between the working and middle classes. Depending on their class-based assumptions, various employers treated governesses differently, either as servants or as honorary family members, though lacking certain rights and privileges. In Charlotte Brontë's novel, governess Jane Eyre is treated as an intimate by Mr. Rochester because he loves her, but his fiancée consistently denigrates her with name-calling and exclusionary gestures that are ostensibly justified by class hierarchy.

Cultural historians frequently adopt one-word descriptors to define the Victorian Age, *morality* and *reform* being among the most popular. *Paradox* also fits. Queen Victoria's attitude toward child-rearing is an example. Although she had nine children, was deeply in love with her husband, and publicly mourned his death from 1861 to the end of her life in 1901, she stated that she actually did not like having children. One of her greatest duties as a mother was to marry off her children to appropriate European royalty. Lytton Strachey's biography (1921) portrays the Queen as a cold mother. Similarly, though the tenor of Victorian times is prudish, in fact, prostitution and pornography flourished during this time. Although women were supposed to be angels in their respective houses, the women's movement persisted heroically against enormous setbacks. From proto-feminist Mary Wollstonecraft's publishing of *A Vindication of the Rights of Women* in 1792 to suffragist Emily Davison's dramatic gesture of throwing herself under the King's horse at the Epsom Derby in 1913, feminists and suffragettes put their reputations and their lives on the line.

Paradox is also inherent in British attitudes of superiority (of race, class, gender, and nation) juxtaposed to their spirit of meliorism, their gentlemen's code of honor and fairness, and their sense of duty to help those in need. One of the most fascinating instances of the condescension in Victorian *noblesse oblige* is Britain's certainty that Anglicanism and British culture were the proper religion and culture for all other peoples on the planet. A lasting legacy of nineteenth-century British hegemony is the challenge to former colonial subjects of assuming hybrid identities based on the combination of native and colonizer influences. Postcolonial writers such as Seamus Heaney (Northern Ireland) and Chinua Achebe (Nigeria) are conscious of having hybrid identities that complicate their lives but also enrich them. These writers are both proud and angry to be inheritors of the traditions of British culture.

Genre. The novels in this selection are chosen for their status as the best-known and best-loved novels written during Victoria's reign. Small differences in opinion do exist over which novels belong on this list, but such debates for the most part entail which of the authors' works to include rather than which authors. Anthony Trollope's *The Warden* (1855), Wilkie Collins's *The Moonstone* (1868), and Anne Brontë's *The Tenant of Wildfell Hall* (1848) are the next choices for a longer list. George Meredith's *The Egoist* (1879) and Oscar Wilde's *The Picture of Dorian Gray* (1890) could be added. Although Joseph Conrad published *Heart of Darkness* (1899) a few years before Victoria's death, it belongs, in my opinion, to the modernist category rather than Victorian. Some Dickensians prefer *Bleak House* (1853) and *Little Dorrit* (1857) to the two Dickens novels I chose, *Great Expectations* (1861) and *A Tale of Two Cities* (1859), but the latter pair are far more popular and easier to read. *David Copperfield* (1850) could replace *Great Expectations*, being an autobiographical novel (Dickens's personal favorite of his novels) and an excellent satire on Victorian institutions, but I, for one, would miss Pip's distinctive forms of innocence and drive. Among Hardy's works, *The Mayor of Casterbridge* (1886) could replace *Far from the Madding Crowd* (1874), though I find Bathsheba Everdene a more compelling character than Michael Henchard. And so it goes—we love those works that speak to us most directly, which provide a mirror for our souls.

The contents of this book are arranged in chronological order, partly to demonstrate a historical progression through genres and social issues. This is not to say that all authors of a period use only one genre; in fact, during a single decade, works in a variety of genres and subgenres would be produced, and a single author would mix genre elements within single books. But there is a general trend through the period that ranges from gothic to satire to panoramic realism to social problems to psychological horror, and this trend reflects topical social issues as well as the ongoing development of the novel as a literary form. The Victorian novel is a "loose, baggy monster," according to Henry James, capable of incorporating many elements. A novel might use letters and journals, narrative omniscience, free indirect discourse, interior monologue, or metafictional address to the reader. Most Victorian novels contain subplots and/or parallel plots, such as the Dorothea/Ladislaw and Rosamond/Lydgate romances in *Middlemarch* and the Monica/Widdowson and Rhoda/Barfoot pairings in *The Odd Women*. The Victorian novel may include political/historical events, such as the Great Reform Act in *Middlemarch*, the Battle of Waterloo in *Vanity Fair*, and the French Revolution in *A Tale of Two Cities*. Increasingly through the century we find references to the Continent or the colonies, and some characters live in these foreign territories, such as Jos Sedley in Bengal (*Vanity Fair*) and Angel Clare in Brazil

(*Tess of the D'Urbervilles*). Remaining constant as a topic in most Victorian novels (excepting some, such as Dickens and Stevenson) is the role of women in society. Woman-authored novels, such as *Jane Eyre* and *North and South*, feature protagonists who directly voice the problem of women's limitations in patriarchy—Jane Eyre in her interior monologue about women needing a larger sphere of action, and Margaret Hale in her reflections about a woman having to decide whether to fulfill herself or fulfill society's expectations of women. Man-authored Victorian novels also address the woman question. Bathsheba Everdene (*Far from the Madding Crowd*) tells Gabriel Oak she doesn't want to be the property of a man and values her independence too much to submit to marriage. Mary Barfoot (*The Odd Women*) makes impassioned speeches about the need for women not only to be in the workforce but also to actively fight the patriarchy. The narrator of *Vanity Fair* alternately praises Becky Sharp's ingenuity for circumnavigating the limitations of her gender and condemns her "mermaid" propensity to entrap men for torture and annihilation.

Emily and Charlotte Brontë's novels (1847) contain strong gothic elements—intense romance, doubling, supernatural elements, remote rural settings, and extreme emotional states, including terror, dread, and insanity. These elements echo the high age of gothic romance that began with Horace Walpole's *The Castle of Otranto* (1769) and ended with Jane Austen's parody of the genre in *Northanger Abbey* (1817). The Victorian gothic, on the other hand, starts with a basis in realism and blends in gothic elements such as doubling and terror. The Romantic Age's gothic literature took place in the wilderness, often at an abandoned castle in the mountainous regions of eastern Europe or southern France. After *Wuthering Heights* and *Jane Eyre*, the Victorian gothic moves its setting from the remote countryside to the metropolis, as in the London settings of *Dr. Jekyll and Mr. Hyde* and *The Picture of Dorian Gray*. The presence of horror in the most civilized capital of Europe is doubly unsettling, as it reveals that the horror is actually within us, rather than in the colonial, racial, or historical Other. The same realization comes to the dying Kurtz in *Heart of Darkness*, whose last words, "the horror, the horror!" reflect his sense of evil within himself.

Realism is the major genre of the Victorian novel; Thackeray, Dickens, Gaskell, and Eliot write variations of the mode, such as panoramic, satirical, psychological, and historical realism. Realism is the genre chosen by social reformers such as Dickens or Gaskell, who use real-seeming characters in plausible situations to expose and interrogate the social ills of Victorian England. By making their characters relatable, the writers aim to raise awareness and motivate the reader to resist social injustice. Gaskell's and Eliot's voices are more earnest, whereas those of Thackeray and Dickens are more satirical, coming at the subject with an ironic twist. I mentioned in the Preface that satire is a dangerous mode for a nineteenth-century female writer because within Victorian ideology it is not women's role to criticize society. Instead, she should smooth out problems by helping her menfolk. Women should assist without seeming to lead, never usurping the rightful place of a man. Satire implies an intellectual ability to analyze complex problems and the self-esteem required for stating opinions boldly—both considered masculine traits. Satire is implicitly a critique of patriarchy, so women writers would either withhold judgment, or pull back at the endings of their novels so that the implied critique is withdrawn. For example, *Middlemarch*'s Dorothea Brooke feels bereft of a *métier* at the end of the novel, but the narrator assures the reader that she is doing good for others behind the scenes: "Her full nature … spent itself in channels which had no great name on the earth. But the effect of her being on those around her was incalculably diffusive: for the growing good of the world is partly dependent on unhistoric acts" (838). Ultimately, Eliot relegates Dorothea to the role of Angel in the House rather than the reformer that she once wished to be.

Thomas Hardy's pastoralism—his idealization of rural life—is also a blended genre, for his dark fatalism or environmental determinism overpowers his sentiment about the goodness of Wessex people. The Victorian sexual double standard leads Tess to become a murderer. As much as Angel would like to correct the punitive beliefs of the evangelical church, he is nonetheless destined to judge Tess according to scriptural proclamations about tainted women. Social mores are too deeply ingrained in him to resist. Hardy's cosmic irony makes *Tess* a philosophical novel, but not a novel of ideas (like Gissing's *Odd Women)*, because Hardy's characters and settings are so powerfully drawn that they would make an excellent novel even without the narrator's philosophical musings. Hardy's religious skepticism reflects the heightened tension between Church and science from the time of Darwin's *Origin of Species* (1859) onward. Hardy is a sharp critic of his age, and, like the modernists of the subsequent era, he placed a nostalgic value on antiquity because it seemed to adopt a nobler set of ethics.

George Gissing has a hobbyhorse, and that is the condition of women. On the first page of *The Odd Women*, the narrator sets out the social problem of the book: Dr. Madden (and his ilk) puts his own notions of a genteel reputation above practical consideration of his daughters' material needs. His failure to prepare his daughters for self-support after his death leads to their tragic ends. The "novel of ideas" is a genre that uses characters, plot, and settings in service of a greater purpose than the organic realism of the story; the philosophical or political idea is primary. The novel of ideas is commonly associated with times and places of intense political strife and ideological warfare. The 1890s New Woman—though sometimes portrayed frivolously as one who wears comfortable clothing, adopts new habits such as smoking, and converses about a wider range of subjects—is fundamentally a disturbing challenge to the very roots of patriarchy. The New Woman has the potential to destroy the old ways, including domesticity, the Angel in the House, and separate spheres ideology. She will unbalance the economy, undermine the male ego, and radically change the social structures of the world. Thus, the New Woman is a topical issue for the 1890s and an appropriate subject for a novel of ideas. This is, however, the most difficult genre in which to write well—the author needs to beware that their ideology doesn't overpower the characters, settings, and plot.

The 1890s brought a sense of exhaustion typical of *fin-de-siècle* thinking, a millenarian sense of anxiety about what's coming next (expressed succinctly by Kurtz's phrase, "the horror, the horror!"). After the development of ideas such as biological racism, women's hysteria, eugenics, and genocide, it's understandable that Victorians might have felt a sense of terror about where scientific theorizing would lead next. As Dr. Jekyll reveals, the horror is not necessarily the Other who resides in far-flung colonies, lingers in Newgate Prison, or lurks in a city alley, but the unknown, unconscious self that drives our existence. At the turn of the century, psychology is becoming a popular subject; Sigmund Freud's books* teach about the existence of the unconscious, and Cesare Lombroso's criminology studies liken criminals to nonhuman animals. The women's suffrage movement has turned militant and seems increasingly likely to succeed, while the sixty-three-year reign of an extremely successful sovereign is about to end. Anxieties about these threats to patriarchy, to self-knowledge and religion, even to British superiority, are relayed in the literature of psychological realism, horror, and the urban gothic. Dr. Jekyll's story is a cry for help. Victorian standards of gentility reduce the good doctor to a split personality whose dark side kills and maims with glee, utterly enjoying the atrocities he commits. Jekyll is aware that his own social fears created the monster. The absence of women from the novella is a haunting reminder that the woman question spells trouble—like Hyde, the New Woman is repressed out of (conscious) existence by Jekyll and his circle of genteel professionals.

Collectively, the lectures in this book are meant to give an overview

---

* *Studies on Hysteria* (1895), *The Interpretation of Dreams* (1899), and *The Psychopathology of Everyday Life* (1901) were some of Freud's texts written in laymen's terms. It took about eight years before *The Interpretation of Dreams* was widely read by non-specialists, after which it gained popular success.

of salient issues of Victorian life—cultural, political, social, and psychological—as represented in major literary novels. The lectures about genre are intended to deepen our understanding about ways in which genre is deployed to further the author's rhetorical and political purposes. Appendix A contains additional discussion questions for classrooms or book clubs. In keeping with the themes of this book, I have drafted questions on the subjects of genre, gender, race, and class. These questions are meant to open up discussions about Victorian culture, politics, and identities that readers may compare to current events. Appendix B is a glossary of literary and historical terms intended as a handy reference tool to supplement the lectures. Written in an expansive style, the glossary provides examples from the novels covered in the book. It can be read on its own for an overview of political and literary issues of the Victorian age.

Works Cited

Eliot, George. *Middlemarch*. Penguin, 1994.

James, Henry. Preface. *The Tragic Muse*. Houghton, 1890.

Patmore, Coventry. "The Angel in the House" (1891). https://victorianweb.org/authors/patmore/angel/9.html

Steinbach, Susie. *Understanding the Victorians: Politics, Culture and Society in Nineteenth-Century Britain*. Routledge, 2012.

Walker, Pamela J. *Pulling the Devil's Kingdom Down: The Salvation Army in Victorian Britain*. University of California Press, 2001.

Woolf, Virginia. *Orlando*. Harcourt Brace Jovanovich, 1928; 1956.

I. *WUTHERING HEIGHTS* (1847)

1

Heathcliff's Social Climbing

Question:

Wuthering Heights is a gothic romance with one of the stormiest love affairs in all of British literature. Its strong subtext is Heathcliff's drive to raise his class status, a theme associated much more with the genre of social realism than gothic romance. By contrasting the people at the Grange and the Heights, and demonstrating what it took for a street urchin to eventually gain power, does Emily Brontë intend to critique the British class system?

Synopsis:

An urban gentleman called Lockwood rents Thrushcross Grange in the Yorkshire moors for a year of rest and recreation. Meeting his land-lord, Heathcliff, on a stormy night at the neighboring estate of Wuther-ing Heights, Lockwood accepts the invitation to stay overnight. He has a nightmare that includes a visitation from Cathy-the-First (to differenti-ate from her eponymous daughter), who is Heathcliff's deceased love. As Lockwood slowly recovers from illness, Nelly Dean, the servant, tells him the history of the two families. Thirty years earlier, Mr. Earnshaw, owner of the Heights, brought home a dark-skinned "gipsy" from the streets of Liverpool. Earnshaw favored Heathcliff over his natural children, Cathy-the-First and Hindley, causing violent resentment on Hindley's part. Hindley abused Heathcliff badly, but Cathy fell in love with him for his good looks, his dedication to her, and their shared love of the moors. When Mr. Earnshaw died, Hindley inherited Wuthering Heights. Cathy-the-First married a gentleman, Edgar Linton, and went to live with him and his sis-ter, Isabella, at Thrushcross Grange. Edgar and Cathy had a daughter, also

Commonly believed to be the inspiration for *Wuthering Heights* (photograph by Tim Green [unaltered]. Licensed by Creative Commons. Link: Creative Commons Attribution 2.0 Generic).

called Cathy (hereinafter Cathy-the-Second). Heathcliff ran away, aiming to educate and raise himself above Hindley and Edgar's class-based insults.

Three years later, Heathcliff returns with the clothes and bearing of a gentleman, though he still behaves in a surly manner and uses Yorkshire dialect instead of the Queen's English. He moves back into the Heights and slowly bleeds Hindley of his property by lending him money for gambling and drink using the house as collateral. When Hindley dies, the Heights belongs to Heathcliff. Hareton Earnshaw is Hindley's son whom Heathcliff treats badly, replicating in his behavior the condescension that Hindley had shown to him. Heathcliff's third revenge target is Edgar Linton. In return for Edgar's banishing him from the Grange, Heathcliff elopes with Edgar's sister, Isabella. They produce a feeble son called Linton Heathcliff. When Isabella dies, Linton Heathcliff comes to live at the Grange, where Heathcliff torments him mercilessly until he agrees to marry Cathy Linton (Cathy-the-Second), Edgar and Cathy's daughter. Upon Linton Heathcliff's early death from tuberculosis, Heathcliff inherits the Grange. Cathy-the-Second teaches Hareton to read and they fall in love. Heathcliff starts seeing visions of the dead Catherine-the-First. He stops eating, becomes delirious, and wills himself to die so that he can "rejoin her" on the moors. As the novel ends, Cathy-the-Second and Hareton Earnshaw are planning to marry and move into Thrushcross Grange.

Analysis:

To understand an author's intentions—to the extent that such is possible—one should turn first to a consideration of which genre they have selected, because each genre features specific purposes. Social critique usually appears in the genres of satire and/or social realism. Gothic romance, on the other hand, is intended to entertain by horror. Its purpose is neither didactic nor meliorative. The gothic genre flourished in the late eighteenth and early nineteenth centuries but gave way to realism about the time of Victoria's ascension to the throne. *Wuthering Heights* (1847) is a curious instance of gothic romance returning after its heyday. It is possible that Emily Brontë had retreated so far into her own imaginary world that she was removed from social concerns such as literary trends. Her choice is not determined simply by family background (the Brontë family was haunted by death, paternalism, and drug addiction), since her sisters, Charlotte and Anne, chose social realism for their own writing modes. Despite—or because of—its difference from the contemporary norm, Emily's tale of unhappy lovers unable to marry was a commercial success, producing an archetypal Byronic hero and wild woman who became popular cultural icons. In gothic fiction, social critique of gender and class roles is not a primary intention. Rather, the deep layers of myth and psychology predominate thematically. Cathy says she *is* Heathcliff, which today's readers will recognize as a dangerous relinquishment of identity, symptomatic of weak psychic boundaries and a desire to merge with the other. The novel's focus on abnormal psychology, coupled with supernatural elements and the remote, isolated setting of the two houses, are hallmarks of gothic romance, a genre which differs substantially from social realism and social critique.

Consideration of the subtext of social class issues can deepen our experience of the book. I've asked whether Emily Brontë intends such a reading. Poststructural theory posits that an author does not necessarily understand his or her own intentions. Roland Barthes introduced the ideas of "the death of the author" and "the text writes itself." This means that texts are open to numerous, though not unlimited, interpretations due to the overdetermined nature of language and the gap between signifier and signified. Whether or not Emily Brontë *intends* a social critique of British class stratification—which we don't know—I assert that her text does imply a critique because it portrays the tragic outcomes of British class snobbery, which intersects with racism to create multiple barriers to Heathcliff's success.

When Heathcliff returns to the neighborhood with money earned from his three-year self-improvement project, he gradually devises the components of his long-term plan of revenge. He tells Cathy that he at first intended to see Cathy, avenge himself against Hindley, and then kill himself, but upon returning, changed his mind. He remains alive to extend his revenge onto the next generation. After Heathcliff suffers what psychologists call the "primal wound"—separation from his parents (in his case, orphaning)—he goes on to encounter a second wounding at the hands of his adoptive family. This second wounding, the one he wishes to avenge, derives from class-and-race-based prejudice—his own and that of the Earnshaws and Lintons. From childhood onwards, Hindley Earnshaw regards Heathcliff as a "beggarly interloper," Mr. Linton calls him a "little Lascar" (sailor from India or Southeast Asia), and Nelly a "dark-skinned gipsy"; while his ethnicity is uncertain, it's clear he's a "foreigner" who cannot be a deserving member of the Earnshaw family (39). William Empson speculates that Heathcliff may be the illegitimate mixed-race son of Earnshaw's younger brother, thereby explaining why Earnshaw is so affectionate toward Heathcliff and vague in his explanations of their meeting (493).

After initial friendliness, Edgar Linton also rebuffs Heathcliff when the latter states his intention to marry Isabella. Like Hindley, Edgar scorns Heathcliff's "namelessness"—his lack of any family of origin from which to derive a worthwhile status in society (101). Catherine too believes that Heathcliff is too "low" for her and that marrying him would degrade her, a comment that Heathcliff overhears (81). Even Nelly Dean, who appears to be a reliable narrator, judges Heathcliff by his lack of gentlemanly attributes: "Honest people don't hide their deeds," she says, implying that dishonest people are low class (103).

The Victorians insisted that there were distinct moral differences between classes: "British society was fiercely hierarchical…. People at all levels of society believed that the rich and the poor were different beings" (Steinbach 115). Even Cathy (who loves Heathcliff) and Nelly (who initially pities him) consider Heathcliff one of those "different beings" who comes from poverty. This "gipsy"—whose presumed racial difference is hinted at—arrives at a gentleman's home out of nowhere.* British society doesn't

---

  * *Gipsy* was the English spelling until the twentieth century; now *gypsy* is more common. I put "gypsy" and "gipsy" between quotation marks because it is considered a racial slur by many Romani people. Romani are the largest ethnic minority in Europe; they emigrated from northwest India between the ninth and fourteenth centuries. Europeans called them "gypsies" on the mistaken assumption that they were from Egypt because of their dark skin. There are approximately twelve million living in Europe and another one million in the United States. Historians estimate that up to one and a half million Romani were murdered in the Holocaust. Victorians might have used the slur to describe an "unplaceable" poor person with dark skin—like Heathcliff.

accept people out of nowhere; it has a fundamental need to place people in their proper level before deciding how or whether to accept them. As such, *Wuthering Heights* dramatizes the meaning of class for Victorians, making Heathcliff's class injury central to the plot.

Part of the tragedy of Heathcliff's journey from wastrel to gentleman is that he is unable to fit his new niche. His story demonstrates how difficult it is to pass as a gentleman when one isn't born to the role. One area in which he falls short is his relationship to his dependents. Only once do we hear of Wuthering Heights' tenant farmers—the employment of whom marks the difference between being a country squire and merely a farmer. Nelly tells Mr. Lockwood: "the villagers affirmed that Heathcliff was *near*, and a cruel hard landlord" (*near* means cheap and stingy) (197). Many Victorian novelists (such as Eliot, Dickens, and Gaskell) examine the difference between a gentleman by birth and a "true gentleman." The latter has to live up to a certain code of behavior and possess certain innate characteristics—generosity, moderation, temperance, and honor. The duty of *noblesse oblige* requires a country gentleman to care about his tenant farmers and to keep up their cottages. Heathcliff has no more interest in improving the lives of his dependent tenant farmers than he does in teaching Hareton to read.

The ability to "place" people—to instantly gauge which class they belong to—is made possible at first glance by dress and manners, even by one's bearing. As soon as one speaks, one's accent and usage are a dead giveaway. It is interesting to compare Cathy and Heathcliff at the moment of their transformation from wild children to lady and gentleman because Cathy is successful at the performance while Heathcliff is less so. After young Cathy's convalescence at Thrushcross Grange, she returns home and Nelly sees:

> instead of a wild, hatless little savage jumping into the house, and rushing to squeeze us all breathless, there lighted from a handsome black pony a very dignified person, with brown ringlets falling from the cover of a feathered beaver, and a long cloth habit which she was obliged to hold up with both hands that she might sail in [53].

Nelly's impression is that, by virtue of her convalescence at the Grange and intermingling with its inhabitants, Cathy transformed herself from savage to dignified person.

Heathcliff is less successful in performing his new class position convincingly because he lacks the noble characteristics that make one a true gentleman. What Nelly notices at first glance are the exterior aspects, but his controlled facial expression and upright bearing cannot hide the suppressed anger within:

He had grown a tall, athletic, well-formed man.... His upright carriage suggested the idea of his having been in the army. His countenance was much
older in expression and decision of feature than Mr. Linton's; it looked intelligent and retained no marks of former degradation. A half-civilized ferocity
lurked yet in the depressed brows and eyes full of black fire, but it was sub-
dued; and his manner was even dignified, quite divested of roughness though
too stern for grace [96].

This is Heathcliff's best face, prepared to meet the faces of Catherine and
Edgar at his first visit to the Grange after his travels, and yet this face still
expresses his "half-civilization," sternness, anger, and lack of grace. Once
ensconced in his role as Wuthering Heights's master, he will wear the
clothes of a gentleman, but will no longer trouble to adopt gentlemanly
manners, facial expressions, or language. Heathcliff is frightening because
he has some of the forms of a gentleman without the inner essence—a
Romantic "hollow man" par excellence.

Each element of his revenge plan relates to Heathcliff's class-based
envy. Like a horror movie, Heathcliff's step-by-step execution of his lurid
revenge fills the reader with terror. We wonder how far he will go, and
whether he will spare anyone, fearing lest Cathy too will become a target.
First, he had intended to kill Hindley and then himself. Finding himself
admitted to the Grange, he modifies the original plan, deciding to torture
Edgar and Cathy and lead Hindley to his own demise by way of his vices
of drinking and gambling. Instead of dying, it would give him more pleasure to observe the suffering of those who had wounded him. Not content
to torment his main enemies, Heathcliff manipulates the lives of all those
around him. His abusive relationship with Isabella leads to her death. He
refuses to stop at one generation but also tortures their offspring. Like
some latter-day Greek tragic hero, Heathcliff expands his revenge beyond
its initial target, because harming Hindley isn't enough retribution for his
fathomless pain.

Knowing that land ownership is one's entrée to the gentry,
Heathcliff carefully plans the transfer of Wuthering Heights to himself
by gradually mortgaging "every yard" of the estate through numerous
card games which he easily wins against a drunken Hindley (188). Further, he intends to inherit Thrushcross Grange as well—this will be the
real symbol of victory over his oppressors, as it is far grander than the
Heights. Like a spider awaiting its prey, he patiently waits for Isabella,
Edgar, and Linton's deaths so that he can inherit the Grange: "Yes, Nell,
my son is prospective owner of your place, and I should not wish him
to die till I was certain of being his successor. Besides, he's *mine*, and I
want the triumph of seeing *my* descendent fairly lord of their estates; my
child hiring their children, to till their fathers' lands for wages" (208). He

intends to reverse the class status of himself and his son with respect to that of the Grange's owners.

One of the ways in which Heathcliff avenges Hindley in the second generation is to turn Hareton into a brute. Heathcliff taunts Hareton with the differences between himself and Linton, both candidates for Cathy-the-Second's love. Hareton is the only character who loved Heathcliff unconditionally, and whose love could have saved Heathcliff's soul if he had responded positively to it. (I don't count Cathy's as unconditional love because when Heathcliff displeases her, she says she'll just love her idea of him rather than himself.) It is interesting that Heathcliff turns Hareton into a version of his own childhood self in all the particulars: deprived of education, caught in a sexual triangle with Cathy-the-Second and Linton, and blindly loving his tormentor (Heathcliff) as Heathcliff blindly loved his (Cathy-the-First). Grown up to be a strong, capable farmer with a vulnerability mostly hidden behind brutish manners, Hareton must be a painful reminder of Heathcliff's past rather than a relieving revenge of it. Hareton is the true proof of the adage that revenge never heals the wound.

Hareton's occupation of the liminal space between gentry and servant is also reminiscent of Heathcliff's inner conflict over his own class status. Raised by gentry (the land-owning class), but not provided with a refining education or (enough) love, Heathcliff and Hareton lead existences that are dissociated from their class at birth. Heathcliff has raised himself in appearance, but not character, while Hareton, though possessing a better character, has been socially lowered without knowing that he has been wronged. Cathy-the-Second makes Hareton painfully aware that he is neither servant nor master, gentry nor working class, and can't be placed— until she does place him by calling him an idiot. Heathcliff's intention is to bring Hareton lower than Hindley had brought Heathcliff: "He'll never be able to emerge from his bathos of coarseness, and ignorance. I've got him faster than his scoundrel of a father secured me, and lower; for he takes a pride in his brutishness" (219). True avengers wish to hurt their offenders more than their offenders hurt them—only in this way can they feel that they have achieved victory over the enemy.

To conclude, Heathcliff's primal wounding and his revenge are related to the problem of class stratification in British society. Young Hindley vilified Heathcliff not only because he stole Mr. Earnshaw's affections but because he was a dark-skinned interloper from a much lower class—found on the streets of Liverpool. Heathcliff avenged himself, utilizing class as a weapon. He took advantage of Hindley's weaknesses to earn title to his property, depriving him of his last attribute of upper-class status. He damaged Edgar's class pride by marrying his sister and lowering her. He deprived Hareton of his class status by brutalizing him and neglecting his education. Heathcliff uses his own offspring to torment Edgar's daughter and to gain ownership of Thrushcross Grange. Ownership of the Grange is the status symbol that proves—outwardly at least—that he has arrived at the top of the gentry class in this part of West Yorkshire, even though, as soon as he "arrives," Heathcliff seeks his own death by roaming the moors in all weathers looking for Catherine. Throughout the novel, Heathcliff substitutes his objective of attaining class status as compensation for his inability to attain his love object—even though he obtains no enjoyment from the status. *Wuthering Heights* illuminates several ways in which class status can be weaponized to hurt others. Brontë's gothic novel demonstrates the pervasive importance of social class in Victorian society.

Works Cited

Barthes, Roland. "The Death of the Author." *Image, Music, Text.* Fontana, 1977. 142–148.

Brontë, Emily. *Wuthering Heights.* Penguin, 2003.

Empson, William. "Letter to *Punch.*" *Argufying: Essays on Literature and Culture.* University of Iowa, 1987. 493–94.

Steinbach, Susie. "Born into the Lower-Upper-Middle Class." *Understanding the Victorians: Politics, Culture and Society in Nineteenth-Century Britain.* Routledge, 2012. 113–131.

2

Masculine Privilege, Absent Mothers, Merging Lovers: Gender Roles and Love Relationships

Question:

The tangled relationships among members of the two houses are psychologically complex. For instance, Heathcliff and Cathy-the-First seem to challenge or even reverse gender roles. Heathcliff "femininely" self-destructs in reaction to rejection, and Cathy coldly ignores her childhood favorite, switching her love to the man who can give her material possessions. Ultimately, however, Heathcliff performs an exaggerated version of masculinity to gain dominance of both houses. What gender roles do the protagonists play in *Wuthering Heights*, and how do their childhood experiences affect their pursuit of love as adults?

Analysis:

In *Wuthering Heights*, masculine privilege enables Heathcliff to insinuate himself into the West Yorkshire gentry class, using marriage and inheritance laws to his advantage. Heathcliff marries Isabella for two reasons—to torment Edgar and Cathy Linton and to inherit the Grange. He plans carefully in order to fulfill these objectives. The action of the novel takes place between 1770 and 1802, long before the Married Women's Property Acts (1870 and 1882) grant wives the right to keep the wages, inheritance, and other property that they receive before and during marriage. Isabella was the rare nineteenth-century female who was nominated to inherit her father's property in the event that her brother should predecease her. Most fathers would choose even a distant male relation as legatee rather than a daughter. Either Edgar Linton Sr. had no such relative, or he found a legal loophole to allow his daughter, Isabella, to inherit his land in the event that her brother predeceased her. (Edgar Linton Jr. did find such a loophole and was planning to put Cathy-the-Second's property into trust to protect it from her future husband, but he died before executing the document.) Heathcliff hoped to inherit the Grange when Isabella died, but Edgar outlived her and retained ownership. As daughter of the male legatee, Cathy-the-Second becomes the new heir. Heathcliff then forces his son, Linton, to marry Cathy-the-Second, who loses her inheritance (through marriage laws) to her husband. Heathcliff now hastens Linton's death in order to ensure his (Heathcliff's) inheritance of the Grange. Heathcliff's merciless manipulation of his own son provides the driving force and psychological horror of Volume II.

Law and custom favor Heathcliff's plan because he's a man, whereas they limit Cathy-the-First's choices because she's a woman. As a woman in the lower stratum of the upper class, Cathy has two choices: she can either marry and move away or remain in her brother's squalid home. Being an upper class female, she is forbidden by custom to earn her own living, though she can earn wages by teaching or sewing. Cathy is not, however, fit for either job. Before her sojourn at the Grange, Cathy lacks the temperament and gentility to be a governess; she isn't a proper role model for girls. She could be a dressmaker, but the remoteness of the Heights limits the number of customers she'd be able to find. She loves Heathcliff, but he has no prospects for earning a living. In the manner of the Romantic gothic, Emily Brontë isolates the characters within the small circumference around the two estates; she constructs an invisible psychic boundary around them that prevents their movement to, or influence by, other places. This invisible fence represents customary restrictions on women's movement between domestic and public space and in particular the gentry class's restrictions on women's employment and marriage choices. Thus, Edgar Linton's proximity and his love make marriage to him the only possible choice for Cathy's future—unless one is hopelessly romantic and thinks that she would have been happy to continue living with Heathcliff under Hindley's domination at the Heights.

A serious psychological obstacle to Cathy-the-First and Heathcliff's happiness is the absence of a good-enough mother. In this novel, mothers either die or their influence is negligible—in fiction and psychology these are called "absent mothers." Catherine's mother, Mrs. Earnshaw, plays only a minor role in Catherine's upbringing before she dies. Edgar's mother, Mrs. Linton Sr., dies shortly after Catherine recuperates from the dog attack at the Linton home. Isabella dies when her son is twelve. In both generations, biological mothers are either literally or figuratively absent and unavailable to support their growing children. In lieu of such biological mothers, Nelly Dean plays surrogate mother to two generations of Earnshaws—Heathcliff, Hindley, and Cathy-the-First in the first generation, Hareton and Cathy-the-Second in the second. Nelly's ongoing dedication to this role is apparent from her reaction to Cathy-the-Second and Hareton's plan to marry: "the crown of all my wishes will be the union of those two" (316). Nelly is happy because the marriage will end the feud and unite the houses, while Heathcliff's death ends years of terror.

The absence of mothering causes internal conflicts in the main characters that inhibit their ability to find secure identities and happy marriages. In object relations theory,* the term "good-enough mothering" is used to describe the most basic requirement for psychological health. Children don't need a perfect mother in order for them to mature into healthy adults. They need mothers who can provide a sense that the world is benign enough for survival—not so malevolent that all relationships appear threatening. The good-enough mother produces children with the capacity to love others. On the other hand, mothers who are not good enough (either overprotective or neglectful) produce children who lack the security and self-esteem to lead healthy lives. Lack of a good-enough mother negatively influences children's potential for adjustment in later life. They may choose inappropriate love objects, will face anxiety and depression, and are likely to become substance abusers.

In "The Absent Mother in *Wuthering Heights*," Philip Wion addresses the lack of a good-enough mother and comments on the role that the narrator, Lockwood, plays in relation to Cathy-the-First and Heathcliff. According to Wion, Lockwood's own psychological problems serve to dramatize Catherine's and Heathcliff's neuroses by exhibiting the opposite type of defense mechanism. Whereas Catherine and Heathcliff compensate for the absent mother by trying to (unhealthily) merge with each other, Lockwood refuses to engage intimately with any woman. Happily, the second generation of lovers, Cathy-the-Second and Hareton, attain a middle ground between the older generation's two extremes of merger and isolation. In their relationship, they manage to maintain separate identities while being dedicated to each other's happiness.

Lockwood is amusing in his role as naïve and unreliable narrator. He

---

* Object relations theory, developed as an offshoot of psychoanalytic theory in the 1940s and '50s by British psychologists Ronald Fairbairn, Melanie Klein, Donald Winnicott, held that interpersonal relationships in adulthood are affected by family experiences during infancy. We internalize the "objects," or images of family members, especially mothers, and unconsciously use them to predict people's behavior and the relative threat of harm or promise of good that these people present.

lacks understanding of his own nature. In the opening chapter he claims he's very similar to Heathcliff in his misanthropy and reserve, but in reality, his temperament is very different from that of Wuthering Heights's master. With just a few words and gestures from Heathcliff, the reader knows that Lockwood's assessments about both Heathcliff and himself are wrong. Lockwood perceives Heathcliff's problem as one of shyness—"I know, by instinct, his reserve springs from an aversion to showy displays of feeling" (5). This isn't Heathcliff's problem at all. Heathcliff is a depressed man filled with anger and hatred, but a passionate one who has the courage to love a woman. Lockwood may be depressed, but the difference between him and Heathcliff is that Lockwood has never tried to establish intimacy with anyone. Intimacy with Catherine—and revenge against Hindley—are the only things that Heathcliff cares about. Whereas Lockwood retreats from the challenges of loving, Heathcliff throws himself into his plan to win Cathy and avenge Hindley and Edward, albeit in a twisted way that ensures disaster. Lockwood's role in the narrative, according to Wion, is to "dramatize this contrasting reaction to a deep longing for union with the mother" (324).

Cathy-the-First and Heathcliff's desire to merge identities is a problematic psychic reaction to their history and environment. Merging is a defense reaction against their motherless childhoods. For their lack of parental love, they try to compensate with manic protestations of all-consuming love for each other. Of course, they are unable to perform such idealized, unrealistic dedication. According to Wion, Lockwood is another adult who suffers ambivalence toward his mother because of their early relationship. She is a critical parent who once predicted that he would "never have a comfortable home" (6). He proceeds to live out her prophecy. When an innocent young lady at a seaside resort returned Lockwood's desiring gaze, he "shrunk icily into [himself], like a snail," and caused the young lady such embarrassment that she had to shorten her vacation and leave town (6). Likewise, when becoming romantically interested in Cathy-the-Second, Lockwood hesitates to show it: "It may be very possible that *I* should love her; but would she love me? I doubt it too much to venture my tranquility, by running into temptation; and then my home is not here. I'm of the busy world, and into its arms I must return" (256). Poor Lockwood has given up the arms of a woman, substituting the arms of the busy world, in an existence so dull that Brontë leaves most of it offstage. Instead of losing himself in love as Cathy and Heathcliff do, Lockwood fears engulfment by Mother (a mother object or "imago"—an unconscious mental image) and is thus unavailable for intimacy with any other person. Cathy and Heathcliff's impossible love is no healthier than Lockwood's retreat from any possibility of love. The Earnshaw children and Lockwood exhibit two defensive types of relation to love objects. Both behaviors demonstrate that children without nurturance grow up to be adults without the capacity to nurture.

Works Cited

Brontë, Emily. *Wuthering Heights.* Penguin, 2003.

Steinbach, Susie L. "Born into the Lower-Upper-Middle: Class." *Understanding the Victorians: Politics, Culture and Society in Nineteenth-Century Britain.* Routledge, 2012. 113–131.

Wion, Philip. "The Absent Mother in *Wuthering Heights*." *Case Studies in Contemporary Criticism,* Wuthering Heights. Bedford Books, 1992. 315–30.

3

Judging People by Color, Physiognomy, and Phrenology

Question:

Throughout the first half of the novel, a mysterious energy radiates from the attic, haunting Thornfield Hall and implicating Edward Rochester in an inexplicably sinister past. Bertha Mason is Creole, which can (ambiguously) mean either a person of mixed European and Black descent, or else a person of European *or* Black African descent who is born in the West Indies. Given her brother Richard's sallow complexion, it is unlikely that Bertha is Black. But Edward projects his fear of miscegenation onto her, blending categories of insanity, gender, and race into a supremely negative mix. What is the role of race prejudice in *Jane Eyre*?

Synopsis:

Orphaned as a child, Jane Eyre is taken in and abused by her aunt. Accusing her of lying, Mrs. Reed sends Jane away to Lowood Institute. This charitable institution affords orphans the most meager necessities and treats them brutally—a semi-starvation diet, public shaming, extreme cold, and inadequate clothing—all of which weakens their defenses and makes them susceptible to typhoid. Jane vows to study hard and to tame her emotions in emulation of her best friend, Helen Burns, and her admired teacher, Miss Maria Temple. At age eighteen, Jane finds a job teaching a French girl, Adèle Varens, at Thornfield Hall. Although the master of the house, Edward Rochester, is initially severe, Jane's moral integrity impresses him, and they soon fall in love. During a house party at the Hall, Rochester flirts with Blanche Ingram, an aristocrat who is pretty, rich, and cruel. Jane is called away to tend Mrs. Reed, who is dying of a stroke.

Returning to Thornfield Hall, Jane assumes she will have to find another job, since Blanche and Edward are about to marry. Edward finally admits to loving only Jane and proposes marriage. At the altar, Richard Mason reveals that there is an impediment to this marriage, as Edward is already married to Richard's sister, Bertha Mason. Angrily, Edward confesses, and leads the wedding party to the attic where he has confined Bertha for the past ten years. Edward asks Jane to move to southern France with him, but Jane has no desire of becoming another of Edward's mistresses. Before dawn, she boards a coach to Whitcross, a remote crossroads in the moors. Having left her purse behind in the coach, Jane is destitute and begs unsuccessfully for food in the village of Morton. At death's door, she implores the maid of a small country house, Marsh End, for food and shelter. Though Hannah refuses her, the owner, St. John Rivers, returns home just in time to save her life.

In a short time, Jane learns to love St. John and his sisters, Diana and Mary. St. John finds Jane a position teaching in a school for local farm girls. She humbly accepts the tedious work but still pines for Edward. St. John receives word of his uncle's death and discovers Jane's real last name, which she had hidden in order to protect Edward from gossip. St. John reveals that they are cousins, and their Uncle John has died and left her £20,000. She immediately divides the sum into four parts, sharing equally with St. John and his two

Charlotte Brontë. Painted by Evert A. Duyckinck (1873). Courtesy of the University of Texas Libraries, the University of Texas at Austin.

sisters. Jane quits teaching and refurbishes Marsh End, then invites Diana and Mary home from their governess positions, which they are happy to quit. St. John teaches Jane the Hindustani language and asks her to accompany him to India for missionary work—as his wife. Knowing he does not love her, she agrees to go, but refuses to marry him. He treats her coldly for several weeks, which eventually wears down her willpower.

One evening when she is about to give in, Jane hears Edward's voice calling her name across the moors. She visits Thornfield Hall, which is burnt to the ground. The local innkeeper tells her that Bertha Mason started the fire, then jumped off the parapet to her death. Edward had been blinded and maimed while trying to save Bertha. Jane finds Edward living at Ferndean Manor, his second home. He is a changed man, living only for the memory of his true love. They marry and have a son. Happiness helps restore his sight. They place Adèle in a good school and act as her parents. St. John's sisters marry well, but St. John dies of fever in India.

Analysis:

Race prejudice plays a fundamental role in the plot of *Jane Eyre*, though the word *race* is used differently in the book than we use it today. In 1847, the term was broad; it meant "a group of people, a nation or tribe with a common cultural or linguistic inheritance, or a category of humans who shared a particular trait" (Betensky). To the early Victorians, *race* was such a flexible term that it could denote race as we speak of it today, or color, or ethnicity, or religion, or profession, or families, or persons from a specific geographic area, even one that is comparatively small, such as a particular English county. For instance, Yorkshire people were, and continue to be, classified as a particular type. In *Jane Eyre*, Brontë uses the word *race* to denote mental kinship between characters such as Jane and Edward, and also to signify one's family, one's profession, or one's social breeding. For example, Mrs. Fairfax uses "race" to mean family, telling Jane that the Rochesters "had been a violent race" (125). St. John uses the word *race* to denote the human species when he says that missionaries share the glorious ambition of "bettering their race" (431). Mrs. Dent uses *race* derogatorily toward a particular subspecies of the working class, governesses, when she calls them "that anathematized race" (205). Edward tells Jane that the Masons accepted him as Bertha's betrothed because "he was of a good race," and the Penguin endnote by Stevie Davies explains that Edward might mean *either* of good breeding *or* of European race (352, 580). In this and other instances, the reader remains uncertain of the Masons' skin color and ethnicity, but Edward's expressions make clear that he considers them to belong to a particular group of people—colonials—who are corrupt and have degenerated from their "pure" English origins. Thus, their social status "darkens" the impression that Edward and other colonizers receive, insofar as he degrades and down-classes them vis-à-vis his own social position.

Rather than racializing the identities of others, the characters of this novel use shades of skin color to distinguish between themselves and others. Brontë was a great reader who imbibed the popular science and racial prejudices of her time. She doesn't simply buy into a racial hierarchy where white people are superior to all others. Instead, she mixes her middle-class Victorian racial biases with a trendy fascination for exotic "darkness." Her exoticism is derived from the Romantics and their Orientalist notions by which non–Western people are both exoticized for their difference and denigrated for their supposed lack of civilization. Notably, the two characters who flaunt these Orientalist tastes are Edward Rochester and Blanche Ingram, whose wit and erudition are meant to display that they are up to date with the latest intellectual fashion. A pretended attraction to the dark Other is trendy with their set, but Edward's actual experience with Bertha Mason proves him completely unaccepting of the racial, ethnic, or geographic Other. Blanche, on the other hand, uses daring sexual references to dark races and dark deeds as a way of flirting, such as "know that I dote on Corsairs" and "I like black Bothwell [a murderer] … to my mind a man is nothing without a spice of the devil" (298, 297). She calculates her remarks to match Rochester's devilish spirit, but it does not signify that she actually wants an interracial marriage or an affair with a murderer. Rochester, in turn, plays the Orientalist game when he dresses up as an Eastern emir in the charade, and as Mother Bunch, the dark-skinned gypsy who comes to tell fortunes. Color preference is also seen in the contrasts between health and sickness. For Jane and Edward, white doesn't always mean healthy, just as non-white doesn't always mean corrupt. "Sallow complexion" is shorthand, in Victorian literature, for a person with questionable morals. Jane's moral preferences are made clear when she presents physical descriptions upon introducing each new character. Jane's colorist biases combine with phrenological categorizations that help her to place people on a scale of moral worth.

Phrenology, established in the 1790s by Franz Gall and brought to Britain by George Combe, was an extremely popular pseudo-science that was taken seriously by most people in the mid- to late Victorian era. Phrenologists claimed that bumps on the skull were indices of character and abilities. Brontë's acceptance of phrenology was not unusual: "Phrenology was familiar to everyone and accepted by many; it was one of the most widespread sciences in Britain, which is remarkable considering that it was practiced by ordinary people rather than anyone who made professional or institutional claims to expertise" (Steinbach 239). Combe's *Constitution of Man Considered in Relation to External Objects* (1838) was a bestseller and one of the most influential publications of the century; it is clear from Brontë's references to phrenology in the novel that she read it. Combe claimed that the size of various regions of the brain (which is divided into thirty-five "organs") determines a person's behavior and moral stature. Jane often refers to "organs of the brain" as the source of character traits such as curiosity, admiration, and benevolence. Edward also buys into phrenology; when noticing her ability to form an instant bond of affection with Adèle and Mrs. Fairfax, he compliments Jane's "organ of Adhesiveness," the basis of friendship and attachment (288).

Closely related to phrenology is the pseudo-science of physiognomy—the reading of various facial features to denote moral characteristics or propensities. Physiognomy dates back to the ancient Greeks and was still popular during Brontë's time. Jane's habit of describing facial features such as brows and chins indicates her familiarity with the science of physiognomy. Whenever Jane meets a new person, Brontë provides a description of facial features. Particularly noteworthy among meaningful features are low brows and protruding jaws. Lady Ingram and her daughter Blanche have low brows, which denote moral and intellectual degradation. The protruding or hard jaws of Bertha Mason, Georgiana, and Mrs. Reed denote their apish nature caused by inbreeding or low breeding (549). In contrast, the high brows of St. John and Miss Maria Temple are associated with intelligence and goodness. A white high brow is indicative of purity and spiritual ambition. Phrenology and physiognomy were taken seriously during Brontë's time. Both theories were widely used to justify racist views and practices, whether in courts of law, doctors' offices, or social circles. Using physical appearance to categorize and judge others perpetuated the prejudices of the day.

To categorize Jane's (and the author's) colorist, phrenological, and physiognomic biases and Orientalizing propensities, I've made a chart that is divided into three "color" types: white, dark, and in-between (usually sallow, which is variously defined as grey, light brown, or yellowish). Since Jane introduces each character with a color and physiognomic description, then proceeds to delineate their moral and psychological propensities, we may assume that the physical categories of color and physiognomy signify to her the moral character of each person she meets. The chart illuminates biases and stereotypes found in this particular Victorian text and may shed light on our current discourses around racism. Jane's ways of thinking about difference are similar to racism because she essentializes categories of human beings based on the arbitrary markers of color and facial features.

I. Whiteness. White skin color is associated with goodness in the novel, though dark tresses are preferred to blonde.*

1. *Maria Temple* is the benevolent headmistress of Lowood School. On many occasions she acts as Jane's savior. Maria helps Jane clear her reputation after Brocklehurst's slander. Maria demonstrates what teacherly love should look like, inviting emaciated Helen and Jane for tea and cake to reward them for their studies, and carrying on an enlightening conversation about books. Maria lends Helen her own room so that she can die with dignity. Jane feels her "organ of veneration" operating whenever she admires Miss Temple (56). The teacher is tall, dark, and slender—as are all the beautiful ladies in the book—but her intelligence is characterized by her "pale and large forehead" (52). Stevie Davies, annotator of the Penguin edition, remarks that Maria's surname, Temple, is associated with "a sacred sanctuary" (550). Her high white forehead appears to Jane to be the repository of her sanctity.

2. *Diana Rivers* is another benevolent lady who rescues Jane from starvation and educates her. As with Miss Temple, Jane stands in awe of Diana's kindness and positive energy. Diana is the elder of two sisters. (Two sisters and a brother is a favorite sibling configuration in the novel. Other sets are John, Georgiana, and Eliza Reed; and Lord, Blanche, and Mary Ingram. Brontë's own sibling set was composed of three sisters and a brother, after two other sisters died in childhood.) Diana is both stronger-willed and warmer than her reserved sister, Mary. Perhaps her most helpful act is encouraging Jane to resist marriage to St. John. When she first approaches the Rivers house, Jane sees Diana and Mary, framed by their sitting room window, as a picture of domestic bliss. The women are genuinely caring, patient, and studious. They love their home, and don't hesitate to quit their jobs and return to it once Jane comes into money. Diana is "fair complexioned and slenderly made" with a face "full of distinction and intelligence" (384). She enjoys vigorous health: "in her animal spirits there was an affluence of life and certainty of flow, such as excited my wonder" (403).

---

* In early to mid-Victorian times, it was fashionable for a woman to have dark brown hair, whereas blonde hair became chic in the 1880s. Dark brown hair was said to be indicative of "a loyal temperament that cannot be shaken by ill fortune"—an accurate description of Jane's character, as well as Maria and Diana's ("Victorian"). Rochester described Jane's hair as "hazel," which would imply brown with green or amber tints. This implies that Jane is not the perfect beauty of the time, a judgment which is in accordance with her own perception of herself. Rochester learns to love loyalty over beauty; Jane's loyalty transforms her appearance—to him—into beauty.

3. *Rosamond Oliver* has the kind of peaches-and-cream English complexion that an average Englishman (unlike Romantic types such as Edward) finds attractive. Her male counterpart in beauty is St. John, whose features closely resemble the Greek ideal. Like Adèle Varens, Rosamond is aware of her feminine power to attract people and is relatively shallow intellectually, but because of her careful upbringing and good social position, she matures into a companion whom Jane approves. Rosamond enjoys a stainless reputation, suggested by her "white, smooth forehead, which adds such repose to the livelier beauties of tint and ray" (418). Although initially in love with St. John, she finds a far more appropriate match in a titled gentleman from Sheffield.

4. *St. John Rivers* is a perfect specimen of classical male beauty. He has the requisite physiognomy for his upright, stainless character and noble ambition: "His face riveted the eye; it was like a Greek face, very pure in outline" (396). Jane instinctively compares herself: "He might well be a little shocked at the irregularity of my lineaments, his own being so harmonious." Neither Jane nor Edward Rochester shares the category of pure whiteness with these other characters. This signifies two things: first, that Brontë, like her sister Emily, prefers a bit of Romantic rebelliousness in her characters; second, that both Jane and Edward have some growing up to do before reaching maturity. Their growth will purge them of their unruly passions by channeling them into appropriate married love. St. John's coloring is light, as near to white as human skin can be: "His eyes were large and blue, with brown lashes; his high forehead, colourless as ivory, was partially streaked over by careless locks of fair hair" (396). The "colorlessness" of his forehead suggests that not one thought of his—at least at the time she meets him—could be considered ignoble. Later, Jane will realize that his nobility is intellectual and not emotional. He is the color of ivory and has the coldness of marble. St. John Rivers' innermost character is different from what his beautiful features suggest; in an opposite way, Edward Rochester's innermost character is different (and better) than what his ugly features and behavior often suggest. These contradictory discoveries don't, however, put Jane off her pursuit of physiognomic insights.

II. Darkness. In this novel, darkness can be a playful, flirty quality with Orientalist undertones, but Brontë also uses it to denote the madness and violence of a Bertha Mason.

1. *Edward Rochester* is a Romantic sensualist who needs taming, at least within the moral economy of the Victorian woman's novel. Unlike St. John's white temple of a forehead, Edward's olive-hued forehead contains many impure thoughts and memories of past mistakes. His strong libido (and anger at his father's treatment) led him into numerous sexual affairs

with mistresses of various European and non–European races. Given his past, it would be impossible for his forehead to be high and white. Yet Jane sees him as a singularly compelling man:

> My master's colourless, olive face, square, massive brow, broad and jetty eyebrows, deep eyes, strong features, firm, grim mouth—all energy, decision, will—were not beautiful, according to rule; but they were more than beautiful to me: they were full of an interest, an influence that quite mastered me—that took my feelings from my own power and fettered them in his [203].

Jane's response to her master is erotically charged, and she feels both "fettered" and "full of interest." His face is a hybrid of the features that physiognomy calls good and bad—he has the deep eyes, strong features, and dark hair of the good, virile type, but the grim mouth, massive brow, and olive complexion of the bad, suspicious type. Because his coloring is the oxymoronic "colourless olive," I suspect that *colourless* has a metaphorical meaning that isn't strictly about whiteness. Rather, it is the trait he shares with St. John Rivers, who also sports a colorless forehead. Whereas St. John's colorlessness denotes his relative purity (he has briefly harbored fantasies about Rosamond but allows himself only fifteen minutes for the exercise), I think Edward's colorless forehead denotes the potential for correction. Edward's love of Jane is quite pure; he loves her kindred spirit. Although in the past Edward has led a *colorful* life of affairs with women of many countries, his conversion to a remorseful, humbled, and "pure" man is complete by the time Jane returns from Marsh End. After the loss of Jane and Bertha, Edward's brain will gradually live up to the "colourless" purity that Jane's hybrid description suggests him capable of achieving. Edward's olive complexion links him with Bertha Mason and Blanche Ingram as an attractive, romantic, and adventurous character. For the British, there is a hint of sexuality in olive skin that these three main characters share.

2. *Blanche Ingram*: Though her first name means *white*, Blanche is "dark as a Spaniard," and "big, brown and buxom as the ladies of Carthage" (201, 253). Blanche is Edward's match in flirtatious wit, musical talent, and good breeding, but, unlike him, she is shallow and selfish. Her above-quoted comments about Corsairs and murderers suggest that she understands how to pique a man's sexual interest. She is more interested in Edward for the money she thinks he possesses than for the sexual charisma of his ugly but powerful presence. Jane places Blanche in a distinct moral category beneath her own: "Miss Ingram was a mark beneath jealousy; she was too inferior to excite the feeling … her mind was poor, her heart barren … she was not good; she was not original; she never offered, nor had, an opinion of her own" (215–16). So Blanche might be brown on

the outside, but she is void, or "blanched," on the inside. Yet Edward was attracted to her type, which he revealed when describing Bertha as similar in appearance to Blanche.

3. *Bertha Mason* is a Creole woman whose natural skin color (when not enraged) remains unstated. When Jane first sees her rending the bridal veil in her bedchamber, she says, "It was a discoloured face—it was a savage face. I wish I could forget the roll of the red eyes and the fearful blackened inflation of the lineaments!" (327). Stevie Davies's footnote (Penguin edition) indicates that these words "evoke a black person" and that Bertha has the facial attributes of "a maniac" (577). Bertha's features and complexion are transfigured by her bad diet, lack of exercise, rage, and madness. Her face is purple, her lips are swelled and dark, her brow is furrowed, and her visage reminds Jane of a vampire. We do not know, from this or other descriptions by Edward and Jane, whether Bertha is Black, white, or mixed race. Was Brontë reluctant to reveal her race prejudice, or did she intentionally equate madness with blackness? We don't know. If Brontë had moral qualms about making mad Bertha a Black woman, perhaps she allayed them by making her into a bestial figure of destruction instead. When Jane meets her in the attic, she describes Bertha as a non-gendered beast: "*it* grovelled, seemingly, on all fours; *it* snatched and growled like some strange wild animal; but *it* was covered with clothing, and a quantity of dark, grizzled hair, wild as a mane, hid *its* head and face" (338, italics added). When it comes to Bertha, the positive attributes of dark hair have vanished, and it becomes synonymous with animal hair, "wild as a mane." The forehead, which is so important for describing the moral value of the other characters, is hidden by the creature's "mane." Bertha is the degradation, the lowest possible specimen, of the "dark type" that Edward has favored in his love choices.

III. In-betweenness. This is a liminal or hybrid category for characters who don't commit sins or crimes but who lack vitality. They appear sickly and sallow skinned. Richard Mason and Eliza Reed are sallow. This liminal category suggests the ambiguities and paradoxes of skin color as a means of classifying people's moral value. Hybridity dismantles the clarity of Jane's color chart.

1. *Richard Mason* is a curious character who elicits a strong response from Jane and Edward. He is a coward—though he entered Bertha's chamber, he didn't at that time know that she was violent. At Edward and Jane's wedding, he hides in the shadows until his solicitor paves the way for his announcement. He is racially ambiguous, causing Rochester difficulty in placing and trusting him. He is one example of the sallow-faced character type common in Victorian fiction. "Sallow" is from the Old

German *salo*, meaning murky or dirty or gray. In modern English, it means of a sickly yellowish or light brown color. Since its actual hue varies so much in definitions, the word seems to denote a quality more of sickliness than of color. In Victorian texts it signifies moral degeneracy or deficiency of *élan vital*. Jane notes the paradox of Richard's simultaneous attractiveness and repulsiveness: "[You] detected something in his face that displeased," a laxness—"the life looking out of [the eye] was a tame, vacant life" (220). Though ladies admired him, there is something repulsive about Mason—possibly his colonial status. The text suggests he's an Englishman who has inherited wealth from his father's Jamaica sugar plantation, but whose life in the tropics has destroyed his moral character. Rochester doesn't see him as a white man, or one belonging to the same English "race" as himself.

In giving this colonial man a strange accent and displeasing face, Brontë betrays a common prejudice of her time and place. As Steinbach explains, Victorians reserved a special opprobrium for colonial whites: "Once in Britain their skin color allowed these 'fictive Europeans' to move across Britain more freely than people of color, but their colonial accents marked them as socially subordinate, and the British often did not consider white colonials British" (71). Mason is unplaceable, being almost, but not quite, British. Jane notes his strange accent: "His manner was polite; his accent, in speaking, struck me as being somewhat unusual—not precisely foreign, but still not altogether English" (220). Richard Mason and his sister elicit distrust and scorn in Edward and Jane, who consider Richard repulsive and Bertha insane, perhaps due to their colonial Jamaican origins as much as their strange color (Richard sallow, Bertha discolored by rage).

2. *Eliza Reed* sports a sallow complexion and "severe mien," which Jane associates with her hard heart and misguided allegiance to the Catholic faith (263). In a long-standing tradition dating from before King Henry VIII, British Protestants (especially families of clergymen, such as the Brontës) despised Catholics, accusing them of superstition, barbarism, and simony. Brontë displays her dread of Catholics when she typecasts Eliza Reed as a selfish, misguided convert. When Jane visits Gateshead Hall to visit her dying aunt, Eliza's courtesy is merely perfunctory. Eliza derides her sister Georgiana's lazy character and shows no pity for their dying mother, Mrs. Reed. Instead, she looks forward to her mother's death since it will free her to join a French convent and disown her sister forever. Eliza fulfills her duties, but in a mechanical way; Jane believes she lacks the Christian virtues of charity and mercy. Jane's final verdict on Eliza is that "judgment untampered by feeling is too bitter and husky a morsel for human deglutition" (272). Jane can't "swallow" Eliza, just as Eliza never swallowed Jane as the good and charitable person she truly is. (Jane's

charity is amply underlined in this chapter, when she pities and forgives her uncharitable aunt.) With Eliza and St. John, Brontë gives us two negative religious characters to warn of the misuses to which religious fervor can be put. Both St. John and Eliza dedicate their lives to Christ yet are wanting in human sympathy. That St. John is a more attractive character than Eliza may be due to the separate (gendered) spheres in which they're allowed to operate. Manly St. John has a true vocation to convert Indians to Christianity, whereas Eliza, in her female sphere, will serve only herself by hiding from the secular world. For moral vacancy, Eliza merits a "sallow" classification on the color chart.

The "color" chart and physiognomic classifications of Brontë's characters reveal Victorian biases about race, national origin, class, and gender. *Colorism* is a term that means prejudice or discrimination against individuals with a darker skin tone than that of the speaker or person who is discriminating. Since there are no Black people in the text, Jane's categories belong instead to a colorist designation of moral value, in which whiteness denotes potential for moral goodness, darkness throws up a red flag of danger, and the greyness of sallow people denotes that they lack the vitality to be either white or dark—somewhat like Dante's "uncommitted" souls in Hell's vestibule, who neither chose nor rejected God. "Darkness" holds its Romantic charms, but in Rochester's case, exploration of exotic attraction can result only in tragedy and corruption.

Though she shares many of the unexamined prejudices of her times, Brontë endows disenfranchised people with various shades of meaning, rather than making categorical judgments based on their social and cultural origins. The reader follows Jane's progress in becoming a more tolerant person. Like other Victorian Bildungsroman heroines, Jane gains emotional maturity and loses harsh judgment when she becomes a woman. Some of her experiences soften her learned prejudices. For instance, she defends the right of the insane to compassionate treatment, and her departure from Thornfield is at least partially due to a repudiation of Edward's cruel treatment of Bertha: "Sir, you are inexorable for that unfortunate lady: you speak of her with hate—with vindictive antipathy. It is cruel—she cannot help being mad" (347). When Jane goes begging for a piece of bread and a roof to sleep under, she is rebuffed by Hannah, showing how harshly beggars are judged by people lucky enough to have food and shelter. Once recuperated, Jane gives Hannah a lesson about Christianity: "Some of the best people that ever lived have been as destitute as I am; and if you are a Christian, you ought not to consider poverty a crime" (393).

At the start of this lecture I asked, what is the role of race prejudice in *Jane Eyre*? There are no Black characters in the text, but I remarked upon early Victorians' use of the word *race* to include classes and individuals that share a particular trait. I found colorist attitudes among the white characters who judged others on the basis of their skin color, ranging from discolored (Bertha) to olive-complexioned to sallow to alabaster. Closely linked to a discourse of color were the uses of the pseudo-sciences (phrenology and physiognomy) to rank people on a social hierarchy. To answer the question, then—what we commonly call race prejudice today is expressed as an amalgam of color prejudice, nationalism, misogyny, and class snobbery in this Victorian novel. Thus, *Jane Eyre* is a good example of the principle of intersectionality; Bertha's potentially mixed-race, colonial-origin, hereditary-madness, and female identities result in many oppressions, including private incarceration and utter ostracism (except for the ministrations of Grace Poole). Colorism and other ways of stereotyping individuals negatively affect each of the relationships in the novel.

The next lecture will examine the question of race in *Jane Eyre* from the viewpoint of a Creole Caribbean writer. I use *Creole* here in the second sense given in my definition at the top of this lecture: a person of European descent born in the West Indies. Jean Rhys's father was a Welsh doctor and her mother a third-generation Dominican of Scots ancestry. Rhys writes a prequel to *Jane Eyre*, in which Bertha's account of her marriage and sojourn in Yorkshire is juxtaposed to Edward's. In *Wide Sargasso Sea*, race and color are the dominant issues of Rochester and Bertha's relationship, issues that were almost wholly repressed in Charlotte Brontë's rendition.

Works Cited

Betensky, Carolyn. "Casual Racism in Victorian Literature." *Victorian Literature and Culture* November 1, 2019. https://www.cambridge.org/core/journals/victorian-literature-and-culture/article/casual-racism-in-victorian-literature/

Brontë, Charlotte. *Jane Eyre*. Penguin, 2006.

Davies, Stevie. Introduction. *Jane Eyre*. Penguin, 2006. vii–xxx.

Steinbach, Susie. *Understanding the Victorians: Politics, Culture and Society in Nineteenth-Century Britain*. Routledge, 2012.

"Victorian and Edwardian Hair Care." http://www.sewhistorically.com/heat-hair-hair-color-victorian-and-edwardian-hair-care/. November 7, 2015.

4

Wide Sargasso Sea— Dark Secrets of the Caribbean: Hatred, Murder, Madness

Question:

Contagious hatred is the dominant theme of *Wide Sargasso Sea*. The word "hate" appears at least thirty-five times along with related words such as "menace," "hostility," and "contempt." Like a disease, hatred infects the characters and spreads from one to another. In the beginning, Black servants kill a white child. White plantation owner Annette eventually "catches" their hatred and tries to kill her own husband. Her daughter Antoinette catches the hatred and goes mad. Edward catches a virulent strain and vows lifelong vengeance against his wife. Differently from *Wide Sargasso Sea*, race hatred remains mostly off-stage in *Jane Eyre*; there are no characters of color, and the imperialism that enables Rochester's marriage to a Jamaican Creole and St. John's work in colonial India goes unremarked. In *Wide Sargasso Sea*, on the other hand, Rhys brings racism and colonialism center stage. What role does race hatred play in *Wide Sargasso Sea* and how does Rhys negotiate the challenge of fairly portraying the two sides, Black and white?

Synopsis:

Wide Sargasso Sea is a prequel to *Jane Eyre*, written 119 years after the publication of Charlotte Brontë's novel. The author is Jean Rhys, a white Creole born and raised in Dominica in the Windward Islands. Having experienced the aftermath of Caribbean colonialism, Rhys wanted

47

to explore why Bertha (who never speaks in *Jane Eyre*) would have gone mad. Whereas Brontë's protagonist comes of age in the decade 1800–1810, Rhys pushed the setting forward to 1839 because she wanted to examine the effects of emancipation on Jamaica's former slaves. Decades of Jamaican slave rebellions culminated in the Baptist War of 1831, the largest uprising in the British Caribbean. The Slavery Abolition Act (1833) stated that former slaves, though technically free, still owed four to six years of indentured servitude to their former masters. This extension of slavery caused further rebellion. The Act promised compensation to slave-owners for their loss of property, but many families never received these benefits. Antoinette's family was one of these, and her mother, Annette, *had* to remarry in order to survive.

Part I: Antoinette's childhood on Coulibri estate, Jamaica. Antoinette Cosway Mason, white island-born daughter of a deceased sugar plantation owner, is the narrator of Part I. She lives with her widowed mother, Annette, and younger brother, Pierre, at Coulibri. A few Blacks remain on the estate, including Christophine, a "blue-black" Martinique nursemaid who practices *obeah*, a form of black magic. Annette marries a wealthy widowed planter, Mr. Mason. One night, a Black mob sets fire to Pierre's room, killing the child. In her grief, Annette turns against Mr. Mason and tries to kill him. Before leaving his wife, he sets her up in a small house with two angry Black servants. The male servant takes advantage of Annette when she is drunk. Antoinette's nightmares suggest that this is an act of rape—and possibly that Antoinette was also raped in childhood by a Black man, or else that she foresees Edward's eventual use of sex to overpower her, "his face black with hatred" (54). Antoinette's multiple losses—of her innocence, her brother, her mother, and her home—result in a state of despair. She wishes for death. At this time, her stepfather arranges a marriage for her with Mr. Edward Rochester.

Part II: Honeymoon in Dominica, narrated alternately by Antoinette and Edward Rochester. The couple stay at Granbois, her mother's ancestral home. Antoinette loves Edward and hopes that marriage will cure her depression. Edward doesn't love her. His father chose her to be his son's bride only because she had a £30,000 dowry. Edward pulls away from Antoinette because the servants' surly behavior, and Antoinette's friendship with them, begin to alienate him. He receives a letter from Daniel Cosway, who claims to be Antoinette's half-brother. Daniel reveals that Antoinette is a liar, sleeps with her cousin Sandi, and has inherited her mother's madness. Antoinette asks Christophine for an aphrodisiac to make Edward love her. The drug makes him violently ill. Edward sleeps with the Black maid, Amélie, within Antoinette's hearing. Antoinette now turns into "Bertha," the madwoman we know from *Jane Eyre*. She lets herself go—neglecting her appearance, drinking, and swearing obscenities at Rochester. Edward takes Antoinette to Yorkshire, where he locks her up in the attic of Thornfield Hall.

Part III: Takes place at Thornfield Hall, narrated by Antoinette and Grace Poole. Antoinette is now certainly mad. She's not allowed to leave Thornfield Hall and doesn't believe she's in England. Edward avoids her and hires a local woman, Grace Poole, to guard her. On the nights when Grace Poole is inebriated, Antoinette steals the key and roams the mansion. She confuses Thornfield with her memories of Coulibri and Granbois. In her nightmares there are always burning houses, which she takes as a sign. Re-enacting the servants' torching of Coulibri, she burns down the house, thinking it will liberate her. She "flies" off the roof to her death, believing her wild hair will act as wings to save her.

Analysis:

In *Wide Sargasso Sea*, race hatred is a disease that destroys all love and breaks people down. For some, madness is the only refuge from hate, and madness is Antoinette's fate. In the final scene, mad Antoinette no longer knows who or where she is, but she has at least lost her hate. She can be aggressive (for instance, she bites her brother's hand), but she is not intent on Rochester's demise, as she was in *Jane Eyre*. In losing her identity, she loses the ability to hate, underlining the idea that identity, particularly racial identity, is often imbued with devastating hatred. In her madness, Rochester is only "that man who hates me," not the person to whom she owes her catastrophic demise (170). Finding an identity had been a struggle during her childhood because she identified with Black people. She loved and trusted her Black nursemaid, Christophine, and a Black friend, Tia, but distrusted her mother's white friends, and knew her mother was ashamed of her for becoming a "white nigger" (120). This was a term that Blacks used to denote impoverished former slave owners, whereas "real white people" had money (22). Although Christophine does care for Antoinette, this love can't be unconditional because of the race barrier. Antoinette doesn't turn her pain and alienation into hatred until the day that two mixed-race children taunt her in the streets of Spanish Town: "it was then that hate came to me" (45). When isolated at Granbois with Edward, Antoinette reclaims her identification with Blacks, which becomes especially clear in contrast to Edward's dislike and distrust of them. Antoinette likes "their smell, so warm and comforting," but Edward hates it (98). She feels she belongs by Christophine's side instead of Edward's: "This is my place and this is where I belong" (99). She believes that Christophine is her "only friend" (103).

Rather than love, Edward initially feels an attraction to Antoinette's "strangeness," but soon, this quality will become the very aspect that he despises (85). When he learns from Daniel Cosway that she might be partly Black, he codes that strangeness into a racial category, one which he merges with at least three other categories of difference: female sexuality, madness, and Creole origins. Conditioned by Victorian separate spheres ideology that demands that women should feel no passion, Edward despises the female sexual desire that he has awakened in Antoinette. He begins to attribute many racial stereotypes to his wife, such as lying (she's "uncertain about facts") and an exaggerated desire for sex. Edward suspects that secret miscegenation is the rule of the islands, even that Antoinette may be related to the wily Amélie, the younger house servant—"it's probable in this damn place" (115). After a few short weeks of honeymoon, he hates both his wife and the islands, and believes that race hatred—that is, Blacks' hatred of whites—is the underlying "secret" of the place (156). He believes that Antoinette knows this secret and that *obeah* is Blacks' use of poison to kill whites. He suspects that Blacks intend to kill all white islanders: "Always this talk of death. (Is she trying to tell me that is the secret of this place?)" (83). Edward believes that Christophine tried to poison him, though Rhys leaves the reader in the dark, knowing little more about the drug than Edward does, except for Christophine's warning that *obeah* "is not for *béké* [white man]. Bad, bad trouble come when *béké* meddle with that" (102). Either Christophine gave Antoinette an aphrodisiac that was too strong for Edward's white constitution, or it was a poison that would have killed him in a stronger dose.

One of the inexorable effects of the islands' colonial history is that race hatred continues long after emancipation. Memories are long, and most whites continue to have more money and property than Blacks. Rhys's genius is to depict the contagious nature of this hatred, its vicious cycle of revenge. No character is safe from its scourge. Annette and Antoinette both catch it, but Antoinette hates both the white planter class *and* the Blacks who killed her brother, leaving her with no strong social identification. Love of Edward briefly pauses Antoinette's hatred, but once he turns against her, they make hatred into a competition: "We'll see who hates best" (154). In the end, it is Edward who hates best. He uses the word "hate" twice as many times as Antoinette. His revenge is more powerful too, for he first creates a need in her for his loving, then deprives her of it (154). He knows this will break her, which is his reason for doing it. Inciting her madness is his revenge for her having hidden the fact of her mother's insanity. Edward is obsessed with various Victorian notions of "racial" purity having to do with color, national origin, and sanity.

The white characters generalize about Blackness; when speaking of

Black hatred, they assume all Black islanders harbor it. Both whites and Blacks cultivate an us-versus-them mentality in order to protect themselves. The Black indentured servants on the Coulibri estate, the Black "bay people" down the hill, and the Black servants and neighbors at Granbois pose a constant threat to the safety of Antoinette, Annette, and Edward. "The people here hate us," says Annette (29). "I knew that we were hated," says Antoinette (28). They poison Annette's horse and kill her son. The forest for which Granbois is named provides a good cover for machete-wielding killers and is perceived as "the green menace" by Edward (135). Gossip, danger, and the servants' mockery combine with Edward's prejudice to turn him into a hater. By the time he leaves Dominica, his hatred is absolute, spreading outwards and upwards from the people to the land and sky:

> I hated the mountains and the hills, the rivers and the rain. I hated the sunsets of whatever colour, I hated its beauty and its magic and the secret I would never know. I hated its indifference and the cruelty which was part of its loveliness. Above all I hated her [Antoinette]. For she belonged to the magic and the loveliness. She had left me thirsty and all my life would be thirst and longing for *what I had lost before I found it* [156, emphasis added].

"Longing for what I had lost" helps explain why Edward will be so attracted to Jane Eyre when he meets her, for she represents the innocence that he lost when he married Antoinette. At the same time, "before I found it [the magic and loveliness]" implies that, once he has known the beauty of the island and "dark" Antoinette, he will never be satisfied by other lovers. Before proposing to Jane, Rochester sleeps with several "tall, dark, and majestic" European mistresses, having a marked preference for olive-complexioned, dark-haired beauties—dark hair being a sign of beauty in early and mid-century Victorian England (see previous chapter, note 6). Dalliances with German, Italian, and French mistresses don't, however, turn out to be any more fulfilling for Edward than marriage to Antoinette Mason or flirtation with Blanche Ingram.

Rhys is a white author who rises to the inherent challenge of writing about race by giving space and credibility to Black characters Christophine and Daniel Cosway. While race hatred may seem to start with the Black characters and spread to the whites in this novel, in fact this is not precisely true. Rochester's sense of white superiority and race prejudice lay the foundation for his ability to return the hate. If Blacks transmit their hatred to whites in this novel, instead of the other way around, it is due to the historical reality of economic and political power imbalance. Two centuries of undergoing slavery and domination by the white plantocracy entrenched a sense of Black indignation. Years of rebellion taught them to regard all whites as their enemies and torching of their properties as the swiftest means of retaliation. Rhys sensitively represents both sides so that neither Black nor white is morally superior.

Though they inhabit different levels of the social hierarchy, yellow Daniel Cosway and white imperialist Edward Rochester have much in common, psychologically. Being younger sons of rejecting fathers, each nurtures a lifelong bitterness that he appeases by weaponizing race prejudice. The parallel psychological issues of the mixed-race and white character suggest that race prejudice can grow out of an individual sense of loss. The pain of having a rejecting family can easily turn to revenge against the racial Other, as wounded individuals project their pain onto the world. Planting suspicion in Edward's mind, Daniel Cosway is the catalyst for Edward's conversion to a hard-hearted monster. Daniel is a mysterious, racially ambiguous figure. He is a "yellow" color, the code for mixed-race Creole and the sallow hue that I described in the previous lecture as a sign, in British minds, of moral decay. Daniel's first letter to Edward reveals that he and Antoinette share the same white father, Old Man Cosway, but that Daniel's mother was Black. Plotting her own revenge, Amélie tells Edward that *both* Daniel's parents are "colored." If Old Man Cosway was mixed-race, this would mean that Antoinette is mixed-race and passing for white (99). Edward is only too ready to believe this, as he had already remarked her "long, sad, dark alien eyes. Creole of pure English descent she may be, but they are not English or European either" (61).

Using British fear of mixed blood as their strongest weapon, Amélie and Daniel combine to destroy Edward's marriage by "breaking him down," in the lingo of the island, until he cannot trust anyone. Daniel's motive is more specific than a generalized hatred of all whites (116). He has a personal vendetta against his father and Antoinette: "Vengeance is Mine," reads the poster on his kitchen wall (110). In Daniel's telling, Old Man Cosway loved his sister Antoinette better and left her half his estate. Daniel got nothing but small sums of hush money while Cosway Sr. was alive. Daniel was disgusted at his father's cavalier treatment of his several Black mistresses, whom he would abandon after impregnating. Daniel's condemnation of his father is couched in Christian terms; he considers himself a devout Christian and has been a preacher in Spanish Town. He says his father lacks mercy, truthfulness, piety, compassion, and humility: "haughty and proud like that—he walk like he own the earth" (111). Old Man Cosway disowned Daniel when he was sixteen. Lacking family, Daniel has turned into a vengeful gossip who pretends that his "truths" are meant to help other people and save the innocent. The reality is that he wishes to destroy Edward's marriage to Antoinette through racial and sexual innuendoes. He weaponizes white racial prejudice in order to achieve his own goal of hurting the sister who was favored by their father.

Edward Rochester too feels the bitterness of a father's abandonment. Daniel may not know this fact about Edward's personal life, but the reader can appreciate the similarity. Family wounds can devastate any individual's ability to trust. While Daniel suffered from a lower status in his family due to his father's notions of racial purity (it is implied that he prefers Antoinette because she is white), Edward's curse is being second-born. In a society that honors the law of primogeniture (the awarding of the family estate to the eldest son), Rochester's brother inherits Thornfield Hall, so Edward must seek a living elsewhere. In Edward's letter to his father, we see the tension between the rhetoric of a respectful English gentleman and the impassioned words of an embittered second son: "I have a modest competence now. I will never be a disgrace to you or to my dear brother the son you love" (63). Sibling rivalry creates anger toward his father, which Edward expresses sarcastically: "I have sold my soul or you have sold it, and after all is it such a bad bargain? ... The girl is beautiful" (64). Edward's cynicism and coldness toward his wife are traits that Christophine dislikes; she calls him "a damn hard man for a young man" (141). Like Daniel, Edward employs racism as a weapon to defend and justify himself. His prejudice against Creoles (discussed also in the previous lecture) serves to humiliate his wife and justify his emotional abandonment of her. The indeterminacy of Creoles' racial identity, the suspicion that their blood is "polluted" by miscegenation, activates British imperialist racism. Daniel is familiar with this British attitude and uses it to drive Edward from Antoinette with a few well-chosen words. It's not necessary for her to possess "Black features" in order for Edward to distrust her racial purity—sly rumors, different behaviors, and unusual tastes are enough. The fact that Antoinette likes and loves Black people is something that Edward can neither understand nor tolerate.

By comparing Daniel and Edward, I mean to show not only the reciprocity of their racism, but also the ways in which early family wounding might lead to a sense of homelessness, which in turn sets up the desire for an aspirational racial identity. In Amélie's words, Daniel "was a very superior man, always reading the Bible and [living] like white people" (109). When Edward asks what that means, she replies, "that he had a house like white people, with one room only for sitting in. That he had two pictures on the wall of his father and his mother" (109). The possession of a sitting room for reading and hosting guests is a coveted marker of English middle-class respectability. Daniel couldn't get approval from his father, so he seeks it from the society at large by trying to pass as a respectable white man. Likewise, to shore up his own status, Rochester seeks to establish his white superiority over the Black servants in Antoinette's house, as well as exerting his male privilege of controlling his wife by assault and confinement. Since he cannot be favorite son to his father, he compensates by usurping other powers granted by his racial, gendered, and national identity—an attempt to right the balance between himself and his older brother.

At the beginning of the lecture, I asked what role race hatred—a subject omitted from Brontë's text—plays in *Wide Sargasso Sea* and how Rhys negotiates the challenge of representing both sides of race conflict fairly. In my close reading, I noticed that hatred was the predominant emotion of the novel, and that it passed from character to character. Race hatred creates breakdowns in each person and every relationship. Antoinette and her mother break down into insanity—and in so doing they become vulnerable to sexual intercourse with inappropriate men. Edward breaks down morally, when his distrust of Antoinette and the islanders causes him to seek retaliation by having intercourse with their maid. Hatred drives him back to Yorkshire, carrying the burdensome secret that his cruel treatment of his wife led to her breakdown. Christophine's lifelong bond with Antoinette breaks when Edward fires her and reports her to the authorities for practicing obeah. Daniel Cosway is a malicious yellow-skinned man, a casualty of Old Man Cosway's lust and his racist, sexist presumption that plantation owners have rights over Black women's bodies. Daniel mixes a potent cocktail for Edward to drink, playing on Edward's English and male sense of superiority and his fear of the Other. During his honeymoon, Edward is frightened to see how close his lust comes to his hatred. After having sex with Antoinette, he thinks, "It was not a safe game to play—in that place. Desire, Hatred, Life, Death came very close in the darkness" (86). They go to bed in the knowledge that they could be murdered in their sleep, or even during the act of love itself. Edward's flirtation with the Caribbean and its beautiful Creole people is a dangerous dance with death. Hatred ruins the beauty of the island for Edward, for Antoinette, for their servants, and for all the rest of the Black, white, and mixed-race inhabitants.

Race hatred in this novel is not only a disease against which the characters' immunities are insufficient when their bodies and minds experience stress. It is also an epidemic that spreads throughout communities whose cultural institutions, such as colonialism, slavery, and patriarchy, provide favorable conditions for its growth.

Works Cited

Brontë, Charlotte. *Jane Eyre*. Penguin, 2006.
Rhys, Jean. *Wide Sargasso Sea*. Norton, 2016.

5

Race and Empire

Question:

In our time, we are conditioned to read fiction with an awareness of the prejudices of the author. Thackeray's viewpoint on middle- and upper-class Victorians' racism is tricky to pinpoint, partly because his satire of racism and imperialism is humorous; it seems to poke fun at the blindness and prejudice of the speaker. Besides providing entertainment, does Thackeray or his narrator's satire either resist or critique these institutions, and if so, how?

Synopsis:

Astute, pragmatic, and ruthless, Rebecca "Becky" Sharp is the daughter of a poor art teacher (father) and a French opera dancer (mother). She and Amelia "Emmy" Sedley are best friends at Miss Pinkerton's finishing school. When Amelia introduces Becky to her rich brother, Joseph ("Jos"), Becky immediately recognizes an opportunity and tries to wrest a marriage proposal out of him, but Jos, despite his self-aggrandizement, is fundamentally shy and cowardly. Since childhood, Amelia has been affianced to wealthy George Osborne Jr.—dashing, philandering Captain of the –th [*sic*] Regiment. Becky finds employment as governess at the estate of Sir Pitt Crawley, a debauched baronet. She flirts with Sir Pitt but marries his second son, Rawdon, an attractive swashbuckler and impecunious gambler. Becky sets out to improve their finances by flirting with other men to get gifts of jewels and money. All Crawley family members fawn on Sir Pitt's spinster sister, Miss Matilda Crawley, in hopes of inheriting her estate. Angered by Rawdon's marriage to a poor governess, Miss

Crawley bequeaths her estate to the eldest son instead, the pious Mr. Pitt Crawley Jr.

Napoleon's escape from Elba rattles the stock market, and Amelia's father loses all his money. George's loyal school friend, William Dobbin, convinces him that Amelia is a paragon of womanhood and that he must, in honor, marry her despite her misfortune. George marries Amelia over his father's objection and is promptly disinherited. George, Rawdon, and Dobbin are deployed to Brussels in preparation for war. Jos, Rebecca, and Amelia accompany them, enjoying grand balls while awaiting Napoleon's battalions. On the eve of the Battle of Waterloo, George asks Rebecca to run away with him, and she saves the *billet-doux* for later use. The next day, George is killed in battle. Amelia carries the torch for the next fifteen years. She dotes on little Georgy, their son, who grows up as spoiled and self-centered as his father. Dobbin supports the Sedley family with a small annuity. He is in love with Amelia, who thinks of him only as a friend. Dobbin and Jos move to Bengal. Rebecca has a son, Rawdon Jr., whom she neglects. She cultivates the Marquis de Steyne as a patron. Rawdon (her husband) initially accompanies her to parties as she tries to enter high society, but drops out when she takes Miss Briggs, Matilda's former servant, as lady's companion. Pitt Jr. marries the gullible Lady Jane Sheepshanks, who learns to distrust Becky when she witnesses her neglect of Rawdon Jr. and her flirtations with Pitt Jr. One night, Becky and the Marquis arrange to have Rawdon arrested for debt so that they can enjoy an evening of pleasure at home. Rawdon walks in on an intimate moment between them. He calls Steyne a liar and a villain, knocks him to the ground, and throws Becky's diamond necklace in his face. Rawdon and Steyne's seconds are able to prevent a duel. Steyne arranges for Rawdon to become Governor of Coventry Island, a colonial

William Makepeace Thackeray, by Jesse Harrison Whitehurst (1855).

outpost in South America where he will eventually die of yellow fever. Rawdon hands his son over to Lady Jane, and Amelia turns George over to the Osbornes so that he can have a gentleman's upbringing.

Amelia, Dobbin, and teenaged George Osborne Jr. vacation in Pumpernickel (Weimar, Germany) with Jos. They discover Becky making a meager living at the tables, sipping brandy at all hours, and flirting with various degenerate men. The narrator suggests there may be more than flirting. Amelia forgives Becky when the latter tells a story about how the Crawleys ripped her little Rawdon from her breast. Amelia invites Becky to live with her and Jos. When Dobbin balks at the proposal, reminding Amelia of her jealousy of Becky, Amelia becomes indignant and repudiates him. Dobbin accuses Amelia of not being good enough for him and leaves her. At the end of the season, Amelia relents and begs Dobbin's forgiveness, moments before Becky shows her the love note that George passed to her on the eve of Waterloo. This discovery of George's infidelity releases Amelia from her long dedication to an idealized memory of her husband and frees her to appreciate Dobbin's virtues. Amelia and Dobbin marry and have a daughter. Becky manipulates Jos into getting a life insurance policy with her name on it. He dies in suspicious circumstances, and she collects the money. She lives in Bath and Cheltenham but is snubbed by all her old acquaintances, including Dobbin and Amelia. Dobbin is no longer enamored of Amelia but is passionate about their daughter and about his writing project, *A History of the Punjab*.

Analysis:

In appearance and behavior, Jos Sedley, tax collector for Bengal's Boggley Wollah district, is the embodiment of Victorian imperialism. Fat, lazy, cowardly, selfish, foppish, and greedy, Jos is a provincial middle-class Englishman with no perspective on world politics or the existence of those outside his own class and nation. He thinks of his Indian servant as a more primitive version of a human and has no understanding of the opposite sex. In this caricature, Thackeray satirizes British imperialism, but he neither critiques the institution nor suggests an alternative. The text contains numerous instances of casual racism—defined as references to race and racialized characteristics that are incidental to the plot—that indicate Thackeray's participation in Victorian attitudes about the racialized Other. Thackeray's favorite racial targets are the Irish, Indians, Black Caribbeans, French, and Jews. The novelist provides no counterbalance to the characters' bigotry: he neither presents a nonwhite character's viewpoint nor defends an Irish, French, or Jewish person's opinion. Instead, he utilizes stock racial stereotypes to flatten all such characters, hoping to entertain readers who were accustomed to the casual racism in literature and conversation of their times.

Several critics have been interested in Thackeray's attitudes on the subjects of race and empire. I'll provide a brief review of the critical literature. Sandy Norton is perhaps the most forgiving. She believes that the narrator's stance toward racism is ambivalent: the role of the nonwhite characters is to "ridicule the white characters around them while at the same time revealing Thackeray's race and class prejudices" (126–7). Similarly, Corri Zoli says, "while critical of them, Thackeray does not intervene in Victorian discourses of race or empire" (425). Instead, the novelist playfully uses racist tropes because he does not want to alienate readers from their assumptions, though his exaggeration and typecasting "may undermine their beliefs" (426). Nor does Thackeray make a special case for the narrator's moral high ground, for the narrator is a self-admitted snob, like so many of the other characters. Zoli describes the narrator as both an insider and outsider to the English middle class. The narrator both satirizes and shares the beliefs and values of this group.

Charles Heglar remains on the fence about Thackeray's possible racism. His article focuses on Thackeray's treatment of Rhoda Swartz, the mixed-race St. Kitts heiress proposed by Osborne Sr. as a match for his son. Heglar sees Rhoda as an "intensifier of the theme that money is overvalued in Victorian society" (346). At first, she seems morally superior to the Osbornes and Sedleys because she genuinely cares for Amelia and doesn't hesitate to show her feelings. Once she marries into the peerage, however, she drops the bankrupt Amelia as quickly as white aristocrats had done. Since Thackeray's satire offers "no positive alternative to whoever or whatever is satirized negatively, we cannot know Thackeray's racial attitude" (337). I think, on the other hand, that we can, since Thackeray's attitudes are expressed in his nonfictional writings. In a letter to a friend describing his mixed-race niece's visit to London, Thackeray confessed to be ashamed (presumably by her color and illegitimacy) and was relieved when she left. Thackeray's father, Richmond, had a Eurasian mistress with whom he produced a child before his marriage to the author's mother. This fact appears to be something that William can't fully accept. Another indicator of Thackeray's racism is found in his travelogue, *The Irish Sketch Book* (1842). Like other middle-class Englishmen, Thackeray saw people of lower socioeconomic classes as morally inferior to those of the middle and upper classes. Though moved by the sight of Irish poverty before and during the Famine, Thackeray was also repelled by it. Like others of his class, religion, and national origin, he was profoundly anti–Catholic. A visit to an Irish nunnery left him depressed, with a sense of wasted life. He shared Victorian Protestants' view of the Catholic religion—which they called "papacy"—as a pagan, superstitious practice.

Finally, Ed Wiltse focuses on Thackeray's descriptions in the Waterloo chapters as instances of British patriotism and xenophobia. The Battle of Waterloo was a source of immense pride and patriotism to British people. Wellington's victory still lives on in British consciousness, perpetuating national self-regard and exceptionalism. Addressing the surprise twist of the final section, in which Becky's popularity ebbs while Dobbin's moral heroism grows, Wiltse claims that Becky's French blood lowers her in comparison to Dobbin's full-blooded Englishness. Since Becky and Dobbin have similar class origins, the author must instead evaluate their worth according to their national origin—Becky's Frenchness and Dobbin's Englishness (Wiltse 54). Thackeray's patriotism makes Dobbin a characteristically British kind of hero—a good military officer, steadfast lover, chivalric helper of the fair sex—in other words, self-denying, loyal, faithful, generous, and courageous.

Casual racism permeates Victorian literature, in which novelists sprinkle racist epithets like the salt and pepper of everyday seasoning. *Casual racism* doesn't mean insignificant racism; it means gratuitous race references. Adjectival modifiers link to ethnic nouns as predictably as "wine-dark" goes with "sea" in Homer's *Odyssey*. Novelists regularly called Jews "dirty," blacks "dusky," French "depraved," Irish "superstitious," and Arabs "sensual." These epithets constituted a code for racist attitudes expected in the literature of the period. The expressions weren't reserved for satires, in which they might be understood as a condemnation of Britons' racism, but were also prevalent in melodramatic and dramatic genres, where the narrator delivered them straight, without any degree of distance. As we will see in the lecture on anti–Semitism in *Great Expectations*, some members of the targeted groups pushed back. A negative response from Jewish readers caused Dickens to excise many instances of the word "Jew" in later editions of *Oliver Twist*, though Fagin's ethnicity remained the essence of that figure.

Vanity Fair is no exception to this practice of casual racism; it even exceeds the norm, since the novel's geographical range is large, encompassing India, northern Europe, central Germany, Canada, and South America as settings and references. Characters are drawn from several geographical regions and what were understood to be distinct races and ethnicities: Black Caribbeans, Black Indians, and Arabs; also, French, Irish, and Jews. A brief background on Victorians' involvement with these groups of people helps us to understand the genesis of some of these attitudes.

I. **Black Caribbeans**. The British slave trade lasted for two and a half centuries, from the time of Queen Elizabeth's reign until George III's, when it was abolished by the Slave Trade Act of 1807. Initially, British traders supplied slaves to other nations, especially to Portugal and Spain for their colonies in the Caribbean and South America. Eventually Britain entered the competition for sugar, rum, cotton, and tobacco production, acquiring Barbados, Jamaica, and other West Indies islands for plantation of sugar cane. They sent enslaved people from Africa to work in their Caribbean colonies. In the eighteenth century, the transatlantic slave trade, or "Triangle Trade," between West Africa, the Americas, and European ports was the richest part of Britain's trade economy. By 1760, England led other European nations in the volume of its slave trade.*

Until about the 1840s, miscegenation among the white colonizer and the Black native (or slave) inhabitants was common, producing such mixed-race heiresses as Rhoda Swartz, whose father was a German Jew and mother a Black islander. The mixed-race offspring of these unions weren't accepted without prejudice by middle-class English people. As we saw in the *Jane Eyre* lecture, Rochester's racial and national prejudices arose immediately after marrying Antoinette, whose "race" was apparently white (albeit considered tainted because she was French), but whose upbringing by Black servants and whose poverty after the slave revolt had "sullied" her racial purity in the view of her middle-class Yorkshire husband. As Jean Rhys portrays him in *Wide Sargasso Sea*, Rochester was easy prey to Daniel Cosgrove's strategy to cast doubt about Antoinette's racial purity. *Vanity Fair*'s Rhoda Swartz, on the other hand, is visibly mixed-race but undeniably wealthy. Whereas Mr. Osborne Sr. confidently proposes her for his son's bride because he puts wealth before status, George and Mr. Sedley categorically refuse to consider intermarriage of the races. This does not make Mr. Osborne Sr. a better person in the narrator's view, only a greedier one.

Racial stereotypes like those held by George and Mr. Sedley are so well-known and well-accepted by Thackeray's audience that the mere mention of characters' names or provenance is enough to place them socially. This is why epithets are sufficient unto themselves to convey the ways in which nonwhite or non–English characters will be viewed. For instance, George rejects his father's proposal of Rhoda Swartz as a wife by saying, "I don't like the color, sir.... I'm not going to marry a Hottentot Venus" (240).

---

* "British Involvement in the Transatlantic Slave Trade." http://abolition.e2bn.org/slavery.

He's referring to a historical incident of the 1810s, when a Dutch business-man brought a Black South African woman to display in Piccadilly Circus as an example of physical racial differences. British cartoonists exaggerated the size of her buttocks so that she became known as the "Hotten-tot Venus," a racial/sexual slur meant to exoticize and hyper-sexualize all Black African women. George projects these "primitive" qualities onto Rhoda, even though she has the manners and costuming characteristic of young ladies with a London finishing school education, just like his betrothed, Amelia. He feels that the purity of his gentleman status would be threatened by any connection with a mixed-race Caribbean woman, regardless of her wealth.

 II. **"Black" Indians.** The Victorians would use the epithet to distin-guish those of the Indian "race" from the Anglo-Indians, white Britons who were born and bred in India. Before strictures against intermarriage, Anglo-Indians was also the name for offspring of mixed-race marriages between English and Indian partners. Until the early nineteenth century, the Caribbean was the most profitable part of the British Empire. After slave emancipation, India became Britain's richest colonial source of wealth, in the form of spices, textiles, and opium. Because of India's prominence in the empire, it was nicknamed the "Jewel in the Crown." The East India Com-pany had effectively controlled India from 1757 until 1848, at which point the British government assumed direct rule. The British Raj would last another ninety-one years, until 1947. Britain industrialized and "civilized" India by the introduction of railroads, bureaucracies, and educational institutions.

 Despite, or perhaps because of long-term residency in India and fre-quent interactions with Indians, most British colonizers regarded them as an inferior "race," considering them disorganized, dishonest, lazy, and sensual, as well as primitive, provincial, and superstitious. Casual racial epithets about native Indians abound in Thackeray's work; I will select one character as an example. Loll Jewab is Jos's personal valet, who accom-panies him from Bengal to England. Docking in Southampton, the crew and passengers lodge for a night at the George Inn. When Loll Jewab rises before his master to ready his clothes, the sight of him shocks some of the maids: "meeting the dark man in the passages, [they] shrieked, and mis-took him for the devil" (676). These young women are obviously unused to seeing dark-skinned persons in their place of employment, and their immediate association of dark skin with devilry is Thackeray's shorthand way of conveying profound racism—notably, without any comment on its moral tenor. In Brompton, Amelia's landlady suffers a similar "immense sensation" upon meeting Loll Jewab. Not used to the damp weather, he suffers from the cold, and this frightens her: "the shuddering native whose brown face was now livid with cold, and of the colour of a turkey's gizzard ... [was] shaking upon the hall-bench under the coats, moaning in a strange piteous way, and showing his yellow eyeballs and white teeth" (691–92). As discussed in the lecture on colorism in *Jane Eyre*, Victorians judged people by the color of their complexion; here, Loll's dark-red complexion, no less than his yellow eyeballs and white teeth is an indicator of his otherness. "White teeth" are an interesting anomaly, since the color usually associated by white racists with purity becomes, in the context of darker-skinned people's teeth, a sign of otherness.

III. Arabs. Britain's primary economic concern in the Middle East during the nineteenth century was preservation of sea and land routes to its most important colony, India. A land route from Britain through the eastern Mediterranean to the Arabian Sea was far more efficient than a sea route rounding the Cape of Good Hope in South Africa. Following the land route, British colonizers interfaced with people in several Middle Eastern countries. As early as the fifteenth century, a form of cultural imperialism arose, which Edward Said called *Orientalism*—a set of stereotyped portrayals of Islamic countries by which Westerners justified their imperialistic expansion. Travelogues, plays, histories, and novels stereotyped Middle Eastern people as lazy, irrational, sensual, despotic, primitive, and immoral. In *Vanity Fair*, the party scene during which Rebecca performs charades for British aristocrats contains several allusions to Orientalism. At the end of this lecture, I will analyze the charades' deployment of Orientalism to both titillate and frighten the white audience.

IV. Jews. Jewish people have lived and worked in England from the time of the Norman Conquest until the present day. Even during the period of Expulsion, from 1290 to 1656, crypto-Jews remained on the island. Thus, Victorians were familiar with Jews and dependent on their money-lending services; this is why references to them are frequent in Victorian novels. Partly from religious indoctrination, partly from historical distrust of moneylenders, and partly from visible physical differences, Victorian Protestants exaggerated differences that they understood to be "racial" and denigrated Jewish people. *Vanity Fair* is typical in pointing out the Jewishness of those characters associated with financial institutions and roles: the bailiffs are "inexorable Israelites" who seized the Dowager Gaunt's jewels and wardrobe; the creditors who threaten Rawdon are stereotyped as "Moses" or "Levy"; the Hebrew stockbrokers and buyers at the auction have "hooked beaks" and act like "vultures after a battle," according to Becky. In Chapter 53, Rawdon spends the night at "Mr. Moss's mansion in Cursitor Street," a sponging-house for debtors, so-named because the proprietors were known to sponge off their prisoners by charging exorbitant rates for food. There are several coded references to Mr. Moss's Jewishness, including his dark-haired daughter and red-haired son. Red hair was associated with endogamous groups, and red hair along with hooked noses was the shorthand indicator for Jewish characters in British literature. Thackeray repeatedly describes the sponging-house as *dirty*, an adjective long associated with anti–Semitism in the phrase "dirty Jew." The dirtiness of Mr. Moss's house contrasts with the splendor of its accouterments, suggesting that Mr. Moss greedily collects valuable assets from his clients, but because of his low moral status, neglects to keep them clean. Cleanliness is next to Godliness in Victorian ideology:

> Mr Moss's house, though somewhat *dirty*, was splendid throughout. There were *dirty* trays, and wine-coolers en permanence on the sideboard, huge *dirty* gilt cornices, with *dingy* yellow satin hangings to the barred windows … vast and *dirty* gilt picture-frames surrounding pieces sporting and sacred, all of which works were by the greatest masters; and fetched the greatest prices, too, in the bill transactions, in the course of which they were sold and bought over and over again [617, emphasis mine].

In this passage, the dirtiness of the furnishings implies the dirtiness or underhandedness of the money transactions by which they are acquired. To be bought and sold over and over again is the essence of other financial transactions—such as pawnbroking and moneylending—that Victorians associated with their idea of Jewish greed and immorality.

V. Irish. The history of anti–Irish sentiment among English Victorians is well documented. The English stereotyped the Irish as emotional, lazy, superstitious, hot-tempered, effeminate, stupid, and poor. These descriptions are meant to characterize the "papists" as deserving of the colonizers' depredations, such as absentee landlordism, tenant farmer evictions, the Penal Laws, and other practices which culminated in massive starvation during the Irish Potato Famine of 1845–49. Each of the racialized groups I've discussed receives many of the same epithets—laziness, immorality, and stupidity—which says more about the stereotypers than the stereotyped. These epithets represent traits that white Protestant Britons project onto the imagined racial Other. Humans make psychological projections because they are in denial about possessing the same traits in their own psyches. The English saw their national character as being rational, strong, dependable, loyal, and moral. To protect this fragile identity (for who among us can be so good?), they would project the opposite character traits onto groups of different "racial" origins. They define their own national character against others or opposites, needing a Shadow* persona outside of the self in which to deposit their own fears

---

* Carl Gustav Jung described the Shadow archetype as a repository for the psyche's negative images of itself. The psyche rejects (or abjects) these traits from the Self and projects them onto a racialized Other, which can be an individual or a whole race of individuals.

and self-doubts. Therefore, it is not surprising to see immorality, weakness, emotionalism, dishonesty, and unreliability among the racialized characteristics that Britons attribute to Arabs, Jews, Indians, Caribbean Blacks, Irish, and French. Because of their longer association with French, Jewish, and Irish people, British stereotypes of these groups tend to be more particularized and detailed than those of natives of the remoter colonies. From longer association, the British assume they know them better. Mrs. O'Dowd provides an interesting example of an ambivalence that Thackeray felt toward the Irish, for she is both ridiculously provincial and annoyingly garrulous, but also commendably generous and loyal to Amelia and Michael, her husband.

VI. **French.** British animus against the French is also potent and longstanding. France had been Britain's sworn enemy in military conflicts ever since the Norman Conquest of 1066. As with the Irish and Jews, religious difference fuels British bigotry against the French, ostensibly predicated on Catholicism's theological and cultural differences from British Protestantism, but actually more like racial prejudice than theological dispute. Many British people presumed that French Catholics behaved without concern for moral consequences because they could be exonerated from sin and punishment by the Catholic ritual of confession. Accordingly, the French-blooded Marquis de Steyne, whose name sounds like the "stain" of sin, is a shameless fornicator who manipulates women who are in need of money. Becky may have thought that flirtation alone—without sex—was enough to keep this wealthy man in her mermaid's net, but she judged inaccurately. Steyne's abuse of his female relatives underscores his disdain for women. His cruel nature is on display when he tells his daughter-in-law that her only purpose is to produce heirs; nobody likes her, and her opinions are worth nothing in his house. Becky's thieving French maid is another example of the low morals typical of the French, according to English bigotry. And Becky herself is undone by the French blood flowing through her own veins, which makes her Bohemian at heart, and quite happy, in Pumpernickel and elsewhere, living the roving lifestyle of a gambling, whoring trollop.

Orientalism and Typecasting in the Charades Chapter

In Chapter 51, "In which a Charade is acted which may or may not Puzzle the Reader," Thackeray exoticizes Becky as a Greek mythological figure who is willing to kill her husband for the sake of her lover. Clytemnestra's murder of Agamemnon acts as a metaphor for Becky's moral "murdering" of Rawdon and her sacrifice of their marriage. One may also argue that her actions lead to his death because she instigates his posting to the pestilential Coventry Island. The charade also foreshadows Becky's killing of Jos so that she can collect insurance money. Lord Steyne and His Royal Highness the Prince Regent (the real-life George Augustus Frederick was seen by many as debauched and immoral) are particularly excited by Becky's convincing portrayal of Clytemnestra, and Steyne takes it as evidence that she will sleep with him and betray Rawdon: "By ---, she'd do it too," he said after the performance (598).

As wicked as Becky's role is in the first charade as Clytemnestra, her performance as the victimized Philomela in the second is the reverse, for Philomela is a Greek mythological figure who is raped and has her tongue cut out by her sister's husband. Metamorphosized into a nightingale, she sings beautifully of her tragedy. But rather than express the horror of the rape and mayhem, Becky sings her song from *Le Rossignol* in an "innocent and youthful" manner, and her air of girlishness earns approval from the Prince, the Marquis, and other noblemen. Underlying their attraction to Becky is the Freudian virgin/whore complex, in which men make their lovers into either the virgin or the whore because they feel a strong Oedipal need to separate "motherly" nurturance from female sexual desire. But Becky offers double satisfaction, playing each role sequentially. The combination proves irresistible to the debauched tastes and mental instability of members of the Hanoverian line and the Steyne family. Her erotic charms outshine even the beauty of the prettier Mrs. Winkworth who had played the concubine in the first charade. Becky reigns as queen of the night—her last enchanted moment before an inexorable fall.

The chapter title is intriguing ("Charade … may Puzzle the Reader"), as it does not specify which of the charades is more puzzling, leaving us to speculate whether it is Becky as murderess or Becky as rape victim that should surprise us. In retrospect, neither role is out of character, as seen in the many performances that she stages in her quest to find financial and social stability. In dalliances with various powerful men, she repeatedly sacrifices her husband's honor. The narrator hints that she also kills Jos. But Becky doesn't see herself as evil. In fact, she frequently portrays herself as a victim, as when she describes to Pitt the events leading to Steyne and Rawdon's confrontation, or when she explains to Amelia why Rawdon Jr. no longer lives with her.

The charades foreshadow Becky's betrayals and also provide interesting cultural information about ways in which the British middle and upper classes Orientalized the myths and legends of the eastern Mediterranean. By exoticizing her identity and behavior, the charades both denigrate and glamorize Becky. In myth, Clytemnestra conspires with her lover, Aegisthus, to murder her husband, Agamemnon, upon his return from the Trojan War. Paralleling Becky with Clytemnestra gives the act of spouse-killing a mythological allure. Transposing an ambitious woman's ugly deeds to a literary rendering in a distant setting may function to remove her behavior from British moral norms. This distancing may momentarily distract the reader from the legend's very real application to her current intrigue with Lord Steyne, even though he and the Prince immediately interpret her character's willingness to murder as a sign of Becky's sexual availability to themselves. In their minds, she "kills" Rawdon on stage to show that she's willing to betray him sexually with them.

Fundamental to Britons' othering of the East is their sense of strangeness about the Islamic religion. One of the most alien features to them is polygamy; by traditional law, Muslims may be married to several women at once. In the charades, the Aga's possession of concubines is considered exotic. Combined with implications of his sadism, the Aga's promiscuity frightens, but also titillates, the English audience. The elaborately costumed players and their rich tableaux highlight the exotic accouterments and practices of this "strange" religion, Islam. In the first charade, the "true believers" still wear the immense plumed headdress of yore. In the second, the Turks turn their heads eastward at sunrise and bow to the sand, a Muslim prayer ritual. Despite their piety, the officers of the Ottoman Empire are deemed particularly cruel. Thackeray utilizes two Orientalist myths, which the notes to the Penguin edition claim are not based in fact (844, 851). The curtain falls just when Kislar Aga, grinning horribly, pulls out a bowstring. According to myth, the Sultan's henchmen used bowstrings as garrotes for strangling victims at his command (597). The Kislar Aga is about to kill the Hassan, who cries "mercy" when the curtain falls. The second myth is that the Sultan punishes the concubines who displease him by having them sewn into sacks and dumped into the Nile. The ladies in the audience whisper that Bedwin Sand's Black slave (whom they find "hideous") has "tilted ever so many odalisques" into the Nile (596). Epithets attached to the Aga include "odious Mahometan," "obdurate Hassan," and the "Turkish voluptuary," while the Black slave is "hideous," "unprepossessing" and, in the role of Kislar Aga, filled with "ghastly joy" when about to kill the Pasha (596, 597). Myths about Black violence and Turkish cruelty merge in this scene of Oriental terror. Yet the fear of death is intertwined with the sexual attractiveness of the new concubine, Zuleika, who sinks to the floor in "an attitude of most beautiful despair" at the thought of her prostitution, for she has been sold to the Aga as a sex slave (597). Playing to another myth about female sexuality, the next scene has her "perfectly reconciled" to her "Hassan," as though his masterful sexual performance has completely satisfied her. The scenes combine sexist, racist, and specifically Orientalist myths to simultaneously scare and attract the white British audience.

Conclusion:

In reviewing examples of racial epithets attached to several groups of people, I conclude, with most other critics, that Thackeray depicts racism and imperialism satirically but without casting moral judgment on the perpetrators. His narrator shares with other characters a sense of English superiority to nonwhite and non–English Others. This view underpins England's justification for imperialism—the white man's burden is to civilize the heathens—about which Thackeray has nothing morally negative to say. Thackeray is more critical of class distinctions than those based on race, but his narrator admits that he himself is a class snob. This class snobbery is the object of the author's most trenchant satire, but the narrator, who is very close to the author, repeatedly tells the reader in direct address that all humans share the desire to better themselves at the expense of others. Amelia and Dobbin alone escape this characterization, though they do harbor other vain desires. Even with its conventional ending of marriage between two good people, the expected contentment of the partners is undermined by Dobbin's falling out of love with Amelia. This unexpected element is Thackeray's last attempt to prove his thesis that all humans are alike—even "good" ones—in their weakness and in the futility of their desires. It would require a more optimistic or idealistic Victorian than Thackeray to challenge the status quo of racial, sexual, and national prejudices of his time.

Works Cited

Heglar, Charles. "Rhoda Swartz in *Vanity Fair*: A Doll Without Admirers." *CLA Journal* 37.3 (1994). 336–47.
Norton, Sandy Morey. "The Ex-Collector of Boggley-Wollah: Colonialism in the Empire of *Vanity Fair*." *Narrative* 1:2 (1993). 124–137.
Said, Edward W. *Orientalism*. Vintage, 1979.
Thackeray, William Makepeace. *Vanity Fair*. Penguin, 2001.
Wiltse, Ed. "'The shout of the beef-eating British': Nation and Genre in *Vanity Fair*." *CEA Critic* 67.3 (2005). 41–64.
Zoli, Corri. "Black Holes of Calcutta and London." *Victorian Literature and Culture* 35.2 (2007). 417–449.

6

Aporia, Metafiction, and the Narrator

Question:

The narrator plays a prominent role in *Vanity Fair* as commentator, moralist, satirist, and participant, using direct address to the reader and other metafictional elements. Though he often contradicts himself, are we able to discern a moral character in this narrator? What might be Thackeray's purpose in making the narrator's observations contradictory?

Analysis:

Fiction narrators carry the burden of translating the characters' actions into meaning. Depending on how omniscient, intrusive, or objective the author wishes their narrator to be, this character—who is both a storyteller and something more—usually provides a guide to the moral messages of the text. Genre conventions determine the role a narrator will play, and metafictional narrators may speak directly to their readers. For instance, the narrator of John Bunyan's allegorical *Pilgrim's Progress* (1678) plays the role of preacher to the reader. He explains the moral meaning of Christian's journey, frequently citing scripture as his tale directly illustrates the Bible's teachings. He clearly states in direct address that his purpose is to improve the reader: "May I not write in such a style as this? / In such a method, too, and yet not miss / My end—thy good?" (4). In another metafictional novel, the narrator of Laurence Sterne's *Tristram Shandy* (1759) also directly addresses the reader and comments on the nature of the text. But this narrator's purpose is to entertain, rather than to preach. In the dedication to Mr. Pitt, the author states that his purpose is to create mirth, because laughing has the effect of lengthening one's life span. He writes, "if I am ever told, it has made you smile; or can conceive it has beguiled you of one moment's pain—I shall think myself as happy as a minister of state" (2). (I wonder if Sterne intended to raise the question whether a minister of state is capable of being happy, given the burdens of such a job.) *Vanity Fair*'s narrator seems to combine these two purposes, to teach and to entertain, but the didactic function is ambiguous.

In addition to their memorable narrators, *Pilgrim's Progress* and *Tristram Shandy* are central to Thackeray's conception of his own novel in other ways. He borrows his title from a section in Bunyan's allegory (which some critics consider the first English novel) in which Christian and Faithful offend the merchants of Vanity Fair because they won't buy any of the things on offer, including preferment, titles, social status, and the services of prostitutes. For their offense, they go to trial, and Faithful is punished for his honest defense by torture and death, while Christian remains free to continue his journey through terrestrial places before his own ascension to heaven. Thackeray's adoption of the setting and concept of Bunyan's text is both serious and comic, for Thackeray's novelistic world is bereft of a God and of true believers, even though there are plenty of characters who pose as believers for purposes of social advancement. The serious side of the Bunyan allusion is the fact that Thackeray's narrator does condemn—albeit lightly, satirically, and sympathetically—the vanities of his own characters. "*Vanitas Vanitatum, omnia vanitas*"—Vanity of vanities, all is vanity (*Ecclesiastes* 1:2)—the quotation, with its reference to Bunyan's fair, opens and closes Thackeray's novel. Thackeray reaps both comedic and dramatic value from the literary comparison to Bunyan, as James Joyce draws both inspiration and comedy from *Ulysses*'s implied comparison to Homer's *Odyssey*.

In style, Thackeray's novel resembles *Tristram Shandy* far more than *Pilgrim's Progress* because of the frequent intrusions of its comical narrator. Both Sterne and Thackeray use metafictional devices to comment upon the conventions of genre and the relationship between fiction and life. Metafiction calls attention to the constructedness of fiction, using direct address to the reader and remarking on the difficulties of obeying generic conventions. Metafictional narrators seem to be striving to crawl out of their fictions and talk to us directly about their own feelings, yet at the same time, their apparent honesty is subject to the same biases, blind spots, and self-deceptions to which all human nature is prone. A cunning author is well aware that his narrator is flawed, and the author achieves comic flourish by presenting these weaknesses to the reader. The readers' interpretations of the narrator will also depend on their own positions as subjects who may live in a different time, place, and culture than the author's. Here's one example: The narrator describes Becky as a mermaid with pretty hair and a sultry voice that attracts men, but beneath the water level, he sees a slimy tail, which represents her "hideous" true nature as a "fiendish marine cannibal reveling and feasting on [her] wretched pickled victims" (747–48). As in the charade scene described in the previous lecture, Thackeray presents Becky as a seducing murderess who first cajoles men into intimacy and then, having "pickled" them, goes in for the attack. Today's readers may question why Becky's sexual nature troubles the narrator. In the quoted passage, we recognize the dramatic break from his usual ironic tone when he displays an exaggerated revulsion at the thought of female sexuality. The quoted sentence is the only time he savages Becky in the entire novel; yet, since he refuses to commit to a statement that Becky has sex with her "victims," the mermaid denunciation seems to be more a reflection of the narrator's own generalized fears about female sexuality than of Becky herself. Elsewhere, the narrator defends Becky's actions as a necessary way to earn her and Rawdon's living.

This and other moralistic comments point to states of aporia in which the narrator cannot explain his own contradictions. *Aporia* is an irresolvable conflict or logical disjunction—a paradox. As a philosophical device, it derives from Plato's early dialogues in which Socrates sets up a challenge to the philosophers, asking them to define abstract terms such as *virtue* or *courage*. After much discourse, Socrates's student will realize his own confusion: he actually doesn't know what he's talking about. In classical rhetoric, aporia was a claim, often feigned, of not knowing something, which could be used to stimulate the audience to participate in the quest for truth—much like Socrates's strategy. I suggest that the narrator of *Vanity Fair* either uses aporia, or is overwhelmed by it, when questions of his own moral beliefs arise. In the remainder of this lecture, I'll analyze several passages in which the narrator either contradicts himself or claims not to know the answer to his own questions, with the aim of understanding whether the narrator has any moral purpose beyond the stated claim of showing that earthly desires are vain. In other words, what are we to make of the theme that *all* participants at the "fair" of life are self-centered and act in vain, and that *anyone* would commit the sins of a Becky or a Rawdon if their economic circumstances required it? If all people are corrupt, why write a novel of manners and morals? Does the self-proclaimed "moralist" narrator have a discernible moral standard?

I. "Never have feelings which may make you uncomfortable, or make any promises which you cannot at any required moment command and withdraw" (201).

Sympathizing with Amelia's despair at losing George when his father prohibits their love match, the narrator delivers the above *bon mot* that teaches young ladies how to avoid painful feelings of rejection. Almost certainly it is not heartfelt advice because it asks the impossible: the repression of all natural, loving, and hopeful feelings in young women looking for partners. He also advises them to avoid committing to engagements, ostensibly until the intention and wealth of the suitor are ascertained and guaranteed. This advice, if not impossible, may be inadvisable, since the marriage market is portrayed as a fierce competition in most Victorian novels, and such delay could result in losing the prize. So clearly the narrator's advice is mere hyperbole, and his intention is something else. In fact, his real meaning is the opposite; he actually values Amelia's sentimentalism, and her ability to be loyal to her feelings, but he also pities her for them. More than once he tells the reader that a woman martyred to her man or children (which Amelia is, to both) is the most "affecting" sight: "I know few things more affecting than that timorous debasement and self-humiliation of a woman. How she owns that it is she and not the man who is guilty: how she takes all the faults on her side: how she courts in a manner punishment for the wrongs which she has not committed, and persists in shielding the real culprit!" (582–93). This description of Amelia's self-sacrifice to her ungrateful and patronizing son "affects" the narrator because of its pathos. On the other hand, he derides Amelia for her lack of wisdom in blindly loving George Osborne, a man who belittles and betrays her. It's not clear whether the narrator admires women capable of wholeheartedly devoting themselves to men and children or whether he finds them pitiably lacking in judgment. The answer seems to be both, which makes the narrator very human in his changeability but also unreliable as a judge of character.

II. "The novelist knows everything" (419).

The narrator's uneasy occupation of the omniscient role becomes apparent when he proclaims midway through the novel that "the novelist knows everything" and proceeds to demonstrate this truism by a rendering of the Rawdon Crawleys' finances. This is an ironic perversion of the status of omniscience, which usually refers to the narrator's prerogative to know the inner conflicts of his characters, rather than focusing on the things that they own or the debts that they owe. Critic Cynthia Wolff remarked that the narrator loses confidence in his moralist role about half-way through the book. The strange assertion that the "the novelist knows everything" signals that turning point. After the Battle of Waterloo, the dramatic action is falling, and so is the characters' youthful potential. The die is cast—from the midpoint onward we'll see in meticulous detail how Rawdon and Becky make their living out of cheating other (good) people, and how Amelia's moral backbone weakens when she relinquishes her child to his rich grandfather. Defending each of his characters becomes more difficult the more they age and habituate themselves to courses of conduct that range from dull (Amelia) to despicable (Becky).

In contrast to the narrator's prideful assertion that he knows everything, more and more things arise that he doesn't know, such as whether Becky slept with Lord Steyne and whether she killed Jos Sedley. Whereas the narrator pretends that these questions don't matter, they have to matter fundamentally in a novel, no matter its genre, and so I agree with Cynthia Wolff that the narrator loses control of the complex morality of the story after Waterloo. The narrator's confident tone doesn't fool the reader. As Wolff writes, "The narrator's playful, flippant, mocking tone becomes an elaborate device which seeks to hide the fact that he cannot support his own preferred moral position and that he has no direct answer for strong evidence to the contrary" (197). I think Wolff means that the narrator's tolerance of Becky's peccadillos (and, in this instance, her coldness as a mother) is unsupportable if indeed, as he claims, he is a moralist. If he truly values warmth of feeling as the most admirable trait, as described in the previous example, then how can he approve of Becky when he describes her as "a stone"? In this context, the narrator's refusal to mention whether Steyne and Becky "went all the way" is not mere Victorian reluctance to refer to sexual intercourse, but the narrator's refusal to topple the scaffolding of his puppet show. Becky is meant to be a likable character (she's kind and generous) and at the same time has dishonest and harmful traits (manipulation and self-interest) that the narrator has decided to excuse in order to maintain the theme of universal vanity—everyone has vain and trivial desires, so we should try to excuse them or else be hypocrites. The worse Becky's behavior gets, however—and murder is her final destination—the more the thesis falters.

III. "Which, I wonder, brother reader, is the better lot, to die prosperous and famous, or poor and disappointed?" (710)

Upon his deathbed, Mr. Sedley has forgiven both his daughter and George Osborne Sr.—and even Fortune herself for ruining his opportunities. There follows a two-page digression by the narrator about whether it would not be better to be like Mr. Sedley, "after all"—that is, by acknowledging one's poverty, mistakes, and stupidity, humbling oneself and asking for Divine Mercy instead of leaving this world as a proud rich man does, "defying any man to find anything against [his] character" (711). The narrator chooses Sedley's, rather than the rich man's, as the better way to go. Yet there is nothing in the novel to prepare us for this choice, for the narrator emphatically does not evaluate people according to how they will be appraised on Judgment Day. It is a novel about "a set of people living without God in the world … greedy pompous mean," as Thackeray wrote in a letter to his mother (Carey xiii). Although some of the characters believe in an afterlife, there is no indication until this point in the text that the narrator actually does (we do have evidence, however, that its author had "*some sort* of belief in immortality," as he wrote to his dogmatically religious mother) (xx). The qualifying words "some sort" perfectly reflect the hesitations and moral ambiguity of his narrator.

For me, this moment in the text is the most striking aporia, presenting such a contradiction to the narrator's previous irreligious status that it hints at unconscious motivations. This is not to say that the only motivation for acting ethically is religious belief—this is far from the truth. But Victorian writers regularly rely on their readers' shared belief in a moral code to appeal to common assumptions of right behavior—Dickens, Eliot, and Gaskell are strong examples. *Vanity Fair* is an unusual Victorian novel in its narrator's distance from religion. If Vanity Fair is a world without God, then by what standard should a reader judge the characters' actions? How does the narrator achieve a moral vision if he lacks a standard? In the absence of religion, which ethical standard does he adopt, and does he consistently apply it? Finally, the narrator is forced by his own plot to state a moral standard that will justify, explain, and beautify the complex events of the novel. I suggest that the narrator's moral standard is derivable from his notion of a "true gentleman"—that "rare personage" whose "aims are generous, whose truth is constant, and not only constant in its kind but elevated in its degree; whose want of meanness makes [him] simple; who can look the world honestly in the face with an equal manly sympathy for the great and the small" (728). Just after arriving at his definition, the narrator realizes he has described Dobbin, a man who is generous, truthful, and kind—but he realizes these important values only in the final section of the book.

This answer, however, raises several questions. Are women, whom he has described as crueler than men, exempt from this "true gentleman" standard (377)? Since only rare personages attain this inner-gentleman status, are the rest of us doomed to burn in hell? If this is "A Novel Without a Hero" (its subtitle), then how does he justify Dobbin's newfound heroic status? If Dobbin is a gentleman, and possibly a hero, then why not reward him with happiness in his wife as well as love for his daughter and satisfaction with his work? The narrator's final epigram, "Which of us has his desire? Or, having it, is satisfied?" clearly applies to Dobbins's cooled feelings toward Amelia, made clear in his breakup speech at Pumpernickel (809). The love that he lost then simply was not retrievable: "That sort of regard, which he had proffered to her for so many faithful years, can't be flung down and shattered and mended so as to show no scars" (797). Thackeray's realism in this instance is laudable; he avoids the cloying happy ending of the domestic comedy genre that he has been resisting throughout. His ending suggests, rather, that even goodness is not fully rewarded in the godless Vanity Fair of Thackeray's world (unlike Bunyan's). As such, Thackeray's social realist novel is far closer to twentieth-century absurdism or to Laurence Sterne's metafiction than to his Victorian rivals, Charles Dickens and George Eliot, each of whom has a lucid moral vision.

Conclusion

In the discussion question at the beginning of this lecture, I asked what purpose Thackeray might have had in making his narrator aporetic—frequently at an impasse how to resolve contradictions or paradoxes. Perhaps Cynthia Wolff is right, and the narrator's loss of control of the material after Waterloo implies Thackeray's same loss of control. On the other hand, if Thackeray intends to make his narrator as foolish and inconsistent as the other characters, then those questions that the narrator answers flippantly, while the reader takes them seriously, constitute an intentional stratagem. The narrator's unreliability reminds the reader that we all pretend to obey a moral order, one which we may not, however, really understand or be able to articulate. We may condemn Becky or Steyne or any number of other sinners, but we may also be prompted to hold up a mirror to our own clownish image, like the puppeteer on the cover page of Thackeray's first edition.

Works Cited

Bunyan, John. *Pilgrim's Progress*. Project Gutenberg. https://www.gutenberg.org/files/39270/39270-h/39270-h.htm.

Carey, John. "Introduction." *Vanity Fair*. Penguin, 2001.

Sterne, Laurence. *The Life and Opinions of Tristram Shandy, Gentleman*. Project Gutenberg. https://www.gutenberg.org/files/131/131-h/131-h.htm.

Thackeray, William Makepeace. *Vanity Fair*. Introduction by John Carey. Penguin, 2001.

Wolff, Cynthia Griffin. "Who Is the Narrator of *Vanity Fair* and Where Is He Standing?" *College Literature* 1.3 (1974). 190–203.

7

Roman Daughter
and Milquetoast Father

> "Poor Margaret! All that afternoon she had to act
> the part of a Roman daughter and give strength
> out of her own scanty stock to her father."
> —Narrator, *North and South*

Question:

Margaret Hale is a strong-minded, intelligent mid-century woman living in a middle-class family. How does such a strong woman cope with the requirements of the separate spheres doctrine, Angel in the House, and the demands of bourgeois respectability?

Synopsis:

Margaret is the eighteen-year-old daughter of Richard Hale, the parson of Helstone, a village in bucolic Hampshire. Attorney Henry Lennox proposes to Margaret, who is startled by his desire and turns him down. When required to profess his allegiance to the Thirty-nine Articles of Religion (doctrines of the Church of England), Richard Hale takes exception and renounces his position. The family moves to Milton (real-life Manchester), a northern cotton-manufacturing city, where Richard earns a living by tutoring businessmen in the classics. One of his students is John Thornton, imperious owner of Marlborough Mills, a successful cotton textile manufacturing mill. Thornton is attracted to Margaret, but she takes offence at his brusque manners, though she recognizes that people in trade have different social codes than the genteel class to which she proudly belongs. For his part, John has many prejudices about southerners, gentry, and educated people.

Margaret befriends a millworker, Nicholas Higgins, and his daughter, Bessy. Through them, she learns about the millworkers' union and their planned strike. On the day of the strike, Margaret is visiting the Thorntons. When workers riot in front of his house, Margaret exhorts John to face his workers like a man, but when they throw stones at him, she embraces him, interposing her body between him and the crowd. After the riot, Thornton gradually learns more about his workers and begins to transform his attitude about labor rela-

Elizabeth Gaskell by George Richmond, 1851 (frontispiece, Ellis H. Chadwick's *Ms. Gaskell: Haunts, Homes and Stories* [London, 1913]).

tions. He builds workers a dining hall and shares meals with them, getting to know his "hands."

Margaret's brother, Frederick, joined a mutiny while serving on a British ship; thus, he is living in permanent exile in Spain. If apprehended in England, he would be executed. When Margaret's mother nears death, she asks Margaret to invite Frederick home for a final visit. During this visit Margaret does her best to hide Frederick, but Thornton sees them together at the railway station, and he assumes Frederick is Margaret's lover. Frederick is recognized by a fellow seaman, Leonards, a drunkard who threatens to turn him in to the authorities. During a tussle, Frederick pushes Leonards onto the train tracks. Leonards dies of his alcoholism (not the fall) shortly after the accident. The police interrogate Margaret, who was present at the scene of the crime. To protect her brother's identity, she denies to the police that she was present at the scene. When Thornton learns of her lie, Margaret is deeply disturbed, as she now wants his good opinion. After the deaths of her mother and father, Margaret requests Mr.

Bell, an intimate family friend, to explain to Thornton the truth about the night she was seen at the station, thus clearing the way for the lovers to forgive and unite. When Mr. Bell dies, he leaves Margaret his estate, and she invests most of it in Marlborough Mills, saving it from failure. Margaret and John proclaim their love. Each has overcome their pride and prejudice through attraction to the best qualities of the other.

Analysis:

Margaret's use of her body to comfort her father and protect Thornton from assault evokes the Roman story of Cimon and his daughter, Pero. The Roman Daughter is an ancient story in which an adult Pero suckles her imprisoned father, who's been sentenced to death by starvation. Pero's breastfeeding is seen by some as filial piety, by others as perversity. Painters through the centuries have represented it in varying degrees of salacious or pure intent. In a curious reversal of parental and filial roles, several paintings at Pompeii depict father and daughter gazing into each other's eyes while father feeds at daughter's breast.

In several scenes, Gaskell paints Margaret as a Pero-like figure to Mr. Hale. Due to his wife's prolonged illness and his own anxiety about the risk of Frederick's Milton visit, Mr. Hale succumbs to melancholy, and the narrator comments: "Poor Margaret! All that afternoon she had to act the part of a Roman daughter, and give strength out of her own scanty stock to her father" (238). The author seems to have illustrations of Roman Charity in mind when she arranges father and daughter in the following tableau: "He lay across the table, helpless as ever; but she had the spell by which to rouse him…. 'Papa,' said she, throwing her arms fondly round his neck; pulling his weary head up in fact with her gentle violence, till it rested in her arms, and she could look into his eyes, and let them gain strength and assurance from hers" (240). With her characteristic "gentle violence," Margaret literally pulls her father up and offers strength through her gaze—which stands in for the breast milk in the Roman story. The fortitude conveyed by this gaze extends her father's life long enough to see Frederick and to survive Maria's death by a few weeks. In this gesture, Margaret plays daughter, wife, and mother to her own father, filling all the roles which the other members of the household fail to perform. If Margaret is an overperformer, it's because her father, mother and brother typically underperform. Even gallant Frederick weakens upon the death of his mother. The Victorian separate spheres doctrine allows, even encourages, such an imbalance to occur in family relations, so that the apparent role reversal may actually be a standard paradigm.

Separate spheres ideology not only limits the kinds of activities that Victorian women can do outside the home. It also imposes many activities upon them that require all their time and energy unless they actively resist the imposition. In the Hale family, these requirements are particularly burdensome upon Margaret, who by default shoulders responsibilities in both the male and female spheres. Margaret's situation may not be unusual; in fact, it's a hidden cost of separate spheres—the Angel in the House has far more work, often of a more demanding nature, than her male counterpart. The angel has no time for herself unless she becomes ill or burns the midnight oil. Margaret's father fails to do nearly as much as the male role requires, and her mother is an invalid who responds negatively to her husband's needs for her to be the resident angel. Like Margaret, many middle-class Victorian daughters remained unmarried because of their all-consuming duties to their family.

Resentful of Hale's relinquishment of the parson's job at Helstone, and particularly of his choice of grimy Milton as their new residence, his wife, Maria, responds by losing interest in the world around her. She becomes peevish and sickly. Persistent strain leads to her final illness—cancer—the word that doctor and family alike are afraid to utter. Seeing that Richard isn't strong enough to accept it, the doctor entrusts Margaret, rather than her father, with the diagnosis.

Richard Hale is frequently likened to a woman because of his cowardice, unworldliness, and physical and emotional weakness. Incidentally, this comparison is inaccurate, since many of the women in Victorian novels are stronger than the men when it comes to emotional matters. Richard's dereliction of duty leaves Margaret to take household matters, spiritual problems, and even financial concerns into her own hands. She must shoulder major responsibilities such as telling her mother of her father's decision to leave the Church, finding a new home, storing furniture, arranging for Frederick's visit and finding him a lawyer, planning her mother's funeral, and informing Mrs. Boucher of her husband's suicide when both Nicholas Higgins and Richard Hale are too weak to do so. This last job is particularly ironic in a culture where middle-class women are not invited to funerals because they're considered too weak to manage grief. Margaret says, "Women of our class don't go [to funerals], because they have no power over their emotions, and yet are ashamed of showing them" (261). The Catch-22 is that women are relied on for their emotions as a resource yet condemned if they display emotions (or ideas) in ways not accepted by the social code. For women, crying and breakdown are acceptable, but anger, independence, and defiance are definitely not.

Margaret is expected to do the aforementioned "male jobs" while maintaining the fiction that her father is in control, confirming that patriarchy in and outside the Hale home remains secure. In order to retain the family's social standing, it must not appear that Margaret has shared the male role in either the business or the domestic sphere. A particularly complex conflict occurs between Margaret's spiritual duties to herself and filial duties to her father when she must support him in his apostasy although she herself remains faithful. When Richard tells Margaret of his decision, she is torn: "'And may He restore you to His Church,' responded she, out of the fulness of her heart. The next moment she feared lest this answer to his blessing might be irreverent, wrong—might hurt him as coming from his daughter, and she threw her arms round his neck" (41). Even in a question of faith, a daughter must submit to her father in order to protect his pride and standing. Since she loves her family deeply, these requirements don't trouble Margaret to any conscious degree, though she does feel remarkably relieved when Mr. Hale leaves her alone for a few days while visiting Oxford. Unburdened of the duty to be cheerful for her father's sake, Margaret indulges in the luxury of feeling her own feelings: "what seemed worth more than all the other privileges—she might be unhappy if she liked" (336).

In the novel's climactic scene, Margaret's ongoing battle with separate spheres ideology is put to the test. Margaret claims that she is acting "like any woman" when she throws her body against Thornton's to protect him from hurled objects, but the reactions of Fanny, the servants, and Mrs. Thornton prove that she has overstepped the bounds of femininity (193). They can only see her in the role of a traditional woman, with such a woman's typical motives. We, the reader, know that Margaret wasn't staking a claim over her lover's body to force him into a marriage proposal. But to the small minds of his sister and servants, and the Oedipal perspective of his mother, sexual possession seems to be the motive for Margaret's action. Her speech and gestures are a graphic violation of separate spheres—an exhortation to Thornton to face the workers "like a man," and then her insertion of her own body to protect him (175).

The scene focuses the theme of Margaret's courage in a cinematic manner. In symbolic intensity, the scene rivals Hester Prynne's three days on the scaffold in punishment for a sin she shared with a clergyman who was too afraid to confess his own part in it. Rather than gratitude from his family for saving Thornton from harm and defusing the riot, Margaret's sacrifice garners disapproval for its supposed sexual aggressiveness. In both scenes (Hester on the scaffold in *The Scarlet Letter*, Margaret on the Thornton doorstep in *North and South*), the women are brave and truthful, while their men remain "behind" their women—literally, in the case of Thornton, when Margaret "made her body into a shield from the fierce people beyond" (177). Margaret takes the hit of the stone meant for

Thornton, while Hester takes the hit of stones thrown by children and the public scorn that should have been shared by the minister who impregnated her. In both cases, the woman is nobler than the man.

Despite her independent nature, Margaret internalizes the rules of gentility and suffers as a result of her brave action. Bourgeois respectability forbids a woman from touching a man unless she is married to him—Margaret's genteel southern upbringing even forbade handshakes between men and women. The scandal over Margaret's rescue of Thornton reveals the intersection of class and gender biases. Her middle-class female body enjoys immunity from harm because "it was supposed unthinkable for a man to strike a middle-class woman," though "violence against working-class women is not similarly regarded" (Ingham 438). It is interesting to note that Bessy Higgins, who worships Margaret and emulates her actions, likewise interposes herself between Boucher and her father when they prepare to fight (199). As a working-class woman, Bessy did not shock her family. Regardless of the protection implied by her class status, however, Margaret did take a blow on the face from a hurled stone, though it had been intended for Thornton.

In addition to the prohibition against touching, Margaret also internalizes general prohibitions against female desire—and to such an extent that she denies her own attraction to Thornton, causing her to rudely rebuff his overture of gratitude. She tells Thornton, "Why, there was not a man—not a poor desperate man in all that crowd—for whom I had not more sympathy—for whom I should not have done what little I could more heartily" (193). She could have made the point more tactfully without pretending that she valued every other man more than she valued Thornton. A combination of Margaret's personal pride and her society's condemnation of female lust causes her to insult Thornton and even to tell a small, albeit unconscious, lie—that she would prefer to help any other man than him. The reader may wink at the juxtaposition between Margaret's dread of lying and her own self-deception. Despite her abhorrence of falsehoods, she will proceed to lie to herself daily for more than two years regarding her feelings for Mr. Thornton. Although the modern reader recognizes its cost to the psyche, Victorian repression of female sexuality serves at least one good purpose—to extend a serialized novel and increase sexual tension until the marriage proposal finally occurs on the penultimate page. But repression costs the heroine precious energy and self-esteem as she veers back and forth between blaming herself for stepping outside her proper sphere, and faulting Thornton for presuming to care for her in a sexual way.

Another nicety required of Victorian women is to avoid expressing strong feelings and to feel guilty whenever they experience them. Nor are they expected to listen to the expression of strong feelings by men. This is why some proposals in Victorian novels end with the woman becoming offended that the man expressed his desire and admiration. Although Margaret becomes upset when both Henry Lennox and John Thornton profess their love, she wishes that she could speak of her own strong feelings and could invite the expression of Thornton's feelings—albeit only the negative ones—so that she could humble and redeem herself: "Oh! I wish I were a man, that I could go and force him to express his disapprobation, and tell him honestly that I knew I deserved it" (302). Thornton also recognizes the unspoken rule of gender difference when he claims, "I am a man. I claim the right of expressing my feelings," and defends the male privilege of saying he loves her (193). Fulfilling gentility and gender roles requires restraint. In some areas of etiquette, men and women are equally restrained. But in self-expression, men are afforded a greater "right" to feeling, as Thornton remarks.

Requiring a woman to be the repository of the family's feelings while at the same time prohibiting her expression of them sets up an internal conflict. Patricia Ingham describes Margaret as the repository of others' feelings. Discussing the scene where Margaret struggles with her own faith because her father is renouncing his, she writes: "this is one of the many instances when she becomes the crucible for every painful and disturbing experience in the narrative" (429). The crucible is an effective image, because in addition to her own passionate feelings about everything from workers' rights to religion, Margaret assumes responsibility for the feelings of her parents, including her mother's depression and her father's despair. The epithet Angel in the House* makes the woman's role seem ethereal, whereas in reality, it is a crucible—a severe trial in which disparate elements are heated at extreme temperatures in order to meld them. Margaret's job is to create harmony and cheer among the disappointed (Richard and Maria) and law-breaking (Frederick) elements of her family, while postponing her own fulfillment and neglecting her own passionate feelings. Both John Thornton and Mr. Bell could attest that Margaret was not available for a relationship with a man before the death of her parents and the safe arrangement of Frederick's affairs, because Margaret would always put her family's interests before her own. She would not leave her father's home while he was still alive and would have flown to Frederick's side if he had needed her.

---

* Angel in the House is an ideal closely related to the separate spheres doctrine. It derives its name from Coventry Patmore's 1854 poem of the same name and denotes a woman (usually mother, wife, or eldest daughter) who is entirely virtuous, self-sacrificing, and benevolent. She is the helpmate to her husband or father and a spiritual role model to other family members.

Carrying such large responsibilities to others, it is no wonder that many Victorian middle-class daughters lacked time and space to pursue their own affairs of the heart, let alone occupations that would bring purely personal rewards, such as writing and other arts. The Roman daughter in the Hale family has her hands full and her duty spelled out: she will ignore her own sexuality in order to nurture her family. As in the Roman legend, Margaret nurses her father when he has received his own death sentence—which is the demise of his wife. The ending of the novel opens the question whether Margaret and John's marriage will defy the gender imbalance of the Victorian home, as they enter into a business partnership of sorts. The reader hopes that they will work together to bring back Marlborough Mills to its old prominence while incorporating new methods to unite master and worker in common cause. With Margaret as investor, John as owner/manager, and both as progressive innovators, the distinctness of the separate spheres may be lessened, though certainly not broken.

How does a strong woman like Margaret Hale cope with the requirements of separate spheres ideology and the demands of bourgeois respectability? Margaret coped by taking these demands and duties to heart, performing or even overperforming them. She also extended her realm of action into the community by helping the Higgins family and Mr. Thornton, which ultimately led to Nicholas and John meeting regularly. Once Thornton began to incorporate her ideas into his work, other workers felt the effects. Margaret went beyond Angel in the House to become Angel of Frances Street (the Higgins's dwelling place) and Angel of Marlborough Mills as well—it was she who planted the idea in Thornton's mind that he must "cultivate some intercourse with the hands beyond the mere cash nexus" (420).

Once removed from Milton, which had given her a fitting sphere of action because of her growing interest in the working classes, Margaret struggles to find a new plan. She tells her cousin, "as I have neither husband nor child to give me natural duties, I must make myself some, in addition to ordering my gowns" (407). During her seaside meditations at Cromer, she vows to do something important, though the exact project remains indistinct until she consults with Henry Lennox: "she had learnt in those solemn hours of thought that she herself must one day answer for her own life, and what she had done with it: and she tried to settle that most difficult problem for women, how much was to be utterly merged in obedience to authority, and how much might be set apart for freedom in working" (406).

At the novel's ending, is Margaret really free in her work? We could denigrate Margaret's contribution to factory working conditions by pointing out that it was only through the acquisition and investment of money that she was able to obtain influence in the male sphere of commerce. Trivializing her contribution would, however, deny the sexual chemistry between her and Thornton, which Gaskell convincingly portrays. If we believe in the promise of their mutual love and admiration, we might also believe that the new Marlborough Mills will be a collaborative operation. If Thornton is willing, Margaret might become its moral beacon.

Works Cited

Gaskell, Elizabeth. *North and South*. Penguin, 1995.
Ingham, Patricia. "Introduction." *North and South*. Penguin, 1995. xii–xxviii.

8

Regional and Class Prejudice

"North and South has met and made a kind o' friends in
this big smoky place."
                                        —Nicholas Higgins

Question:

Many heroines of nineteenth-century novels—such as Jane Eyre, Tess
Durbeyfield, and Dorothea Brooke—are morally purer than the men who
pursue them; this purity entails honesty and selflessness as well as sexual chastity. Part of the satisfaction in reading these works is to see the
male characters reform themselves in order to be accepted in marriage by
their noble counterparts. Elizabeth Gaskell adds piquancy to the formula
because Margaret Hale is flawed in ways similar to her lover. What makes
Margaret's and John Thornton's trajectories from flawed to better people
so satisfactory?

Analysis:

Of all the noble, reforming Victorian heroines, Margaret Hale may be
the only one who possesses both charisma and a glaring personal flaw—
her shameless class snobbery. As a plot device, this serves well, as it provides a concrete trajectory for the book: Margaret must overcome this bias
if she is to be more successful as a heroine! What differentiates *North and
South* from other Victorian novels is that the heroine matures not only
through a challenging romance with a flawed male character, but also
and equally as a result of her friendship with a family of a lower class,
the Higginses. An interesting comparison can be made with Jane Austen's

Pride and Prejudice, in which Elizabeth Bennett overcomes her prejudice about Fitzwilliam Darcy's arrogant personality as she learns more about his inner life—his secrets, good deeds, and psychological conflicts. On the other hand, Margaret Hale and John Thornton's rapprochement occurs at the level of political and philosophical issues as well as personal affinities. Gaskell's characters cross more hard-drawn class boundaries than do Elizabeth and Darcy, who are members of more proximate strata, the professional and gentry classes (her father, as parson and educator, is high in status, but low in income). Margaret, on the other hand, overcomes two barriers—one upwards, and one downwards on the income scale. The first is her genteel aversion to people in trade (even though the Thorntons are initially much wealthier than her own family), the other her difference from people who work in factories for a living. Margaret's friendship with Bessy, and John's with Nicholas, prove to them that social relationships can exist between members of different classes. Such bridges have broader implications for achieving a more equitable society—a project that Victorians began to pursue, and that we continue to work for in the twenty-first century. My own theory is that until such interclass personal relationships start to occur on a larger scale, race/class prejudice and inequities will remain difficult to dismantle.

Margaret's progress is satisfying to the reader because of its complexity—she has the kind of layered biases we associate with the discourse of identity. As she gets to know the Thorntons and Higginses, Margaret begins to disentangle her sense of class superiority from her regionalist racism, the latter perhaps more acceptable as a topic in polite drawing rooms. As long as her class prejudice is couched in geographical terms, it appears to be a bias that members of all classes can share—a preference for countryside over city, for agrarian over industrial culture. In fact, it is a thinly disguised bias of the gentry (landowning) and genteel (the learned professions) against the businessmen (those "in trade"). In the beginning of the novel, and especially from our twenty-first-century American point of view, Margaret has two distinct prejudices to overcome: (1) her scorn of tradesmen, based on the classist assumption that those who earn their money in commerce are "lower" (not only socially but morally) than those who gain it in the professions (law, medicine, church, military), or by land management (the gentry), or through inheritance, and (2) her assumption that working class people have nothing to offer her in the way of inspiration, education, or friendship, based on the classist belief that the working class is a different race. Susie Steinbach likens the hard lines between classes in Victorian Britain with those between races in the United States. She accentuates the alienation between the classes: "People at all levels of society believed that the rich and the poor were different beings," and "There was a strong feeling on the part of most people that people of different classes and races are fundamentally unlike one another" (114).

Softening Margaret's rough edges in both directions—upward to "new money" and downward to working-class low income—makes this novel more engaging and less predictable than some of its contemporaries. Through Margaret's own intimacy with the Higginses she inspires Thornton to know Nicholas. John and Margaret's class ranks are closer socioeconomically than either is to the Higginses'; separately but at the same time, they learn to recognize the personal value of working people. This is the effort—though executed individually—that finally unites the lovers across their prejudice toward each other as members of different sub-classes: the professional (Margaret) and commercial (John).

In the disparaging words of Mrs. Thornton, Margaret is only a poor country clergyman's daughter. Yet to Margaret and her mother, their family is higher than the Thorntons because Richard belonged to "one of the three learned professions," whereas the Thorntons earn their living in trade (20). When we first meet the heroine, Gaskell portrays her class snobbery as an amusing attribute of character. Since her mother is the daughter of Lady Jane and ward of Sir John Beresford—a fact she often reminds people of—we could say that Margaret comes by the snobbery honestly, or at least, from her upbringing. Margaret may have internalized her mother's sense of disappointment at having "married down," and this may account for Margaret's antipathy to marrying a man "in trade." She rejects her mother's offer to introduce the Gormans, who made their fortune in coach building, saying, "I don't like shoppy people.... I like all people whose occupations have to do with land; I like soldiers and sailors, and the three learned professions, as they call them. I'm sure you don't want me to admire butchers and bakers, and candlestick-makers, do you, mamma?" (20)

Margaret likes to keep social categories pure and separate. When she learns of her father's new job as tutor to Milton manufacturers, she asks, "What in the world do manufacturers want with the classics, or literature, or the accomplishments of a gentleman?" (40). She obviously has not come into contact with the many tradesmen who want very much to acquire culture, sometimes as a strategy to attain gentility through marriage, but often because they're hungry for knowledge and beauty. When she begins to like Thornton, she defends him, though with all the condescension of her class: "as to Mr Thornton's being in trade, why he can't help that now, poor fellow. I don't suppose his education would fit him for much else" (77). It is only when Thornton confesses his hard upbringing—his father lost all his assets on speculation and then committed suicide—that

Margaret begins to regard him with more sympathy, which she does by separating his behavior from others of his class: "Mr. Thornton made his confession of having been a shop-boy ... with so little of the pretence that makes the vulgarity of shop-people ... that I was less likely to leave the room" (87). For Margaret, the "taint" of trade means "testing everything by the standard of wealth" (88).

The turning point for Margaret's attitude to John and tradesmen is attending the Thorntons' dinner party, where she begins to feel a thrill for the manufacturers' energy: "She liked the exultation in the sense of power which these Milton men had.... They seemed to defy the old limits of possibility, in a kind of fine intoxication" (162). Mr. Hale too admired the drive and imagination of the mill owners: "there was something dazzling to Mr Hale in the energy which conquered immense difficulties with ease; the power of the machinery of Milton, the power of the men of Milton impressed him with a sense of grandeur" (70). Margaret perceived a similarly energizing life force among the workers, and she is particularly impressed by their organization of unions. Her changed perceptions become clear when she convinces Nicholas Higgins not to go south for work, as she is sure he would miss having comradeship with his mates and that his mind would wilt from lack of stimulation. Effectively she is stating that union organization is the breath of life for the working poor, and that her beloved agrarian south is stagnant in comparison to the industrial north. Of southern workers she says, "The hard spade-work robs their brain of life; they don't care to meet to talk over thoughts and speculations.... You could not stir them up into any companionship, which you get in a town as plentiful as the air you breathe" (299). Again, it's pleasing to see Margaret reverse her regional prejudices based on her perceptions of the life of the general populace, rather than merely upon her attraction to one handsome bachelor of the north.

Thornton's reversals of opinion are just as compelling—and perhaps more so, since he has a broader sphere in which to put new ideas into action. But Margaret remains the protagonist and moving force of the novel; it is her influence that causes such changes in Thornton. The mill owner is not as categorical as Margaret in his distinctions between commerce and gentry; after all, he chose to take lessons in classical Greek and Roman from a retired curate of the professional class. But Margaret's snobbery causes him to reassess his position. He defensively makes distinctions between "men" and "gentlemen," appropriating the nobler qualities of masculinity to the commercial class: "A man is to me a higher and a completer being than a gentleman" (163). Since Thornton's definition is relevant to discussion of the intersection of class and gender roles, I quote it in full:

I take it that "gentleman" is a term that only describes a person in his relation to others; but when we speak of him as "a man," we consider him not merely with regard to his fellow-men, but in relation to himself—to life—to time—to eternity. A cast-away as lonely as Robinson Crusoe—a prisoner immured in a dungeon for life—nay, even a saint in Patmos, has *his endurance, his strength, his faith*, best described by being spoken of as "a man." I am rather weary of this word "gentlemanly," which seems to me to be often inappropriately used, and often, too, with such exaggerated distortion of meaning ... that I am induced to class it with the cant of the day [163, italics mine].

For Thornton, manliness comes down to the will to live well despite challenging circumstances, like Robinson Crusoe making life as comfortable as he can on his deserted island. But, of course, men *are* also judged by their relations with their fellow men and women. Thornton's true manliness is tested by a woman—Margaret—when his workers strike, and he must decide how to react. In the days and weeks following the riot, he gradually changes his view of what constitutes both a man and a master. He endeavors to break down the communication barrier by getting to know his workers through several efforts: creating a workers' dining hall on the factory grounds, eating dinner with the workers, learning of their concerns, and understanding their needs. He becomes so committed to his idea of "intercourse beyond the cash nexus" that, after his business fails, he refuses a profitable partnership with another factory owner whom he knows to be conservative in his views of employment relations. Thornton is beginning to live up to his idea of masculinity by enacting his ideals of *endurance, strength, and faith*—qualities, incidentally, that would make a good woman too, and that Margaret possesses. He has the *faith* to remain loyal to Margaret even when he mistakenly believes that Frederick and Henry Lennox are her suitors. He has the *strength* to resist Watson's risky investment that could make him rich but would compromise his conscience. He finds the *endurance* to accept his business loss as an opportunity to start afresh and implement his new approach to management. By the end of the novel, Thornton would rather work *for* another man with similar principles than compromise his own principles for the sake of being boss. In other words, Margaret's idea of the fundamental necessity of communication between management and workers has completely won him over.

Although their means of implementation are as yet unspecified—other than the dining hall—Thornton is clear about the principles that drive his "experiments" in labor relations. At the Lennoxes' dinner party, Thornton expresses his ideas to the inquiring MP, Mr. Colthurst. Margaret's ideas of charity, her Christian sense of universal fraternity, have infiltrated Thornton's mind and speech: "No mere institutions, however wise, … can attach class to class as they should be attached, unless the working out of such institutions bring the individuals of the different classes into actual personal contact" (421). In describing his friendship with Nicholas, Thornton explains that one bridge will lead to others: "Starting from a kind of friendship with one, I was becoming acquainted with many. The advantages were mutual; we were both unconsciously and consciously teaching each other" (420). Workers and managers have not only common economic interests to share, but a common humanity: "Once brought face to face, man to man, with an individual of the masses around him, and out of the character of master and workman, … they had each begun to recognize that 'we have all of us one human heart'" (409). The last phrase is William Wordsworth's; showing off his education, John quotes the best English literary communicator of the democratic sentiment (whereas Walt Whitman fills that role among American poets).

One must be careful not to exaggerate the effects of Margaret and John's efforts on the Milton manufacturing community. As Ingham notes, they've not begun a social revolution: "Only so much has been achieved, and that not for certain" (xxvii) and "Milton as a whole is unchanged" (xxvi). On the other hand, ideas have been exchanged across the aisle of class and gender difference, and this seems to me to be the starting point of any social change. Margaret and John have advocated their new ideas and implementation for one generation of millworkers, the effects of which will be passed down to their inheritors.

As Ingham writes, "[Milton] destabilizes [Margaret's] sense of class as a constituent of her identity" (xvii). The operative word is "destabilizes"—not "destroys"—for Margaret will not, nor should she, jettison the teachings and values of her genteel upbringing. What she learns in the course of her Milton sojourn is that she has more in common with the Other than she was brought up to believe. The boundaries between herself and workers, and between herself and manufacturers, are now more permeable. The principle of reciprocity between self and other, regardless of class, is nicely expressed by Bessy when she says to Margaret that, despite the differences between those who are "pre-elected to sumptuous feasts" and those who "toil and moil all their lives long," she loves Margaret: "I'll come across the great gulf to yo' just for th' thought o' what yo've been to me here" (149). After leaving Milton, Margaret's own version of crossing the gulf is to commit herself to "natural duties" and "freedom in working" that implicitly involve the improvement of conditions for the working class (407, 406).

Margaret's meditations at Cromer lead to a vague resolve to "work" that might be less than completely satisfying to the reader because her future job remains unspecified. The narrator's voice intrudes when Margaret thinks of her situation within a feminist framework: "she tried to settle that most difficult problem for women, how much was to be utterly merged in obedience to authority, and how much might be set apart for freedom in working" (406). Margaret is concerned not only about limitations on women's ability to work, but on limitations of the social intercourse between classes, a type of exchange which had given her Milton experience such vitality and meaning. Returning to Harley Street after living in Milton, Margaret becomes dissatisfied with the gentry's requirement of separate spheres for the classes:

> There might be toilers and moilers there in London, but she never saw them; the very servants lived in an underground world of their own, of which she knew neither the hopes nor the fears; they only seemed to start into existence when some want or whim of their master and mistress needed them. There was a strange unsatisfied vacuum in Margaret's heart and mode of life [364].

Like Thornton, Margaret has acquired a need for contact with the working class in order to feel fulfilled. But Margaret may be unfulfilled in her role as John's wife and an investor in Marlborough Mills. Will she continue to influence her husband, encouraging him to continue his social experiments? Thornton might grant her the power to initiate projects that increase worker/manager contact, such as the dining hall that he once planned with Higgins. Alternatively, he might thank her for the financial contribution and then dismiss her input, defaulting to the more comfortable framework of separate spheres for men and women. Perhaps John Thornton will realize the parallels in gender and class oppressions. He has seen that separation of class spheres causes volatility at the factory; will he see that separation of gender spheres contributes to developing frivolous women like his sister Fanny? Will he appreciate that following separate spheres ideology would prevent his intelligent wife from being fulfilled? At the end of the book, he has completely committed to breaking down the separation of the classes, at least those of worker and master. It might, however, be a more difficult prospect to relinquish his male privileges by allowing his wife into the male public sphere.

North and South is not unique among Victorian novels for leaving uncertain the future of its intense, ambitious female protagonist. *Middlemarch*'s heroine, Dorothea Brooke, is similar to Margaret in terms of her intelligence, will power, and intention to do good for the needy of her community. At the end of the novel, Dorothea marries a good man, Will Ladislaw, but gives up the charitable work she had been doing in the community. *Middlemarch*'s narrator recognizes that it takes more than a great spirit to fulfill a woman's potential amidst social limitations of gender and class: "For there is no creature whose inward being is so strong that it is not greatly determined by what lies outside it" (838). In *North and*

South, Margaret and John may succumb to this determinism, or they may fight it.

Let's return to the discussion question: what makes John and Margaret's changes satisfactory to the reader? Regardless of how they run the mill, or whether they will share the duties traditionally relegated to separate spheres, this couple has overcome entrenched class prejudice by falling in love. Each has turned 180 degrees from the views with which their story begins. Margaret learns that "shoppy people" may be a fitter description for specific personalities than for how a class of people earns a living. She admires the intelligence, ambition, and goodness of her friends Bessy and Nicholas Higgins, and she sees their plight within the wider framework of working-class conditions in the cotton industry. Bessy's lung disease is a cost of weaving cotton; Nicholas's union work is necessary to support the out-of-work families that are even poorer than his own. Striking is the only way for workers to increase wages and reduce their poverty.

John Thornton also reverses his opinion of learned people living on inheritance or the professions. The life of the mind doesn't have to be a competitive accumulation of irrelevant facts of bygone eras; John actually considers Hale's assigned Greek texts as guides to intellectual consideration of what is good and just in his own line of work. Through a combination of Hale's lessons and Margaret's instinctive advocacy for the poor, John learns that business doesn't have to be seen as a Malthusian struggle for existence that inevitably destroys the weaker competitors. Nor do the interests of labor and management have to be in opposition.

Whatever the future of Marlborough Mills' management, there is at least one clear benefit of Margaret's move to Milton: "North and South has met and made a kind o' friends in this big smoky place."

Works Cited

Eliot, George. *Middlemarch*. Penguin, 1994.
Gaskell, Elizabeth. *North and South*. Penguin, 1995.
Ingham, Patricia. Introduction. *North and South*. Penguin, 1995. xii–xxviii.
Steinbach, Susie. *Understanding the Victorians: Politics, Culture and Society in Nineteenth-Century Britain*. Routledge, 2012.

9

London versus Paris: Is This a Competition?

Question:

The title of the novel implies a comparison of London and Paris as they are at the time of its setting (1775–1793). It's clear that the cities, for Dickens, represent the national cultures of England and France. Given that Dickens is notoriously satirical about Victorian institutions, we might assume that he would resist any urge to esteem London over Paris. Does Dickens portray one culture as morally superior and/or more politically advanced?

Synopsis:

Dr. Alexandre Manette leaves French prison after eighteen years of incarceration and is hiding in an apartment over Thérèse and Ernest Defarge's wine shop in St. Antoine, Paris. His daughter, Lucie, who is unknown to him, learns of his whereabouts, takes him back to England, and helps him recover from the trance he lives in as a consequence of trauma. Meanwhile, Frenchman Charles Darnay is tried for treason against the British crown. He's acquitted when barrister Sydney Carton uses their nearly identical appearance to discredit the witness who is "sure" he saw Darnay engaged in compromising discussions with French soldiers. Back in Paris, the arrogant Marquis St. Evrémonde runs over a peasant child in the street and tosses a coin to his father to compensate him for his loss. The father attaches himself to the underside of the Marquis's carriage, penetrates his castle, and murders him in his bed. We learn that Darnay is the Marquis's nephew, but that he has repudiated his aristocratic rank and title, anglicized his name, and moved to London to work as a tutor. In London, Darnay marries Lucie without revealing his past identity.

In Paris, shop owner Ernest Defarge leads a group of rabid revolution- aries in the Storming of the Bastille and searches Manette's cell, finding the prisoner's letters. Madame Defarge leads the revolu- tionary women, who mur- der aristocrats and pillage their residences. When Darnay returns to Paris to help one of his family's ser- vants get out of prison, he is seized by the new French authorities, arrested for being a returned emigrant, and jailed in La Force

Charles Dickens, by Jeremiah Gurney (1867–68).

Prison. A year later, Darnay is tried for being an aristocrat. The prose- cution uses a letter written by Dr. Manette that was found in his cell by Ernest Defarge. The letter describes a female patient whom the Evré- monde brothers raped, and her brother, who died of injuries received by them. When the doctor couldn't save their lives, the aristocrats offered him a bribe to keep quiet about their crimes, but Manette turned it down. In prison, he wrote an account of the Evrémondes' crimes, and condemned them and their descendants for all time. The prosecu- tion would not let Dr. Manette retract this evidence, even though Dar- nay was now his son-in-law and had nothing to do with his father and uncle's crimes. Darnay is sentenced to execution by guillotine. Sydney Carton, wishing to help Lucie and Charles, makes a plan to substitute himself for Charles at the execution. Lucie, Charles, little Lucie (their child), and Alexandre flee to London as Sydney martyrs himself for the Frenchman.

Analysis:

The short answer to my question is that, in the book, London is better than France both politically and morally—though its institutions are nevertheless rife with corruption. In the famous opening passage of the novel ("It was the best of times, it was the worst of times…"), Dickens sardonically compares British and French corruptions in 1775, accentuating their similarities. Although France was "less favored on the whole as to matters spiritual," in England, "there was scarcely an amount of order and protection to justify much national boasting" (7, 8). Each country used outmoded, violent legal procedures and inflicted cruel punishments. There was no reasonable standard of justice in either place. Part of the appeal of the story as it progresses (at least to Anglophiles) is to gradually reveal the heroic propensities of the British characters as they rescue the French (Sydney Carton saves Charles Darnay; Miss Pross eradicates The Vengeance and saves Lucie).

A brief historical background will help contextualize elements that gave the British a sense of superiority vis-à-vis their neighbors across the Channel. Both nations suffered from the inequities of feudalism—excessive taxation, immunity for clergy, lack of legal standing for commoners. These inequities had been a major issue in England since the Magna Carta was signed in 1215. However, the parliamentary reforms that the French revolutionaries fought for in 1789 had been achieved one hundred years earlier by the English. France's trio of events—the Revolution, the Reign of Terror, and Napoleon's dictatorship—involved massive bloodshed. In contrast, England's 1688 revolution was nicknamed "The Bloodless Revolution" because of the non-violent way that it occurred (except in Scotland and Ireland). On the other hand, the English Civil Wars of 1642–1651 (involving England, Scotland, and Ireland) were some of the bloodiest in the history of the British Isles. After the Glorious, or Bloodless Revolution, King William and Queen Mary signed the English Declaration of Rights (1689), which restricted the power of the monarch and extended the rights of the people, granting free elections, freedom of speech, and regular Parliaments. (Freedom of religion was not granted at this time; the Declaration forbade the monarchy from being Catholic.)

Meantime, in France, the *ancien régime* (old rule) abused power by overtaxing the third estate (all those who were not clergy or nobility), refusing to tax clergy or nobility, employing *droits de seigneur* (a landowner's right to rape a vassal's bride), and extending other privileges to nobility. One hundred years after England's rulers had signed a Declaration of Rights, France still ran on an outmoded feudal system that lacked any concept of individual human rights. Excessive taxation created revenue for France's military expenditure in the Seven Years' War and the American Revolution, but it impoverished the peasants. Famine swept the land—Dickens's descriptions of the allegorized "Hunger" in Book the Second are probably no exaggeration.

Despite her Declaration of Rights, England was no paradise either. As Dickens's famous opening sentences suggest, England shared France's problems of power abuse and social inequity. The "king with a large jaw and queen with a plain face" in England is equivalent to the "king with a large jaw and queen with a fair face" in France (7). In the eighteenth century, English monarchs (George III and IV) and French monarchs (Louis XIV, XV, and XVI) were alike corrupt, but the privileges of nobility had been revoked a century earlier in Britain. In contrast to the French, who lived in fear of their despotic monarch and his court, the English grew to revere their monarch. By Victorian times, the monarchy and the House of Lords were considered the "dignified parts" of British government, the House of Commons being the "efficient part" (Steinbach quoting Walter Bagehot, 32). "Dignity" was an epithet never possible for the French government, given the excesses and absolutism of the succession of Kings Louis that preceded the French Revolution.

Although England is morally superior to France by the end of *A Tale of Two Cities*, this is true only in relative terms. Dickens attacks English institutions hard. In particular, its legal system is outmoded and unfair, with punishments that far exceed the crimes. Drawing and quartering is still practiced, and the death penalty applies to petty theft as well as murder. The English people readily become a bloodthirsty mob at public executions. Other English institutions also practice tyranny of rank, creating a typical Dickensian London in which social injustice affects people of all levels. In a bizarre comparison, banks "kill" their employees by harsh training and overwork, just as the Law kills its offenders by execution (56): "at that time, putting to death was a recipe much in vogue with all trades and professions, and not least of all with Tellson's.... When they took a young man into Tellson's London house, they hid him somewhere till he was old" (56).

The difference between the two cities is—in a word—blood. Dickens's satire of English institutions emphasizes disparity in wealth, power, and status, but also acknowledges the positive business morals of honesty and integrity—as in the case of Tellson's. The Bank trains its servants to uphold the honesty and reliability of the institution. Such training is harsh but also capable of producing good men such as Jarvis Lorry. On the other hand, French institutions are so morally corrupt that radical retaliation is the people's only answer. The French monarchy trains its courtiers to reproduce its savage disregard for the wellbeing of the Third Estate, which in turn results in the savage mentalities of revolutionaries such as Madame Defarge and The Vengeance. (The issue of why women are portrayed as more bloodthirsty than men—in Dickens, Shakespeare, and other popular writers—is matter for another discussion.)

French and English institutions may both be corrupt in this novel, but despite his love of France, Dickens emphasizes the negative stereotypes of French national character and subtly prefers the English character. According to Albert Hutter, author of "Nation and Generation in *A Tale of Two Cities*," the novel contrasts the British ability to control impulses and pull for the common good (the superego function) with the French ability to lose oneself in one's passions (what the id does). Englishman Sydney Carton's supremely noble sacrifice contrasts sharply with the Evrémonde brothers' sinful indulgences (rape, kidnapping, casual murders, the desire for absolute control). Hutter argues that while British citizens "turn external tyranny into internal censorship and control," French citizens cannot or will not do so. Because their external political repression under the *ancien régime* is so extreme, the French are denied psychic integration. In France, "unrestrained selfishness and anarchy tear the country apart" (452). Where political repression is so strong, political retaliation is equally brutal. The atrocities committed by the revolutionaries during the Reign of Terror are the inevitable result of those committed by the monarch and aristocracy of the *ancien régime*. The violence of Madame Defarge and the *sans-culottes* matches that of Evrémonde and other noblemen.

There are historical and psychological reasons why Dickens and Hutter may believe in English moral superiority. True, the English Civil Wars of 1642–1651 were extremely bloody, taking nearly 200,000 lives, but the fact that England is a hundred years ahead of France in the shift from monarchy to representative government makes it look more progressive, enlightened, and reasonable. Psychologically, English national character is often portrayed in literature and oratory as one of self-sacrifice; the Englishman submits his passions to reason and the code of duty—the very core of Enlightenment philosophy. The eighteenth-century Enlightenment period gave rise to the modern political ideology of natural human rights. France and England both produced Enlightenment intellectuals who influenced one another; it was a cosmopolitan movement in which neither nation could claim precedence. Even though Britain wanted to play the role of Reason opposite France's designated role of Passion, the *philosophes* made just as good theorists as the British philosophers. On the British side, Edmund Burke (Anglo-Irish), Thomas Hobbes, David Hume (Scottish), John Locke, and Adam Smith (Scottish) were well matched by Frenchmen Baron de Montesquieu, Voltaire,

Jean-Jacques Rousseau, and Denis Diderot in their contributions to Enlightenment philosophy.

Moral uniformity and equality between the nations would not, however, have produced a good novel, especially from Dickens, who is beloved for his melodramatic exaggerations. In *A Tale of Two Cities*, England must come out on top. In Book the Third, Chapter 14, Miss Pross reiterates to Madame Defarge (who doesn't understand English) that she (Miss Pross) will prevail against Madame Defarge because she is an English person, and therefore on the side of right. Sacrificing herself for a good cause (saving Lucie's life) is Pross' unswerving intention, and she considers it a quality inseparable from her Englishness: "I am a Briton. I am desperate. I don't care an English Twopence for myself" (364). On the other hand, Defarge is evil, in Pross' view, because she is French: "If those eyes of yours were bed-winches and I was an English four-poster, they shouldn't loose a splinter of me. No, you wicked foreign woman; I am your match" (364). Pross assumes that her English moral superiority lends her the strength to claim a physical advantage over a French madwoman. Pross expresses Dickens's bias for his own country; in essence, she believes she is good because she is English, and that God assists the good in any fight. Dickens takes care to make Defarge's death accidental so that Pross (a woman, after all) is saved from committing murder: the Frenchwoman is killed by a gunshot from her own pistol during a scuffle with the Englishwoman.

In contrast to the virtuous English characters (Sydney Carton, Jarvis Lorry, and Miss Pross), the virtuous French ones (Charles Darnay, Alexandre and Lucie Manette) have to emigrate or be killed, suggesting that they are anomalies rather than true representations of French moral character. The revolutionaries are monomaniacal about the purity of identity; any taint of connection to the aristocracy is purged by execution. Despite his love of France (his most frequent vacation destination and the place where he supported his English mistress) and his acerbic satire of English hypocrisies, Dickens presents England as the more tolerant, evolved, and noble of the two nations—as we might expect from a writer who would one day have tea with Queen Victoria.

Works Cited

Dickens, Charles. *A Tale of Two Cities*. Barnes & Noble, 2004.

Hutter, Albert D. "Nation and Generation in *A Tale of Two Cities*." *PMLA* 93.3 (1978). 448–62.

Steinbach, Susie. *Understanding the Victorians*. Chapter 2, "Discussions on the Subject of Reform." Routledge, 2012. 31–58.

Tomalin, Claire. *Charles Dickens: A Life*. Penguin, 2012.

10

Allegory and Personification

Question:

A Tale of Two Cities is historical fiction in a social realist style with aspects of allegory. Some of the characters are actually a collective entity rather than individuals, or in some cases, an individual as well as a collective by the same name. Why does Dickens use allegory and personification, and how do they fit in with the main genre of the novel, which is realism?

Analysis:

Allegory is one of the first literary devices ever used—it's closely related to parable, which is a key rhetorical mode found in the Bible. The messages that allegories convey are usually moral ones. *Merriam-Webster's* definition of allegory is "the expression by means of symbolic fictional figures and actions of truths or generalizations about human existence." Allegory is an extended metaphor that pervades the whole story in which it's found. The most famous example of the genre is Plato's "Allegory of the Cave." In this compelling story, prisoners are living in an underground cave with their heads chained so that they must look at a wall. A row of fires burns in back of them, and figures move in front of these fires (but in back of the prisoners), casting shadows on the wall. Since they see only the wall in front of them, the prisoners take these shadows to be solid beings, i.e., reality. One special prisoner, called The Philosopher, is called to leave the cave and see the sun. At first the light (which represents Truth) blinds him, but once oriented to the real world, he's eager to return to the cave and bring his fellow prisoners up into the light of truth (Fellowship). They resist his efforts (representing Stubborn Ignorance). Plato's allegory means that we get used to whatever limited visions we see and take our illusions for truths. If we are lucky enough to leave our caves of ignorance and see the light, we will initially be blinded. Truth takes some getting used to. We initially resist accepting new truths, but once we believe them, we desire to share them with others.

Besides standing alone as a simple story like Plato's *Allegory of the Cave*, allegory can also be interwoven into novels. *Lord of the Flies* (1954) implicitly likens English schoolboys' cruelty and blood thirst to adult passions that result in the Cold War: a worldwide state of planned mutual annihilation. *The Lottery* represents the ways in which human beings scapegoat innocent people in order to displace their own blame. Orwell's *1984* is an allegory for Russian propaganda and terrorism during the Cold War that led to frightened submission by victims of persecution. *The Crucible* is an allegory for the witch hunts of Senator McCarthy and HUAC (House Un-American Activities Committee) during America's Red Scare of the 1950s. Gillen D'Arcy Wood believes that Dickens's fears of Chartist-fueled revolution in 1855 England inspired his rendition of the French Revolution in *A Tale of Two Cities*, though it lacks a point-to-point correspondence. In short, the allegorical mode in literature is a powerful way to suggest historical repetitions and certain eternal propensities of human nature.

Dickens combines the devices of allegory and personification with those of realism to tell a moral tale about the tragedy of paying back evil with evil, violence with violence, and hatred with more hatred. He develops many personifications of entities such as Wind, Fire, Flood, Hunger, and "the Country." Lucie is known as The Golden Thread for her role in virtuously weaving a family together with the "gold" of her loving personality. The peasant revolutionaries (*sans-culottes*) are all called Jacques, not only because secrecy is fundamental to their success, but also because Dickens wants to imply that, under adverse conditions, this class of people is all alike—that is to say, bloodthirsty. Some of the attackers are called North, South, East, and West (229); their individuality is subsumed in their strategic importance as warriors. In a political reading of literature, one of the dangers of allegory is that it dehistoricizes events, suggesting that its message is good for all time and infusing its realities with a spiritual context. Allegory is good for teaching about history and morality in certain types of fiction, but its form is too general to deal adequately with differences within classes of individuals. It is good for Dickens's purposes of melodrama and satire, but it is too broad-brush to constitute an accurate approach to history.

Dickens uses allegory to depict the generality of the conditions that the novel exposes. His allegorical characters stand in for all those in their group or class. He used the technique often, but it was especially poignant in *Tale of Two Cities,* where he was working from a real-life model. The French revolutionaries actually did substitute allegorical monikers for individual names in order to protect themselves and motivate the people in their struggle (Dickens 389). In this lecture, we'll examine three allegorical figures: Monseigneur, St. Antoine, and The Vengeance. "Monseigneur" refers to two particular noblemen and also to a whole class of individuals—those members of the corrupt aristocracy whose only value is the furtherance of their own power, pride, and pleasure. "Saint Antoine" is the personification and allegorized figure of all the villagers in the Faubourg (neighborhood) St. Antoine. Taken collectively rather than individually, St. Antoine denotes the suffering and indignity that gave rise to revolt. The Vengeance is a friend of Madame Defarge who epitomizes the peasants' murderous intent to avenge themselves on the individuals and the class of people who harmed them. Madame Defarge is quite evil enough on her own ("she was absolutely without pity," 358), but Dickens gives her a sidekick, The Vengeance, perhaps to accentuate the violent capacity of females.

I. Monseigneur. There are two noblemen by this name, one who dwells in the city, one in the country. The nobleman who resides in Paris is easily confused with Marquis Evrémonde because the peasants also call Evrémonde "Monseigneur." The title of Monseigneur, especially in the *ancien régime*, was used to address any eminent person of a rank higher than one's own. It means "My Lord." Monseigneur-in-Town equates himself with God when he bastardizes scripture for his own self-aggrandizement: "The earth and the fullness thereof are mine, saith Monseigneur" (106). We don't learn that the Marquis St. Evrémonde is a distinct character from Monseigneur-in-Town until Evrémonde becomes offended by Monseigneur's cold reception of him. Suddenly, Marquis St. Evrémonde curses the Monseigneur, and drives recklessly away, crushing the peasant child under his carriage wheels (110).

"Monseigneur" is also the name for a collective body. The allegorical Monseigneur is a whole class of noblemen who ignored the socioeconomic problems of their country, abused their serfs and courtiers, and arranged their affairs to garner maximum benefit for themselves. After Chapter 7 ("Monseigneur in Town"), the term "Monseigneur" refers to this collective identity. Dickens mocks their aristocratic pride and self-delusion:

> Monseigneur (often a most worthy individual gentleman) was a national blessing, gave a chivalrous tone to things, was a polite example of luxurious and shining life, and a great deal more to equal purpose; nevertheless, Monseigneur as a class had, somehow or other, brought things to this [the Storming

of the Bastille]. Strange that creation, designed expressly for Monseigneur, should be so soon wrung dry and squeezed out! [224].

After the revolutionaries proclaim martial law and exile the aristocracy (Book 2, Ch. 24), Dickens satirically describes the noblemen's sense of injured pride and incomprehension: "Monseigneur, as a class, had dissociated himself from the phenomenon of his not being appreciated: of his being so little wanted in France, as to incur considerable danger of receiving his dismissal from it, and this life together" (231).

II. Saint Antoine. The neighborhood in east Paris next to the Bastille, St. Antoine is the famine-stricken hotbed of the uprising, with the Defarges' wine shop at its political core. In Christianity, Antoine is the patron saint of lost things. In this case, his namesake village has lost everything—their livelihoods, their dignity, and their decency. In the novel, Dickens personifies this neighborhood collectively as a saint who is suffering all the sorrows and celebrating all the joys of its inhabitants. With this allegorical figure, Dickens mocks the people's penchant for excessive wine drinking: "Saint Antoine in this vinous feature of his..." (164). Once they had licked up all the spilt wine from the broken cask, Dickens describes the villagers' return to depression: "And now that the cloud settled on Saint Antoine, which a momentary gleam had driven from his *sacred* countenance, the darkness of it was heavy—cold, dirt, sickness, ignorance, and want, were the lords in waiting on the saintly presence" (33, emphasis mine). This passage reminds us of the beatific character of the villagers' namesake—ironically, given their own eventual bloodthirstiness. During the Storming of the Bastille, the allegorical Saint Antoine became personally invested in Defarge's heroism: "Saint Antoine was clamorous to have its wine-shop keeper foremost in the guard upon the governor who had defended the Bastille" (216). And when they killed Foulon (the nobleman who said, "let them eat grass"), "Saint Antoine so shouted and danced his angry blood up, that it boiled again, on hearing when the day closed in that the son-in-law of the despatched, another of the people's enemies and insulters, was coming into Paris" (223). By turning the "saint of lost things" into a bloodthirsty revolutionary, Dickens reveals his nostalgia for the lost chivalry and romance of an earlier age, both an imagined historical France and the mythic space of the Bible. Paris changes from the world's most beautiful city into a place of bloodbath and terror.

III. The Vengeance. This allegorical character is Madame Defarge's henchwoman: "The short, rather plump wife of a starved grocer, and the mother of two children withal, this lieutenant had already earned the complimentary name of The Vengeance" (218). When vengefulness is considered a compliment, we know that humanitarianism is at stake. The

Vengeance loves and admires her sister in arms, Madame Defarge, and she serves as a kind of aggrandizing mirror to her friend. For instance, when Madame Defarge refuses Lucy's petition for help in saving Charles, The Vengeance repeats Madame's words, like an echo or refrain. Also, when Madame misses the execution of Darnay, The Vengeance is upset because she knows how much her "sister" enjoys feeding La Guillotine a meal of choice aristocrats. When a messenger brings news that Foulon is afoot, and will be tortured, The Vengeance's blood rises: "The Vengeance, uttering terrific shrieks, and flinging her arms about her head like all the forty Furies at once, was tearing from house to house, rousing the women" (219). Whereas Madame Defarge is characterized as calm and collected, La Vengeance acts as her doppelgänger or darker half. It's curious that Dickens doubles the character of the vengeful female; after all, one Lady Macbeth was quite enough for Shakespeare! This instance might relate to a larger pattern of doubles in the novel. For instance, Carton is a dark doppelgänger of Darnay, with similar looks and similar potential for good, but Carton takes a different path through life's obstacle course and ends up disheveled, disenchanted, and finally, suicidal.

To conclude, what is the point of allegorizing and personifying various ideas in this novel when social realism seems to be an adequate genre for historical fiction? First, it's interesting to note that Dickens is imitating a French revolutionary practice of giving groups of people nicknames that collectivize their identities. For the *sans-culottes*, this may have been a form of secrecy that protected their identities from enemy spies. (*Sans-culottes*, or "without pants," was the term for the peasant revolutionaries who wore long trousers instead of the knee breeches worn by nobility). Second, Dickens wanted to be sure to convey the magnitude of hardship suffered by the working class so as to justify their uprising against the nobility. Showing that their trials were common to all members of their class helps drive home the universality of their problems— everyone suffered. Third, Dickens intends for his novels to deliver a moral message, and allegory is one of the traditional vehicles of morality. He writes for the common people, who tend to respond well to his melodramatic and sentimental plots, characters, and messages. Because of their church attendance, this audience is familiar with allegorical ways of sending a message. A lesson attached to an entertaining plot creates a pleasing package for his readers.

Works Cited

Dickens, Charles. *A Tale of Two Cities.* Barnes & Noble, 2004.
Plato. *The Allegory of the Cave.* https://www.gutenberg.org/files/1497/1497-h/1497-h.htm.
Wood, Gillen D'Arcy. Introduction. *A Tale of Two Cities.* Barnes & Noble, 2004. xiii–xxxi.

11

Law and Justice

Question:

In "The Court Was Crowded All Day," Susie Steinbach describes
the disorganized and inequitable nature of the nineteenth-century
English legal system. Upper-class defendants got away with crimes that
their lower-class counterparts would be hanged for. *A Tale of Two Cities* represents both English jurisprudence and French vigilante justice
during the Revolution. This lecture builds on the earlier discussion
about Dickens's comparison of London and Paris, with a specific focus
on legal procedure. Although the two trials in the novel are held by different types of judicial bodies—the Old Bailey court versus a tribunal
during the French Revolution—Dickens uses them to compare English
and French justice *at that time*. What do the two trial scenes at the
beginning and end of the novel reveal about the relative fairness of the
judicial practices in these two nations during the period of the novel,
1775–1793?

I. The Old Bailey Trial of Charles Darnay for Treason

Given the sarcastic tone of the chapters on the Old Bailey trial (Bk. 2,
Ch. 2 and 3), we know that Dickens finds fault with many aspects of London society, particularly the bloodthirstiness of its people (though, unlike
the French peasants, the English crowds only wish to observe quarterings,
not administer them). Jerry Cruncher likes to watch the tortures committed in the Old Bailey yard. He believes that the term "quartering" includes
other punishments as well: "half-hanging, being sliced up before his [the
convict's] own face, burning of his insides, decapitation, and then being
quartered, or cut in fours" (63). Dickens calls the Londoners' voyeurism

"ogreish" (65). People who relish watching atrocities being committed on others are monsters.

Dickens's next critique of the legal system is the bombastic nature of English barristers. Counselor Stryver struts his pompous figure, his learned vocabulary, and his practiced rhetoric in front of the jury, exaggerating and orating for effect. In contrast, Charles Darnay maintains a serious mien, convincing the reader that he is innocent. His calm temperament and quiet manner appear noble in contrast to his counselor's legal grandstanding.

A third object of Dickens's satire in the trial scene is punishments that far exceed the crimes. The whipping post, pillory, and practice of blood-money (in which people are rewarded for bringing in criminals) turn the Old Bailey proceedings into a spectacle that people pay to attend. A spotlight is created by a mirror placed upon the ceiling so as to reflect light directly onto the defendant's face. This use of bright light to intimidate a victim is reminiscent of the interrogation lights shone upon detainees to scare them into confession—a trope of espionage and thriller films.

The Old Bailey's procedural rules are unsophisticated, and they violate due process. To prove the prosecutor's charge—that Darnay passed English military information to King Louis XVI—the Attorney General relies exclusively on the testimony of Roger Cly, who says he saw the prisoner at various times talking to Frenchmen and passing them lists with names of troops and planned military maneuvers. Counsel for the Defense, Mr. Stryver, destroys the character and credibility of the prosecution's witness. Using Sydney Carton's brilliant strategy, Stryver reveals that Carton's appearance is uncannily like that of the prisoner, thereby "smashing" the prosecution witness's testimony that he saw Darnay in the places and times that he claimed.

The Attorney General (acting as prosecutor) says many things that would be inadmissible in an American court of law in our time. He presumes the guilt of the defendant, leads the witnesses, and ignores the necessity of verifying Darnay's handwriting—"these lists could not be proved to be in the prisoner's handwriting, *but it was all the same*" (68, emphasis mine). The prosecution makes an obvious emotional appeal to the guilty conscience of the jury by claiming they'll never be able to lay their heads on their pillows unless the prisoner's head is taken off (68). The hyperbole and polarization of the Attorney General's characterizations would not engender the trust of a jury today. He describes Barsad to the jury as so noble and patriotic that there should be a public statue of his likeness. Yet they are looking at a witness whom Dickens describes as "sinister." At least *some* members of the jury must be able to detect the prosecutor's falsehoods. His examination of Barsad and Cly is a fine satire of

English judicial procedure. The Judge himself is no less partial than the prosecutor: "Lastly, came my Lord himself, turning the suit of clothes, now inside out, now outside in, but on the whole decidedly trimming and shaping them into graveclothes for the prisoner" (77). Under rules of due process, the judge is not permitted to "trim" or "shape" the evidence to favor the prosecution.

Given the length of time that the prosecution's witnesses are on the stand, and the fact that the case for the defense rests solely on discrediting the witness's identification of the defendant, the reader feels throughout the scene that Darnay is going to be convicted. Fortunately for Charles, however, the jury finds Stryver's argument convincing. The beyond-a-reasonable-doubt standard of proof for criminal convictions did not develop until the mid–1780s, just slightly after Darnay's trial. Nonetheless, in deliberation, this jury must have considered not only whether Cly's testimony was convincing but whether there was any reasonable doubt about its truth and accuracy. Part of the momentum of this chapter is created by building suspense around what the jury's decision will be. Given Dickens's cynical tone, we feel that Darnay will almost certainly be convicted. Therefore, we're greatly relieved when he's acquitted. By carefully orchestrating our emotions, Dickens maintains an entertaining ebb and flow of tension within the scene.

II. The Paris Tribunal Trial of Charles Darnay for "Being an Aristocrat"

As discussed in the lecture entitled "London versus Paris," Dickens presents a sharp contrast between British rationalism and French passion. If the London trial contains procedures and evidentiary standards that give the reader pause, Dickens makes the Paris trial so lawless that London seems positively a model of justice in comparison. On the other hand, since the trial of Darnay in Paris is by tribunal rather than a court of law, the comparison is somewhat skewed. Dickens's point remains, however, that notions of fairness and due process were suspended in the time of the Revolution, and the Paris Tribunal illustrates the point dramatically. A "tribunal" is a judicial body with a lesser degree of formality than a court, in which the normal rules of evidence and procedure may not apply, and whose presiding officers are frequently neither judges nor magistrates. I have likened it to a "kangaroo court," defined by Free Dictionary as "an unfair, biased, or hasty judicial proceeding that ends in a harsh punishment; an unauthorized trial conducted by individuals who have taken the law into their own hands." Charles Darnay's French trial is put on by vigilantes as a sham procedure to rouse the blood of the crowds as their victims proceed to the La Guillotine to provide her daily ration. As such, it is a parody of justice; the tribunal doesn't pretend to offer a fair trial.

In the French Tribunal, all playful satire is gone, and Dickens uses strong words that leave no doubt about his interpretation: "Before that unjust Tribunal, there was little or no order of procedure, ensuring to any accused person any reasonable hearing" (313). In the French system of justice at the time of the newborn Republic, all safeguards against miscarriage of justice are missing. There is no separation of powers, and the head of state serves as judge. The jury is packed with ruthless revolutionaries. The charge is one of belonging to a certain race or class, not of actions per se. In fact, when the Evrémonde brothers' crimes are revealed by the reading of Manette's letter, we learn that the crimes are not his own; they are the actions (rape and murder) of Darnay's relatives. He is to be executed for the crimes of his father and uncle, a practice considered illegal by all legitimate judicial systems. Worse—he is convicted for belonging to a certain class.

With the tyrannical President of the Republic serving as judge and the bloodthirsty revolutionaries serving as jurors, Darnay has no chance. Jacques Three is "a life-thirsting, cannibal-looking, bloody-minded juryman" and "the whole jury is as a jury of dogs empanelled to try the deer" (313). Dickens's wonderful simile accentuates the predatory nature and pack mentality of the jurors. This "trial" makes a mockery of the law and a farce of justice. The charge is "being an Aristocrat, one of a family of tyrants, one of a race proscribed" (314). Dickens describes the prisoner before the trial as "Dead in Law"—not only presumed guilty, but already convicted and doomed and deemed dead, like the people named in Madame's knitted register. At the trial, Darnay's fate rests in the hands of a political president, five judges, a prosecutor, and a jury. There is no defense counsel, and the witness presumed for the defense (Manette) is switched to the prosecutor's side by declaration of the President. Manette is not allowed to explain or refute his prison letter; attempting to do so would put him in contempt of court and result in execution. The President warns him, "Citizen Manette, be tranquil. To fail in submission to the authority of the Tribunal would be to put yourself out of Law.... If the Republic should demand of you the sacrifice of your child herself, you would have no duty but to sacrifice her" (314). In other words, any shred of evidence for the defense is effectively silenced by the threat of defamation and death. This is a totalitarian government.

A final deprivation of due process is the way that the jury members cast their votes. Instead of deliberating and voting behind closed doors—thereby preserving their anonymity and protecting them from influence—these jurors vote publicly, one by one. There is neither anonymity nor

protection. Jurors know that a vote of "guilty" is required if they are to survive the day.

A comparison of the trial scenes implies that, in the novel, English
jurisprudence is fairer and more civilized than French, even though we're
comparing apples and oranges—a law trial during peacetime and a tribunal during revolution. If Gillen D'Arcy Wood is correct, Dickens's novel is
partly a warning about the potential for a Chartist revolution in England.
In this regard, the Tribunal scene emphasizes the point that revolution
entails the total loss of law and order. By sharply contrasting the Old Bailey trial and the French Tribunal, Dickens demonstrates some pride in an
English system of law which, however flawed, is at least more just than
a kangaroo court. With his background in legal journalism (one of his
first jobs was court reporter) and his contempt for legal bureaucracy (dis-
played especially in *Little Dorrit* and *Bleak House*), writing in detail about
legal procedures in these two scenes draws on both his technical specialty
and his allegorical penchant. The French Tribunal stands for the chaos
and mayhem of the French revolution. The opposite outcomes of Darnay's
English and French trials symbolize the respective order and chaos of the
nations at the time.

In the Old Bailey trial, Dickens satirizes the torture-loving crowd,
the bombastic nature of the prosecutor's argument, his disregard of evidentiary rules, and the Judge's prejudice. Despite these drawbacks, justice is served when the innocent defendant is acquitted. Defense counsel
is allowed to be present and is given an equal opportunity to present evidence and give final arguments. The jury deliberates in private and returns
a verdict, not a public vote. In contrast, at the French Tribunal, a political
figure administers the trial, the jury is packed, there is no defense counsel, and the defense witness cannot speak, on penalty of death. The criminal charge is the perceived "race" (aristocratic) and class of the defendant,
not his actions. No wonder the scene reminds us of Black Lives Matter
and our current issues of social injustice. Darnay is being treated in a suspect way based on an attribute of his birth that has nothing to do with his
moral character. He is "breathing while aristocratic," to adapt a current
phrase from race relations discourse. Darnay is being profiled and presumed guilty of criminal acts he did not commit.

Dickens's portrayal of the violence of the French Revolution in the
same period that America was drafting her constitution on Enlightenment
principles invites comparison, but one should do so with full historical
knowledge of the facts. Despite its promising rhetoric, America's constitution did not provide equal rights to women or slaves. While France was
creating a Republic without any pretense of democracy or constitutional
rights, America was pretending to democracy but creating a systemic

inequality that remains today. French and British Enlightenment principles provided the human rights discourse upon which the American constitution is based, but actually enacting and enforcing these ideals took,
and continues to take, a very long time—in America, France, and Britain.
Dickens's inbred sense of British moral superiority is an aspect of Victorian ideology that made him popular with his readers, but today's audiences may contextualize his work within the perspective of later history
and social theories.

Works Cited

Dickens, Charles. *A Tale of Two Cities*. Barnes and Noble, 2004.
Steinbach, Susie. "The Court Was Crowded All Day: Law." *Understanding the Victorians: Politics, Culture and Society in Nineteenth-Century Britain*. Routledge, 2012. 160–174.
Wood, Gillen D'Arcy. Introduction. *A Tale of Two Cities*. Barnes & Noble, 2004. xiii–xxxi.

12

Little Pip's Outsized Guilt

Question:

As an adolescent, Pip makes some choices that are morally question-able, including the exclusion of his family from his newfound social circle and the belief that he is superior to them. As a child, however, Pip appears to be the innocent victim of Mrs. Joe's wrath. Despite his goodness, he is shadowed by a vague but powerful sense of guilt. Why does innocent young Pip feel so guilty?

Synopsis:

Pip was orphaned at birth and reared by his older sister, Mrs. Joe, who constantly beats and berates him. Her husband, Joe Gargery, loves Pip and calls him "best friend," but fails to protect him from his sister's abuse. Pip is seven when he meets an escaped convict, Abel Magwitch, at Pip's family plot in the local churchyard. Magwitch demands that Pip bring him food and a file with which to remove his leg-irons. Magwitch is arrested and transported to Australia to finish his prison sentence. A strange reclusive lady, Miss Havisham, requests Pip's attendance on her and her adopted child, Estella, with the intention of making Pip fall in love with the girl. Miss Havisham was jilted at the altar twenty-five years ago and conse-quently planned revenge on all the male sex by raising Estella to attract, abuse, and abandon suitors. Pip falls hard for Estella even though she is cruel and scorns his low-class status. When Pip learns that he will receive a fortune from a mysterious benefactor upon his age of majority, and will receive financial support until that time, he assumes that Miss Havisham has done the good deed for the purpose of preparing him to marry Estella.

Pip moves to London to get an education. He rooms with a kind and cheerful young man, Herbert Pocket, who teaches him manners with which to ease his way into "gentle" company. On reaching his majority, Pip visits Miss Havisham to thank her for her presumed support. She displays a grown-up Estella, who has acquired grace and manners of her own. Now Pip feels a man's attraction to the beautiful creature. One night, a knock comes at Pip's door. It is Magwitch, returned from Australia, where he has made a fortune as a sheep farmer. Magwitch reveals that he is Pip's benefactor. Having broken the terms of his sentence of permanent exile, he is also a wanted man. Pip learns that Jaggers's housekeeper, Molly, is Estella's mother, and Magwitch her father. Herbert and Pip arrange a secret escape for Magwitch, but just as he is about to board a steamer for Hamburg, an old accomplice, Mr. Compeyson, intervenes. He has brought the authorities to capture Magwitch, but the two criminals assault each other, falling overboard in their fight. Compeyson drowns, and Magwitch's injuries from the steamship blades will also prove fatal. As Magwitch is lingering in the prison infirmary, Pip tells him that his daughter, Estella, is alive and well, and also that he loves him as a true father. When Magwitch dies, Pip contracts a fever. Joe tends him through a long convalescence. Pip plans to propose to Biddy, but she reveals that she is about to marry Joe. Pip goes to Cairo to be Herbert Pocket's clerk and lives with him and his wife. One final chance encounter with Estella proves to him that she finally appreciates his faithful love. Together, holding hands, they leave the dilapidated Satis House for the last time.

Analysis:

The first installment of the three-volume novel presents Pip's early life at the forge, his relationships with Joe and Mrs. Joe, his meeting with Magwitch, his initiation into the weird rites of Satis House, and Jaggers's announcement of his "great expectations" (financial support from an anonymous source). Among the many strange events in these chapters, the recurring references to Pip's strong sense of guilt command our attention—indeed, Pip may possess "one of the guiltiest consciences in literature" (Moynahan 60). But why should innocent little Pip feel guilty? He is the victim of his sister's abuse, not a bully of other people. Pip's faults as a child are the usual ones—small lies and concealments are the worst of these, and his are not severe. He is not without fault in his adolescence, however, and we do see his moral weakness emerge toward the end of Volume I. In the week between learning of his great expectations and leaving for London, his pretensions of social grandeur go to his head. He scorns

Joe because of his lack of genteel manners and succumbs to the flattery of even such an obvious imposter as Pumblechook. Before learning of his great expectations, Pip had exhibited none of these aspects of pride or ambition. In fact, Pip notably does *not* express hatred of his sister. The narrator (grown-up Pip) instead punctuates the telling with satirical barbs, such as "Mrs. Joe was a very clean housekeeper, but had an exquisite art of making her cleanliness more uncomfortable and unacceptable than dirt itself" (23). From his adult perspective, Pip sees that the injustices perpetrated on him by his sister had a profound effect on his character, making him "morally timid and very sensitive" and "in a perpetual conflict with injustice" (63). Pip's self-diagnosed moral timidity goes a long way to explaining why he can't or won't judge Estella and Miss Havisham accurately and escape from their wicked grasp.

In this lecture, I will explore reasons for Pip's outsized sense of guilt and discuss where it leads him. First and foremost, it is an internalization of his sister's brutal treatment of him. Second, the early deaths of seven of his family members set up the conditions for survivor guilt. Third, a shared sense of guilt forms a powerful bond between himself and Joe. Pip's sense of guilt leads inexorably to his choice of a bad love object. He loves Estella not so much because she is beautiful as because she is a familiar type, a prettified version of Mrs. Joe. Both Estella and Pip repeat the patterns of abuse and masochism that they inherited from their parents and guardians. Pip's destiny of living with his best friend and his wife, instead of forming his own home and family, may be seen alternately as the sad "alienation" of a criminal (as Julian Moynahan sees it) or as a fulfilling resolution of his personal needs (as I see it). In sharing Herbert and Clara's Cairo home, Pip is living in the bosom of loving friends and has a good job—as such, the ending may be seen as a recreation of his idealized (and corrected) childhood home: the steady work, the love of a caring male comrade, the absence of the bad mother figure. Depending on one's temperament, the ending may be read as punishment or redemption. I read it as a good, stable situation for Pip, even with the possibility of Estella's friendship. Some readers may hope that he doesn't marry the reformed Estella, not quite believing in her avowed transformation. In any case, Pip ends up better off than he started—and that's all one should look for in the realist, as opposed to romantic, genre.

Great Expectations is considered by many to be Dickens's most successful novel, especially because Pip is a complex hero rather than the flat characters which are Dickens's specialty. Christopher Ricks characterized Pip as just frank enough to be attractive, without either "pandering to the reader's sympathy" or "garnering our disdain at his faults" (Trotter vii). It is precisely because adult Pip narrates his childhood with a fond but evaluating eye that we are able to consider Pip's defection from home as excusable folly rather than contemptible arrogance. Readers admire a narrator who can humbly reflect on his past follies.

In this novel, Dickens reaches psychological depths that he hasn't previously achieved. Specifically, he understands the role of childhood trauma in creating sensitive and proud adults (like himself). Decades before Freud's era, Dickens is aware of the role of the unconscious in creating self-threatening behaviors, or neuroses, as defense mechanisms against perceived harm. Pip's neurosis is caused by the internalization of his sister's criticisms, which creates a strong unconscious sense of his own unworthiness. He also suffers survivor guilt over the deaths of his mother, father, and five brothers. Mrs. Joe, his sister, has told him and her friends that she often wished that Pip had died too. Given his family history, it's easy to understand why Pip identifies strongly with outcasts such as Magwitch—figures unclaimed by either family or community. Since he is accustomed to being thought criminal without having done anything wrong, he may assume that real criminals are good people too.

As Michal Ginsburg points out, Pip's strong sense of guilt actually predates his "sin" of stealing food from Mrs. Joe (both Pip and Joe thought all the food and possessions in the house belonged to her). It starts at birth. The second paragraph of the novel establishes cause for his gloomy temperament, as Pip visits the graves of his father, his mother, and five little brothers who "gave up trying to get a living exceedingly early in that universal struggle" (3). Ginsburg suggests Pip feels responsible for his father's death, as orphans often do. I would add that Pip may have survivor's guilt toward his five brothers as well. Pip must wonder why he and his sister should have survived—he may think there was nothing particularly worthwhile in his sister, and this may cause him to question why it should be her and him, rather than any of the five remaining brothers, who are saved. Amid his ruminations, the text flows seamlessly from gloomy graves to the marshes that are just as desolate. An ominous black gibbet (gallows) is framed in stark relief against the gray evening sky, a detail that filmmakers have utilized to dramatize Pip's fears of execution.* Pip projects his sense of guilt onto objects in his surroundings, such as gates, dykes, and signposts, which then accuse him of stealing and conspiring with criminals. The cattle are strongly personified; they follow him with their judging eyes and condemn him when he steals (though they respect him later when he is granted his "great expectations"). Children tend to

---

* Both David Lean in the 1944 adaptation and Julian Jarrold in the 1999 BBC television version use expressionistic low angle shots of the dark gibbet against the gray sky to good effect. In the novel a pirate was recently hanged on this gibbet, and Pip feels that he could easily be the next victim.

populate the world with spirits and omniscient beings; the bleak marshes afford cattle as the most sentient thing with which Pip can imbue this type of knowledge. The adult Pip looks back with sad fondness on his childish assumptions.

Mrs. Joe is the first reason for Pip's oversized childhood guilt. Pip's sister hates him, or resents her responsibility, which amounts to much the same thing. He might rightly wonder why his sister hates him so much, yet he appears to accept her reasons at face value. Bringing him up had been hard work, because he did all the things a boy normally does—go exploring, fall down, become injured, and sometimes get sick. Being denigrated is bad enough, but to hear she wishes him dead is a degree of cruelty that goes beyond normal sibling rivalry, especially when this wish is shared with her friends. His sister tells her friends of "all the times she had wished [him] in [his] grave, and [he] had contumaciously refused to go there" (28). Sibling rivalry is a strong feeling that can long outlast infancy, and it often entails the wish for the death of the sibling, but Mrs. Joe is acting in the role of mother rather than sister (she's twenty years older than Pip). Her hatred is something more generalized than sibling rivalry, for she denigrates her husband in the same breath and to the same degree as her brother. The only compensation for Mrs. Joe's hatred is Joe's kindness, but that too has its limits. Pip doesn't appreciate it when Joe criticizes his paltry appearance as a babe: "if you could have been aware how small and flabby and mean you was, dear me, you'd have formed the most contemptible opinions of yourself!" (48). Reading between the lines of Joe's story, however, Pip detects that Joe married his sister mainly in order to take care of Pip. After this discovery, Pip realizes that Joe is a noble, self-sacrificing character and begins "looking up to [him] in [his] heart" (50).

While Joe certainly makes life at home tolerable, even a benevolent brother-in-law is not enough to mitigate the effects of the Terrible Mother* which is Mrs. Joe. Dickens establishes Joe's strength and courage in a scene where he fights with Orlick. Yet Joe is unwilling to hit his wife because he's afraid of repeating the pattern of abuse of his own father upon his mother: "I see so much in my poor mother, of a woman drudging and slaving and breaking her honest hart and never getting no peace in her mortal days, that I'm dead afeerd of going wrong in the way of not doing what's right

---

* The Terrible Mother is a Jungian archetype that represents the child's fear of an evil mother, or a mother who sometimes does bad things. To infants and toddlers, mothers are all-powerful; their absolute control over the infant's life seems arbitrary and potentially dangerous. The infant feels powerless to assert its needs against such a monolithic force. A Terrible Mother is in some ways worse than a Bad Father because "femaleness" is supposed to be nurturing and a woman is in fact the literal nurturer when she breastfeeds. In object relations theory, the Terrible Mother archetype becomes an introjected "object" in the infant psyche called the Bad Breast.

by a woman" (50). So Joe refuses to protect Pip from the Tickler, the cane that Mrs. Joe uses on Pip whenever she's "in a Rampage"—which is most of the time. But Pip knows that Joe silently takes his side and that they are "equals." As an equal (more a brother than a father), Joe seems to share Pip's sense of guilt (possibly because of his own mother's victimization), and consequently also shares Pip's identification with criminals. When the posse catches him on the marshes, Magwitch confesses that he stole the blacksmith's food. But Joe doesn't begrudge a poor man a bit of food: "we wouldn't have you starved to death for it, poor miserable fellow-creatur" (40). Living with the Tickler and she who wields it, Joe shares Pip's affinity with accused criminals.

Mrs. Joe's criticisms of Pip don't stop with the complaint that he creates extra work for her. Specifically, she thinks he is ungrateful for her efforts. She has complained so often to her friends—the Hubbles, Mr. Wopsle, and Mr. Pumblechook—that they take it upon themselves to rally to her cause. "Be grateful, boy, to them which brought you up by hand" is Pumblechook's mantra at Christmas dinner and at every other meeting with Pip until he comes into his great expectations. Yet the idiom "brought up by hand" barely masks its real meaning: to be brought up by hand in Pip's case is not to be bottle fed, but to be disciplined daily by Mrs. Joe's slapping, tapping, tweaking, pummeling hands. It is difficult to imagine that a boy who is so abused would *not* develop a severe inferiority complex that would manifest as pride or ambition as soon as he found a way to raise himself up and out of the family. Julian Moynahan claims that Pip's ambition (and repudiation of Joe) is as sinful as murder itself, but I strongly disagree. I believe that the revenge fantasies he unconsciously harbors against Miss Havisham and Mrs. Joe are completely natural and inevitable, given his treatment. An abused child rarely walks away from his family with benevolence toward mankind and faith in his heart. Such a child's great expectations are more likely to entail a good career than a solid belief in a great marriage. He will try to get what is best for himself, since his parents are not his best advocates. (Mrs. Joe supported Pip's patronage by Miss Havisham only because of the money she might get from it, and to get Pip off her hands.) Under these circumstances, Pip's repudiation of his well-meaning brother-in-law is understandable and forgivable—negligent rather than malicious, it hurts no one so much as Pip himself.

Pip does more than experience a vague guilt about living; he actually identifies with Magwitch, a criminal. Michal Ginsburg suggests that when Pip sees Magwitch rise up out of Pip's father's grave, she believes it is the return of his father—and a manifestation of Oedipal guilt. Since Mrs. Joe's characteristics are masculine, she plays the role of bad father rather than mother. Ginsburg believes that Pip combines his dead father, Mrs. Joe, and Magwitch in his imagination to form a ghost that haunts his dreams and threatens to kill him. The ghost represents Pip's generalized guilt for surviving his father and harboring murderous fantasies toward Mrs. Joe and Miss Havisham. I find this a plausible reading of Pip's unconscious fears and wishes. I would also suggest another reason for Pip's identification with Magwitch: that Mrs. Joe treats him, Pip, like a criminal. Mrs. Joe's constant complaints about Pip being a burden to raise lead all of her friends to suspect him of having a bad nature. When Pumblechook hosts a reading of the popular murder mystery *George Barnwell*, Pip assumes that the adults identify him with Barnwell as the killer of his own relative. When Pip learns of Mrs. Joe's attack, he believes the adults consider him guilty, which makes him momentarily believe it himself: "I was at first disposed to believe that *I* must have had some hand in the attack upon my sister" (120). As if reading Pip's mind, Orlick also accuses Pip of attacking his sister, saying Pip was the instigator who *made* Orlick do it. Anyone who had witnessed Mrs. Joe's treatment of Pip would expect him to harbor resentment, so for Orlick to torment Pip in this way was psychologically effective.

Mrs. Joe's criminalization of Pip leads to his instinctive identification with Magwitch. At first, Pip is afraid of Magwitch, but his fear quickly turns to curiosity and pity. When he joins the search for the fugitive, Pip identifies with Magwitch rather than with the adult world represented by soldiers, policemen, or Mrs. Joe's circle of friends. He serves Magwitch without disdain for his criminal condition, being afraid only of Mrs. Joe's rage. Pip does not make distinctions between convicts and free men, perhaps because his sister treats him, and sometimes Joe, like convicts. His crime, in her mind, was simply to be born: "I think my sister must have had some general idea that I was a young offender whom an Accoucheur Policeman had taken up on my birthday and delivered over to her, to be dealt with according to the outraged majesty of the law" (23). The Accoucheur (French for childbirth, or lying-in) Policeman is Dickens's humorous way of suggesting that the midwife saw Pip's badness as soon as he came out of his mother's womb. An original sinner, Pip at birth had already outraged the "majesty of the law," which was his imperious sister. So Pip has a natural affinity for men like Magwitch.

Curiously, Pip puts on his best manners to accommodate Magwitch. In these circumstances, many boys would have told their parents about the fugitive's demand. Most would run away from the fugitive after fulfilling his demands. But Pip is intrigued by his fellow creature. He stays for the meal and tries to compliment Magwitch. Seeing him wolf down the food practically without chewing, Pip assumes gentlemanly manners and says, in all seriousness, "I'm glad you enjoy it, sir" (19). He behaves as though

Magwitch is a gentleman who would want to share the meal, reminding Magwitch that Compeyson is hungry too. Although both men are outlaws to whom most would not extend courtesy, Pip tries to be as polite as he can (19). When the soldiers chase Magwitch, Pip takes responsibility for the fugitive's wellbeing—"I had no doubt I had murdered him somewhere" (28). That evening in bed, Pip worries about "my fugitive friend" (33). In befriending a friendless man, Pip is attempting to compensate for the injustice in his own home, where his sister is the representative of an arbitrary law. She runs her household by intimidation and manipulation (for example, she challenges Joe's masculinity to force him to fight Orlick). In this environment, Pip is the outlaw, Mrs. Joe the lawgiver. Even though his conscience often bothers him in a vague, unexamined way, Pip (and the reader) knows himself to be good. In short, he is living like a criminal in his own home, so he easily relates to an actual adult criminal.

Though identifying with Magwitch in his childhood, Pip rebuffs him in his adolescence. Assuming the trappings of a gentleman, Pip feels he needs to dissociate himself from his humble origins. He is afraid that association with a criminal would disgrace him in Estella's eyes. Later, when Magwitch needs his help to evade the authorities, Pip reverses course once again—a sure sign of his maturation and strong character. From this point forward, he refuses to spurn the man who elevated him from lower- to upper-middle class. Assisting Magwitch in his escape and consoling him during his last illness, Pip learns what good parental love looks like—oddly enough, in the form of a thief and vagrant who has decided to love Pip even at the cost of exposure and execution. Arguably, Magwitch's fatherly love is superior, or at least different in kind, to Joe's brotherly love. Magwitch risks his life to be with Pip, whereas Joe will not even risk his wife's disapproval by defending him. With Estella lost to him, Pip can now make his own moral judgments instead of borrowing those of another person. He calls Magwitch his "second father," and in doing so, partially redeems himself from his sin of ambition.

But before Pip can be redeemed completely, he must live out to the bitter end his infatuation with Estella. We may wonder why Pip, who has experienced abuse from a Terrible Mother figure, would choose a love object with so many of the same qualities (coldness, selfishness, aggression, and pride) and one who shares the attitude that Pip is essentially worthless. Yet it is precisely Pip's relationship with Mrs. Joe that leads inexorably to his choice of a bad love object who will reinforce his internalized sense of essential worthlessness. He loves Estella not so much because she is beautiful as because she is familiar by virtue of her similarity to Mrs. Joe. Her complaints may be different—in the first meeting she calls him a "common labouring-boy" with coarse hands, thick boots, and a countrified diction. But the essence of the two women's complaints is the same—Pip is unworthy of their regard and should not expect kindness or warmth from them. Mercilessly mocking Pip's desire for acceptance and natural kindness, Estella is a beautiful, gentrified version of Mrs. Joe. Since she is cruel, Pip may not actually love Estella so much for her beauty as for her confidence. He contrasts Estella to himself, saying she seems much older than he is, because "she is a girl, and beautiful and self-possessed" (56). Estella has what Pip needs most, a sense of self-worth, a conviction that she deserves fair treatment and the respect of adults.

As in so many other Dickens novels, the orphaned child whose fate depends on chance is a central feature of *Great Expectations*. In this novel, there are three orphans, each of whom fares differently in their family placement. Biddy does the best of the three, despite the unlikely odds. She is brought up by Mr. Wopsle's great-aunt, a vacant-minded shopkeeper with a drinking problem who pretends to run a night school. But Biddy cultivates her inner resources, resulting in a calm demeanor, an accurate evaluation of other people, and loyalty to friends who treat her well. Biddy has the self-possession that Pip desperately lacks. Pip is the second orphan; we have already examined the positives (Joe) and negatives (Mrs. Joe) of Pip's family placement. As for Estella, she was "orphaned" when her mother, Molly, was acquitted of murder but still living as a vagrant, and her father, Magwitch, was transported to Australia. Estella was fortunate that Molly's lawyer placed her in a wealthy household, but much less fortunate in the character of her guardian, Miss Havisham, who selfishly used the child for her own evil plans of revenge "against all of the male sex." Estella's monstrous narcissism is well explained by her upbringing. She is Pip's foil, insofar as she is more damaged by her guardian's abuse than he is by Mrs. Joe's. Like Pip, Estella also chooses a bad love object, Bentley Drummle, who will abuse her once they are married (Jaggers recognizes in him the "violent criminal type"). Pip would gladly have followed the same path and chosen Estella as a mate who would continue abusing him. Fortunately for Pip, however, Estella didn't want him. Magwitch broke Pip's pattern of abuse when he showed him the nature of true love and paved Pip's way back to his own family.

Dickens knew from experience that abusive families create abusive children who abuse their own children, who in turn repeat the vicious cycle. The author carried forward the results of his parents' cold treatment of him, which affected his ability to be a good husband and father. Insofar as it elucidates his understanding of family dysfunction, I'll provide a few details about Dickens's home life. He was sometimes a good father, especially when providing delightful entertainment for his favorite children and loving some of them in his own way. He expressed, however, a sense of frustration and regret that he'd had so many children (ten) and tended to neglect them. On the other hand, he lavished attention on the "adopted daughters" of Urania Cottage, a charitable institution he founded with Angela Burdett-Coutts to rehabilitate prostitutes and other fallen women (Hartley). Dickens didn't demonstrate a strong paternal attachment to his own children, which biographers attribute to the fact that they lacked his stellar ambition and application (with the exception of Henry, who attended Cambridge and became a lawyer). Largely deciding their careers for them, he dispatched five of his sons to the far corners of the empire. When he separated from his wife in 1858, he published a statement to clear his reputation by placing blame on her. He expelled her from his house and tried to alienate the affections of the children from their mother. Dickens's fictional happy families are thus a product of his wishes rather than a reflection of his own home (at least after the initial honeymoon and young family period was over). *Great Expectations* reflects Dickens's awareness of the nature of abusive and/or neglecting families.

Pip's strange love of the abusive Estella is due not only to familiarity—her resemblance in behavior to Mrs. Joe—but also to an unconscious recognition of her orphan status and her abuse by Miss Havisham. Joe's father beat Joe's mother, and Joe had to consciously vow to stop that cycle with regard to his own wife, but at the same time, Joe's "moral timidity" (to use Pip's term about himself) stopped him from defending Pip from daily beatings by his sister. Aware of the injustices perpetrated upon him by his sister, Pip may worry that stopping the cycle and refusing to beat another person is "unmanly" passivity. Would Pip have become an abuser in a marriage to Estella? Would they have formed a codependent relationship in a miserable marriage that perpetuated aspects of the abuse in each one's childhood home?

On reading the proofs of the manuscript, Dickens's writer friend Edward Bulwer-Lytton recommended a new ending for *Great Expectations* because the original one might be "disappointing" to readers. Dickens decided to adopt Bulwer-Lytton's ending in the interests of maintaining his popularity. In both endings, Dickens presents an Estella who has been softened through suffering. After her painful marriage to Drummle, she proclaims she now knows and values what she lost—Pip's love. In the original ending, they part after her revelation. In the published ending, Estella goes much further, begging Pip's forgiveness and asking for his friendship. They leave "the ruined place" (Satis House) together, hand in hand, and Pip muses, "in all the broad expanse of tranquil light.... I saw the shadow of no parting from her" (484). We might quibble over semantics here: does this mean there would be a shadow if Pip did *not* part from Estella? Or does it mean he saw no possibility of parting from her? Either way, Pip may be in for a rough ride. David Lean's 1944 film adaptation gives us a full Hollywood ending, replete with romantic great expectations. But I find Dickens's original ending much better. It's more in keeping with the genre of realism, with the tone of the novel, and with our knowledge of human nature. In the original ending, Estella remains somewhat aloof and sad, but ever her bossy self: "I thought you would like to shake hands with Estella too, Pip. Lift up that pretty child and let me kiss it!" (509). She does not explain how she has changed through suffering, but nevertheless Pip reads the change in her voice and touch. The resolution in this original ending is truer—it redeems Pip's tortured love by having Estella acknowledge its worth. The original ending does not, however, promise the fulfillment of what was essentially a child's fairy tale dream in the first place. Where attraction was initially based on Pip's history of abuse, future fulfillment does not seem to lie in his pairing with a woman who has not yet proven her worthiness. Thanks to Dickens's meticulous exposition and astute psychological comprehension of family dynamics, Pip remains, through the passing of ages, a fully realized character whose complexities remind the reader of real life. That realism includes not knowing whether Estella is a good enough mate for Pip.

Works Cited

Dickens, Charles. *Great Expectations*. Penguin, 1996.
Moynahan, Julian. The Hero's Guilt: The Case of *Great Expectations. Essays in Criticism* 10:1 (1960). 60–79.
Ginsburg, Michal Peled. "Dickens and the Uncanny: Repression and Displacement in *Great Expectations." Dickens Studies Annual* 13 (1984). 119–132.
Hartley, Jenny. *Charles Dickens and the House of Fallen Women*. Methuen, 2008.
Tomalin, Clare. *Charles Dickens: A Life*. Penguin, 2012.
Trotter, David. Introduction. *Great Expectations*. Penguin, 1996. vii–xx.

13

Jack Maggs—
Magwitch Writes Back

Question:

Jack Maggs, by Peter Carey (1997), is a neo–Victorian rewriting of *Great Expectations* from Magwitch's point of view. Maggs aspires to regain his English identity after his fall from grace as a convict and lifelong exile to Australia. Peter Carey's version makes Pip evil and brings Charles Dickens himself into the events as a principal character. How does the rewriting shed light on psychological issues presented or avoided in the original text, such as Pip's guilt and Magwitch's motivations?

Synopsis:

In Peter Carey's retelling of *Great Expectations*, Magwitch reappears as a protagonist called Jack Maggs. The novel explores Maggs's inferiority complex as an Australian ex-convict who attempts to combat the shame of transportation and of his childhood as a Thames mudlark and silver thief brought up by an abortionist. After serving a seven-year sentence and then becoming rich in Australia as a brick factory owner, Jack Maggs violates the terms of his lifelong exile by returning to England in 1837. He aims to move in with his protégé, Henry Phipps. Similarly to Pip, all that four-year-old orphan Phipps ever did for Maggs was give him food when he was in chains, but Maggs is so impressed by Phipps's "innocence," that he vows to "weave him a nest so strong that no one can hurt his goodness" (287). Consequently, Maggs pays for Phipps's education and buys him a house at 27 Great Queen Street in London's posh Holborn neighborhood.

Upon his return to London, Maggs finds Phipps's house empty, so he hires on as footman in the house of *arriviste* Percy Buckle next door. In the evenings, Maggs crosses the rooftops to break into Phipps's abandoned house, where he writes letters in invisible ink to explain his personal history to his "son," Henry Phipps.

As a child, Maggs had been abandoned with the mud larks—scavengers for items of small value in the Thames mudflats. Ringleader of a gang of child thieves, Silas Smith found and brought the infant Maggs to an abortionist, Mary "Ma" Britten, to raise. Silas trained Maggs to enter wealthy homes through the chimneys to steal silver. At age fifteen, Maggs loved and impregnated Silas's other ward, Sophina. Afraid of losing her "golden geese," Mary Britten aborted Sophina's fetus. Tom, Ma Britten's biological child, reported Sophina and Jack to the police for theft. At Sophina's trial, Maggs claimed that he, rather than Sophina, was the thief, but he was convicted of perjury and burglary, and was unable to spare his beloved.

Returning to the present time, Maggs meets writer Tobias "Toby" Oates (a character based on Charles Dickens) who claims to have mesmeric powers that can magnetize the thoughts out of his clients. Recognizing the value of Maggs's "Criminal Mind" to help him create more realistic characters, Oates cuts a deal: Maggs will allow fourteen mesmeric sessions in return for an introduction to the "Thief-taker" Wilfred Partridge, who will locate Henry Phipps. During the mesmeric sessions, Oates drags memories out of Maggs's unconscious mind, but also implants ideas of his own, such as the Phantom. This figure is a composite of the tormentors that Maggs has known in his life, a shapeshifter whose final form is a blonde, blue-eyed soldier. The Phantom appears in flashbacks of Maggs's past traumas, including abuse by prison officials, floggers, and his foster brother, Tom; and a flash-forward to his "son," Henry Phipps, who will attempt to murder Maggs. Angered that Oates is using his story for personal gain, and afraid that Oates might turn him in, Maggs threatens to disclose Oates's own darkest secret—that he has impregnated his wife's sister, Lizzie. Their knowledge of the other's worst sin and crime entwines them in a pact of secrecy. In self-defense, Maggs kills the Thief-taker whom Oates has revealed as a fraud. Maggs handcuffs Oates and brings him home to treat Lizzie with abortion pills procured from Mary Britten.

Meantime, Percy Buckle dismisses his maid, Mercy Larkin, on discovering that she has had intimate conversations with Maggs. Buckle had rescued Mercy as a child from the prostitution career that her mother was planning for her. In return for his patronage, Mercy sleeps with him. Realizing she prefers Maggs to himself, Buckle plans Maggs's death. Buckle convinces Henry Phipps to "lawfully" shoot Maggs, by pretending that he has discovered Maggs intruding in his own house. As Lizzie is dying from hemorrhaging brought on by the abortion pills, Henry Phipps shoots at Maggs with a pistol but misses because Mercy Larkin puts her hand in front of the muzzle. Maggs realizes his "son" hates him and is finally able to correct his misconception of Phipps's temperament. Mercy convinces Maggs to marry her and return to Australia to raise his two biological sons who are in foster care in Sydney. The family multiplies and prospers. Back in London, Oates is so traumatized by Lizzie's death that he doesn't finish his novel, *The Death of Jack Maggs*, until 1860.

Analysis:

In the past twenty years, postcolonial scholars have been reframing their discourse of colonizer/colonized relations from a model of center and periphery to an emphasis on ways in which the two are mutually constitutive. *Jack Maggs* provides a good example of this mutuality by intertwining the identities and needs of the Australian ex-convict, Jack Maggs, with the British writer, Tobias Oates. Australia is the colony where Maggs has been exiled for life, and London is the center of empire where he wants to return, find Phipps, and become a gentleman. During the course of their meetings, Australian ex-con Maggs and British gentleman-writer Oates find out they have more in common than they or anyone else would expect.

Fictional adaptations of canonical texts in which minor colonial characters become protagonists are said to be "writing back to empire" insofar as they interrogate and critique Eurocentric notions of language, literature, and power.* In this novel, Jack Maggs (via Australian writer Peter Carey) writes back to the British Empire to dramatize the long-term psychic costs of the transportation experience, including sadistic abuse by prison wardens, lifelong exile to a remote location, and the effects of both conditions on the ex-convict's psyche. As Mercy tells Jack, "it were the King who lashed you," effectively charging the ruler of empire with the offense of prison flogging because his regime allowed and encouraged this widespread practice (346). Carey's novel creates sympathy for a "criminal" by showing a child raised to be a thief through no fault of his own. Carey also critiques the legal system: transportation, a seven-year sentence, and lifelong exile for burglary are excessive and cruel punishments

---

* Salman Rushdie coined the phrase in an article, "The Empire Writes Back with a Vengeance," in the *London Times*, July 3, 1982. *The Empire Writes Back: Theory and Practice in Post-Colonial Literature* (eds. Bill Ashcroft, Gareth Griffiths, and Helen Tiffin; Routledge, 1989) is the first major theoretical work addressing a wide range of postcolonial texts and their relationship to issues of postcolonial culture.

that exceed what the crime deserves. The previous lecture addressed the question of Pip's guilt—why an innocent child would have such a troubled conscience—concluding that his internalization of his sister's criticisms caused him to consider himself not only worthless but a criminal. The idea of criminality, however, had a special meaning to Pip. When Magwitch appeared on the scene, Pip not only respected but identified with him. In Pip's house, the "outlaw" was a kinder role than the lawgiver's, played by Mrs. Joe. Carey's rendition of Magwitch as Maggs carries forward this notion of the thief who is kinder than the lawgivers who punish him.

Peter Carey's modern adaptation sheds light on the question of Pip's guilt by shifting the focus from guilt to shame, from child to adult psychology, and from moral absolutes to moral ambivalence in each of the characters (except for Phipps, who is pure selfishness). Jack Maggs is a complex protagonist who is both loving and violent. His psychic life is permeated with shame at being considered an Australian, which, in the early nineteenth century, was synonymous with convict or ex-con: "I am not of that race, the Australian race," he protests (340). In returning to London, he hopes to establish a life among the English gentry. This requires that he disown his colonial experience: "I am a fucking Englishman.... I am not to live my life with all that vermin [Australians]. I am here in London where I belong" (140). Though he aspires to Englishness, Maggs cannot hide his identity, which shows in his accent, his rough mien, and his scarred back. Carey's novel addresses the consequences of early Victorian England's "solution" to many social problems, from fallen women to petty criminals clogging the prisons—send them as far away as possible and prevent their return. Like Freud's "return of the repressed," Maggs's past cannot be buried. He comes back to claim what he believes is rightly his— Phipps's love and his own English birthright—and inadvertently confronts his repressed terrors through mesmeric sessions with a Charles Dickens stand-in.

To understand the novel's complex psychological resonances, it's helpful to distinguish between guilt and shame. Guilt is the feeling that one has done something to harm others, whereas shame is a pervading sense of unworthiness that may be unconnected with any specific act but is a condition of the environment in which one grew up or lived as an adult. Maggs may be ashamed of his unsavory childhood experiences in the mudflats, the abortion clinic, and the band of thieves. But he's far more ashamed of his prison-time and his Australian convict identity. On the other hand, Oates is ashamed of his "scoundrel" father (a murderer), his abandonment by his parents, his debts, and his sense of being a fraud whose creative ideas are stolen from others—such as the "Criminal Mind" stories he's plagiarizing from Maggs. Both men are also haunted by guilt.

Oates's sources are much more obvious: his affair with his sister-in-law, his neglect of his wife, and his complicity in Lizzie's death. Guilt and shame are overlapping rather than disparate; especially, repressed guilt can manifest as a pervasive feeling of shame when a person has buried or denied earlier experiences. For instance, under hypnosis Maggs unearths a repressed feeling of guilt that he failed to protect Sophina from Tom's advances and Ma Britten's abortion, which had manifested as generalized shame prior to his mesmeric sessions with Oates.

Like Dickens, Carey inverts class stereotypes so that lower-class characters have nobler traits, such as kindness and loyalty, than those of the upper and rising classes. So, for example, Maggs and Mercy are less selfish than Percy Buckle, Tobias Oates, and Henry Phipps. On the other hand, Carey universalizes the struggle to better oneself, so that even the protagonist Maggs is caught up in attempts to appear more refined than he is. Even a minor character such as Percy Buckle is an amalgam of good and bad, generosity and revenge. Starting out as a poor fishmonger and a rescuer of prostitutes, Percy gradually degenerates when he becomes a "gentleman," ending as an accomplice to murder. Whereas Dickens's sentimentality creates virtuous paragons such as Amy Dorrit and Lucie Manette and unredeemable blackguards such as the Evrémonde brothers, Carey's comparatively cynical outlook distributes positive and negative traits among all characters (except for Phipps, who is thoroughly bad), making his cast truer to twenty-first-century readers' understanding of human complexity.

Carey writes back to *Great Expectations* to examine its psychological mysteries, both manifest and latent. By switching the focus from Pip to Magwitch, Carey examines the latter's extraordinary act of generosity in adopting Pip. In Carey's revision, Jack Maggs is deluded and violent but also kind to many others besides Phipps. But he also has a social ambition that was absent in his Dickens counterpart. In giving Maggs a trait of Dickens's Pip—his social ambition—Carey suggests that it's not simply the possession of the trait but rather the way in which one pursues one's ambition that reflects one's moral worth. In Dickens's novel, it is not Pip's ambition that darkens his soul but his snobbery, the refusal to associate with the loved ones who haven't risen along with him. Although Carey minimizes this aspect of Maggs's history, the fact that he has abandoned two sons in Australia is a major reminder of the cost of his social ambition. The text implies that he abandons them *because* they're Australian, and Maggs is trying to dissociate himself from Australia. Pip's shame about his humble origins transposes, in Carey's novel, into Maggs's shame about being an Australian. As an Australian emigrant himself (Carey moved from Australia to New York in 1990), Carey imagined that Maggs would be embarrassed about his association with the penal colony where he was humiliated in servitude, then freed and given a parcel of infertile land and an unmistakable colonial accent.*

Besides exposing the injustice of transportation, Carey's twenty-first-century "writing back" also reflects contemporary awareness of the effects of trauma on people's behavior and health. Maggs has buried the wounds of his prison experience but its trauma permeates his life in the forms of shame and terror. In letters to Phipps, Maggs tells a detailed story of his childhood. In contrast, his adult history is vague, suggesting that he has blocked adult experiences of which he is ashamed. Memories of his torture at the prison camp spring up in dreams and under hypnosis; the penal experience may have been even more traumatic than his childhood with a sadistic foster mother and brother, and thus, more deeply buried.

Despite a history of abuse, Maggs manages to retain compassion for others which reveals itself in several acts of kindness: saving Edward Constable's job, protecting Tom Britten from Ma's wrath, and consoling Mercy for "losing her da." Although he is often blunt, threatening, or defensive, Maggs has a heart of gold. Like many Dickens characters, he is too gullible for his own safety and pays a price for his trust in other humans. On the other hand, he carries a dagger in his boot and is quick to use it.

Besides his violent temper, Maggs's moral integrity is compromised by his abandonment of his biological sons and his preference for his adopted son—simply because the latter is an English gentleman. As such, Maggs's generosity toward Phipps is accompanied by a selfish motive: to share Phipps's status by moving into his house and social circle. Unlike Dickens, who gradually develops Pip's trajectory of self-improvement, Carey resolves Maggs's moral deficiency in a sudden "fix." In an ending whose sentimentality rivals that of *Great Expectations,* Mercy redeems Maggs by teaching him his duty toward his natural sons and convincing him to return to Australia and raise them. Some readers consider Carey's ending inappropriate, as its sentimentality is unwarranted by the rest of the novel, similar to the happy romantic ending tagged onto *Great Expectations* at Bulwer-Lytton's behest. Carey may have been consciously imitating the master at this point, and/or he may have thought that Maggs deserved a reward for his great, though misdirected, capacity to love.

---

* The normal term of servitude for transported thieves was seven to fourteen years, but Maggs's was for the term of his natural life. "Return from Transportation" was a capital offence. The convict assignment system gave convicts heavy labor on farms or public works such as building roads and harbors. They generally worked in brutal conditions on meager rations. Maggs must have excited the wrath of his masters, for he was flogged. However, he did eventually earn probation and a land grant. After their term of servitude, the British government offered freed convicts the means to stay in Australia to help Britain settle the colony: land, tools, seed, livestock, and even free food for one year (oldbaileyonline.org).

Despite occasional unevenness in tone, Carey's novel does succeed in rendering psychologically accurate characters. He uses parallelism and mirroring to dramatize psychological realities about the nature of shame and trauma. Maggs and Mercy are a pair who share a particular type of child abuse—they were criminalized by their guardians for the guardians' own financial profit, Mercy as a whore, Maggs as a thief. Without discussing their wounds, they instinctively bond through this shared trauma. But it is Maggs and Oates who form the principal parallel and the most fascinating relationship. Oates elicits evidence of Maggs's traumatic wounds and helps to heal them, though this is achieved only obliquely and unintentionally. As a brickmaker and a writer, the men come from different classes and trades, but are more similar than is outwardly apparent. Being abandoned in childhood, Oates and Maggs have both worked hard to arrive at their current property-owning status. Despite his wealth, Maggs still sports the looks and dialect of the Australian ex-convict. After serving his sentence, he earned his living by digging clay out of his land to make bricks, becoming rich in the booming economy of British Australia. Incidentally, there's an interesting continuity between his adult enterprise and his childhood métier of mudlark—both involve digging "treasure" out of seemingly worthless dirt. In the Empire's capital, orphaned Oates rises himself from his humble origins to make a living by the pen. Anxious to accumulate social status, he loves to hobnob with famous writers. With his great aptitude for mimicry, Oates can easily put on the upper-crust dialect of his literary peers and their betters. Maggs wears a red waistcoat, and Oates a green one speckled with yellow and brown: each makes obvious plays for attention.

Maggs and Oates seek validation to combat the shame they feel due to their childhood abuse. Like the actual Dickens, Oates is indignant at his parents' treatment. After placing him in an orphanage until age four, Oates's mother took him in for a year but found the responsibility unpleasant, at which point she fobbed him off on his father, who likewise neglected him. At age five, Oates had to fend for himself. Like Dickens, Oates is a self-made man who compensates for childhood indignity with steely determination to make a name for himself: "He had been cast off, but he would not be flotsam. He had been denied a proper school but he had learned to read and write and he had made himself, by will, a sorcerer of that great city" (170). Dickens never forgave his parents either. He told his best friend, John Forster, that he was a "not particularly-taken-care-of-boy" and didn't understand "how [he] could have been so easily cast away at such an age" (Forster 13, 23). When he was twelve, Dickens's parents got him work at a bootblack factory while the rest of the family lived in the Marshalsea Debtor's Prison. Twisting the knife, his mother wished to keep him working even after they'd been released.

As an adult, Maggs also experiences righteous indignation at his foster mother for using him as her tool. One day during his childhood, he heard Ma tell a jealous Tom that he shouldn't kill Jack—but only because Jack was their breadwinner. Looking back in anger, adult Maggs writes, "It is only now I feel the fury in my furnace: that the bitch would make this speech before a little nipper, letting him know that he had been raised for a base purpose like a hog or a hen" (117). Deprived of motherly love, Oates and Maggs seek other kinds—romantic infatuation, filial devotion, and professional acclaim. Oates needs strokes from his readers and his seventeen-year-old sister-in-law, and Maggs seeks love from a randomly encountered boy whose one small act of generosity he reciprocates with a bountiful supply of love and money.

Because of their persistent sense of shame and unworthiness, Oates and Maggs look for love in the wrong places. Oates had an "unholy thirst for love…. He would not be loved enough, not ever" (43). Finding his wife slow-witted and unattractive, he seeks passion in the arms of his teen-aged sister-in-law. He yearns for public acclaim, becoming as susceptible to flattery and applause as young Pip had been. When he travels to Brighton to write an article about a factory fire, he attends the surgeons' dinner because of his desire to socialize with gentry, even though he has a personal antipathy toward doctors. Succeeding in making them laugh at his impersonations, "he glowed within the circle of their love" (144). Oates needs the limelight in order to feel loved.* After the evening's entertainment is over, he immediately loses his self-esteem and feels deflated: "He was Toby Oates, son of John Oates, a well-known scoundrel" (150). Toby's father was acquitted of a murder charge because the jurors believed he was too small to kill the larger victim, but Toby believes his father did commit the crime. Ironically, the father of the gentleman, Toby, committed a more heinous crime (murder) than the foster father of the convict, Maggs (burglary).

Like Toby Oates, Jack Maggs is aware of his own unholy quest for love, even from the most unlikely source. Writing of his upbringing at Ma Britten's abortion clinic in Pepper Alley Stairs, Maggs muses, "I would have given up all lessons if I could have had Mary Britten love me and call me Son" (102). Recognizing that his childhood wish went unfulfilled, adult Maggs thinks that supporting Phipps will provide the unconditional love that Ma never gave. Despite warnings from Constable and Mercy, Maggs can't understand that his love for Phipps is misplaced until

---

* Like Toby Oates, Dickens loved the immediate ego gratification of public readings, where he mesmerized audiences with his lifelike portrayals of beloved characters. Dickens enjoyed the kind of celebrity that wasn't seen in Britain again until a century later, when idolatrous teenaged girls fainted at Beatles concerts.

the moment he's looking down the muzzle of a gun that his "son" is pointing at him.

Maggs mirrors Oates's faults at a deep unconscious level. In *Great Expectations*, Pip and Magwitch are the symbiotic pair who assist each other's growth. In *Jack Maggs*, Oates and Maggs are such a pair, rather than Maggs and Phipps. The Oates character is a fictional version of Charles Dickens that allows the reader to speculate about Dickens's own shame and guilt and how they might have affected his actions. For instance, Dickens's generous establishment of a home for fallen women, Urania Cottage, may have arisen out of guilt, whether about maintaining a mistress (Ellen Ternan), or possibly using prostitutes' services (we don't know whether or not he did, but some biographers speculate that his frequent nighttime rambles in seedy neighborhoods might have included visits to prostitutes). Dickens's malicious public campaign against his wife (when they separated) may also be an attempt to compensate for guilt about leaving her to be with the beloved mistress—that is, displacing the blame from self to other.

Exploring Oates's shame and guilt is an exercise in understanding Dickens's own psychic economy. Since Dickens is a character in the novel, Carey is allowed to imaginatively explore the complexes of the author and to speculate without committing a biographical fallacy (taking fictional events and personalities as real events and people in the author's life). When Oates plumbs Maggs's unconscious psyche under hypnosis, he reveals the shame and trauma that are experienced by both characters: "For the writer was stumbling through the dark of the convict's past, groping in the shadows, describing what was often a mirror held up to his own turbulent and fearful soul" (86). Putting his client under hypnosis, Oates gets direct access to Maggs's inner monologue, unmediated by tricks and defenses of the conscious mind. When Oates characterizes his activity as learning the Criminal Mind, he is also describing his interest in his own unconscious, the place of unholy desire and overwhelming terror that is currently driving him to commit adultery. Most of the details of Oates's appearance, friendships, hang-ups, and marital problems are borrowed from Dickens's own life. In mixing up the characters and refocusing the story's point of interest, Carey performs a double displacement: first shifting attention from the boy (Pip) to his fugitive friend (Maggs) and then to the author (Dickens), all in the interest of exploring their hidden sources of guilt and shame.

The assumed mutuality of Maggs and Oates's agreement is deceptive; it is in fact a radically unbalanced contract. The deal is that Maggs will undergo fourteen sessions of hypnosis in return for Oates introducing him to the Thief-taker who will find Phipps. Even though Maggs attains temporary relief from his *tic douloureux* while "between the magnets," Oates's potential gains from the deal are far greater than Maggs's. The novel that Oates will construct out of Maggs's story is worth much more than the short character sketches he's been selling to the newspaper for five pounds apiece—he sells the copyright in *The Death of Jack Maggs* for fifty pounds. The project will, however, dredge up so much shame about the events in this period that Oates will be unable to finish it for two decades.*

In Dickens's life, the year 1837 was a professional turning point that Carey's novel dramatizes. *Oliver Twist* (1837) was Dickens's second novel, after *Pickwick Papers*, and showed an advance in Dickens's conception of the novel form. If not quite an exploration of the criminal mind (his psychological insight wasn't yet that developed), it was a shocking exposé of the relationship between hardened criminals, prostitutes, and children that fascinated its author and riveted his audience. Maggs unexpectedly drops into Oates's life at the very moment when the author needs a good story in order to support a growing family. So the deal with Maggs was a substantial professional asset for Oates, moving him to the next creative level. As for Maggs, the deal gave him only an introduction to the Thief-taker, a man who was reputed to be able to find any person in England. Underscoring the flimsiness of Oates's promise is the fact that Buckle, Constable, Mercy, and Oates already know the whereabouts of Henry Phipps, whereas the Thief-taker is a fraud and can't help at all. Their trip to Gloucester to see the Thief-taker proves the unfairness of Oates and Maggs's agreement: Oates has received access to the Criminal Mind, but Maggs has received nothing.

The psychological aspects of the secret-trading pact between Maggs and Oates are, however, more fruitful. Their mutually beneficial exchange of burdensome secrets enables them to witness each other's trauma. The narrator makes several references to the powerful human need of confession—especially of those sins most unspeakable in society. In Victorian times, these would include sodomy, adultery, and abortion. Once again, it transpires that the gentleman's morality is more corrupted than that of the criminal. Maggs was the victim of various forms of abuse, whereas Oates is the perpetrator of many crimes, including incest, adultery, and abortion. When he begins to feel the injustice of the pact, Maggs introduces Oates to the practice of "secret trading" that he had learned in

---

* *The Death of Jack Maggs* is published in the same period as *Great Expectations*, 1860–61, but differs from Dickens's novel in its treatment of the Magwitch character. Because of his resentment for Maggs's contribution to Lizzie's death (directing him to Ma Britten for the abortion pills), Oates avenges himself fictionally by blackening Maggs's character and killing him violently in a raging fire. In contrast, Dickens sweetens Magwitch's end of life with Pip's full devotion and the knowledge that his daughter is alive and well.

prison. Prisoners would trade secrets in order to protect one another from exposure. Sharing a dark secret is simple currency for mutual protection, because a criminal will not usually turn in his fellow offender if it means certain punishment for himself. But prisoners aren't the only people who feel a need to unburden themselves of shameful stories; this is a universal human need. Most characters in the novel do find someone to whom to unburden their woes. For instance, Edward Constable "felt a dangerously strong desire to confess" because he wants to reveal his forbidden homosexuality, his affair with Henry, and Henry's shameful rejection of him: "He had a passion to unburden himself, to disclose that he too had known Henry Phipps, known him in the most personal and private sense" (182).

The desire for confession is so powerful, and confessing is so relieving, that Maggs's painful facial tic subsides as soon as he reveals his dark secrets to Oates under hypnosis. Torn between fear of revelation and the desire to unburden himself, Maggs frequently curses Oates for violating his privacy. Yet Maggs is reaping a benefit beyond pain relief, for his nightly writings reveal greater access to his past and a better understanding of his abuse. Recollections of one trauma (being a prisoner) beget recollections of another (being a child in Ma Britten's house). As a novelist, Oates is more aware than Maggs of the human need for confession, telling his learned friends: "Even the lowest type of renegade has an inner need to give up the truth. Look at those gallows confessions they are still selling on Holborn. It is what our fathers called 'conscience.' We all have it" (33). Yet Oates is unwilling to enter the pact of trading secrets until Maggs threatens him physically during the coach ride to Gloucester. Only then is Oates persuaded to play the convict's game and reveal a secret "twenty times as bad as yours…. It was, in truth, a huge relief to do so" (255). Oates experiences the same degree of relief from confessing his sins as the gallows criminals he described.

What Oates calls our "conscience," twenty-first-century readers informed of trauma theory might call "witnessing." Healing from trauma is promoted by telling the story to a confidante. This confidante stands as witness, so that the teller can begin to process the overwhelming experience instead of repressing it. Finding words for it begins to subject the experience to interpretation, though its horror makes it persistently difficult to comprehend (Caruth). What Oates and Maggs have to share is their shame and guilt about their past and present lives. As for guilt—they have both harmed people in various direct and indirect ways. Maggs harmed rich homeowners by stealing from them and his sons by abandoning them (though this is not on his conscience, nor is his killing of Partridge in self-defense). Oates has harmed his family members by adultery and assisting Lizzie's abortion. As for shame—Oates realizes his reputation as a novelist of manners and morals rests on a flimsy moral basis, since he is not the paragon of a gentleman he appears to be. There is also the shame of the financial debts that threaten his family's wellbeing. In addition to mistreatment by his abusive guardians, Maggs's shame derives from several events. He faults himself for failure to protect Sophina from her mother and the law—though this was impossible under the circumstances, since he was physically restrained by Tom while Ma tortured Sophina, and legally barred in court since the judge did not believe his story. His cruel and unusual treatment in prison could have resulted in shame, since a victim of abuse often internalizes the blame of the abuser. And there is shame at his loathed Australian identity, unmistakable by his accent, manners, and scarred back.

Besides relief from their dark secrets, Oates and Maggs gain other important insights from their strange interaction. Oates learns from Maggs the nature of the Criminal Mind, which is more like his own than he would have expected—a place of fear and anger that gives rise to unsavory acts. Maggs learns from Oates about his repressed fears, symbolized in the Phantom: "I never heard of this Phantom until I met you" (248). Oates teaches Maggs to confront rather than repress the Phantom, much as Oates had learned from his father to confront the things he feared. By confronting the Phantom during his mesmeric sessions, Maggs discovers the root of his shame: he is punishing himself for not having saved Sophina and their child, even though rescue was impossible. He also uncovers a repressed fear that Tom might have raped Sophina. Although the Phantom starts out as the sadistic prison warden who flogged Maggs, this beast eventually takes on the likeness of Henry Phipps. Neither Maggs nor Oates had met Phipps at the time of the mesmeric sessions, yet he appears in Maggs's vision in accurate detail. In this sense, the mesmerism evokes an event that is going to happen in the future: Phipps, dressed in his military uniform, will attempt to kill his benefactor. The Phantom is an amalgamation of the sinister forces that threaten Maggs's life: the faux son, Phipps, and the sadistic flogger in the prison (excessive whipping resulting in death was common in Australian prisons). Without intending to, Oates has functioned as a therapist, witnessing Maggs's traumas and helping him move forward. Realizing that he's idealized Phipps for twenty years, Maggs can walk away from his delusion and become available to love someone else. Mercy is immediately present to fill the void.

In the process of writing back to empire, neo–Victorian writers like to add in the gritty realism left out by Victorian prudery. *Mary Reilly* writes back to *Jekyll and Hyde* the story of incest and child abuse. *Wide Sargasso Sea* writes back to *Jane Eyre* the message of race hatred. *Jack Maggs* writes back to *Great Expectations* about the dark underbelly of Victorian economic and sexual life and the ignominy of transportation as a penalty for nonviolent crime. Horror-inspiring topics, such as child rape, abortion, homosexuality, murder, and torture—all present in *Jack Maggs*—could be addressed by Victorian writers only circumspectly, if at all, and only with regard to thoroughly evil characters. The contemporary novelist, on the other hand, can write about them as directly and graphically as he dares.

Another neo–Victorian practice that "writes back" to the original text is to directly interpret the author's psychic life by inserting them as a character in the revised text. Creating Dickens as a character enables Carey to consider how the author came up with the strong passions and bizarre idiosyncrasies of his own characters. Why does Pip feel so guilty? Why is Magwitch so naïve? Why is Mrs. Joe so merciless? In Toby Oates, Carey has drawn a convincing fictional portrait of the author that reflects Dickens's well-known romantic attachment to his sister-in-law, Georgina, and his mistreatment of his lawfully wedded wife, Catherine. Abused and abandoned as children, Mercy, Maggs, and Oates are reminders of Dickens's own dysfunctional family. Dickens was abandoned and made to support his family at twelve. The shame of the experience was so deep that he refused to talk about it. In *Jack Maggs*, characters do talk about repressed events and their associated shame. A pervasive sense of shame in the neo–Victorian version replicates and expands the theme of Pip's unexplained guilty conscience in the original. By borrowing this theme and disseminating it among many characters, while at the same time increasing their criminality (Phipps a murderer, Maggs a killer in self-defense, Buckle an accomplice to murder and Oates to manslaughter), Carey both explains psychological states that are adumbrated in the original and reveals the greater permissiveness of twenty-first-century culture that allows us to directly confront horror and trauma in literary fiction.

Works Cited

Carey, Peter. *John Maggs*. Vintage, 1998.
Caruth, Cathy. *Unclaimed Experience: Trauma, Narrative, and History*. Johns Hopkins, 1996.
Forster, John. *Life of Charles Dickens*. Diderot, 2006.

14

Refining Fire
and Doppelgänger Devils

Question:

In *Great Expectations*, there are at least two significant scenes involving dangerous fires and fierce antagonists. What is the significance of Pip's exposure to flames while in the threatening presence of his antagonists, Dolge Orlick and Miss Havisham?

Analysis:

Two pivotal scenes symbolically reveal Pip's spiritual tribulation and his refinement in fire. Being a member of the Anglican Church, Dickens didn't believe in the Catholic notion of purgatory, but Protestants do believe in a metaphorical fire that refines sins out of a Christian just as heat brings impurities out of gold: "The purpose of the trial is to draw out our hidden sins so that they may be repented of, and the process of sanctification may be stimulated…. This is the refiner's fire, of which Scripture speaks" (Tautges). In Protestant iconography, the fires that threaten Pip are not those of eternal damnation but those which offer the potential for spiritual redemption by refining or burning out his sins. Accompanying the symbolic flames, Miss Havisham and Orlick appear as devils who torment Pip by mirroring his own faults. In the first scene, a burning Miss Havisham flies at Pip, and he feels he is wrestling with her; their struggle suggests a spiritual reckoning for both characters. The second scene is in the limekiln, where Orlick trusses, threatens, and accuses Pip, who almost dies in the furnace fire. Through strong infernal imagery, these passages highlight Pip's ongoing sense of guilt. The devilish Havisham and Orlick mirror his own shame and self-loathing. Whereas Orlick and Havisham fail to redeem themselves or completely undo their wrongs, Pip grows from these trials by fire into a generous and humble gentleman. I suggest that Dickens, though Anglican, is strongly influenced by literary (especially Dantesque) imagery regarding hellfire and devils.

The first scene takes place during Pip's final visit to Miss Havisham. The encounter has two parts: in the first, Pip witnesses Miss Havisham's shame—her name itself suggests that she is capable of such feelings (have-a-shame). In the second part, Pip rescues her from fire and rolls her in the tablecloth to stifle the flames, emerging from the struggle a changed man. This last visit to Miss Havisham is motivated by Pip's desire to admonish her for her deceptions and to help Herbert—two motives that indicate Pip's growing maturity. When Pip learns the true identity of his benefactor, he decides to ask Miss Havisham for £900, enough to guarantee Herbert's partnership with Clarriker. She writes him a promissory note to give to Herbert, and offers Pip money for himself, which he proudly refuses. After questioning her about Estella's adoption, Pip leaves a much chastened though hysterical Miss Havisham repeating the phrase, "What have I done! What have I done!" and begging Pip's forgiveness.

In the second part of the scene, Pip takes a final tour around the courtyard and outbuildings. At the brewery he sees again that vision of Miss Havisham hanging from a beam that had terrorized him on his first visit some fifteen years earlier. He realizes it's a hallucination, yet it evokes a sense of danger so real that he returns inside to check on Miss Havisham. As he enters the room, she streaks toward him, flaming like a bonfire: "I saw her running at me, shrieking, with a whirl of fire blazing all about her, and soaring at least as many feet above her head as she was high" (402). Pip reacts instinctively, throwing his two coats around her, and yanking the tablecloth from under the molding wedding cake and other paraphernalia never removed since Miss Havisham's wedding day. Pip's decisive action "dragged down the heap of rottenness and all the ugly things that sheltered there" (402). Violently clearing the table puts an end to Miss Havisham's delusions about needing to avenge herself on all men. It performs a similar function for Pip. As the resident beetles and spiders scurry away from the death bed (the wedding table does double duty), Pip continues to "hold her prisoner"—much as she had earlier trapped him in the damaging delusion that she was his benefactor and Estella his future bride. The delusions of both characters are shattered by this dramatic denouement of a woman who was not satisfied merely to freeze her own heart but must also destroy the natural affections of her adopted daughter. The fire melts Miss Havisham's frozen heart, though she doesn't live long enough to rectify her corruption of Estella. The damage is already done.

Leaving Satis House the next morning, Pip's last sight of Miss Havisham is a mummy-like figure swathed in white cotton wool, lying on the wedding/death table and shrouded in a white sheet. Through the night, her speech had wandered, and she now possessed a "phantom air of something that had been and was changed" (403)—signifying remorse for her malicious acts. Like Madame Defarge's unnamed sister in *A Tale of Two Cities*, Miss Havisham attempts to cope with trauma by obsessive repetitions. She repeats three sentences that demonstrate her guilt: (1) "What have I done!" suggests she is only now coming to understand the lifelong effects of her malice toward Pip and Estella. (2) "When she first came, I meant to save her from misery like mine" attests to her realization that she perpetuated her shame and misery rather than protecting Estella from it. (3) "Take the pencil and write under my name, 'I forgive her!'" is her desperate attempt to gain Pip's forgiveness (403). Mirroring Miss Havisham, Pip will beg forgiveness of Joe and Biddy at the end of the book: "pray let me hear you say the words, that I may carry the sound of them away with me, and then I shall be able to believe that you can trust me, and think better of me, in the time to come!" (480). While Pip's final illness burns away his sins, Miss Havisham never recovers from her own trial by fire and dies soon thereafter.

Miss Havisham's lifelong self-deception was the belief that she was justified in using Estella as a tool to avenge herself against all men. At the end of her life, she is disabused of this evil idea. Her realization is a mirror to Pip's own *anagnorisis*. Pip repents his sins in stages. The Satis House fire prefigures the even more frightening one at the limekiln when Pip too is within moments of his own destruction. Pip shares a fault with Miss Havisham—the notion that family members are expendable and should be used to further one's progress toward a personal goal or left behind if they appear to impede that goal. Whereas Miss Havisham uses Estella to exact her revenge, Pip drops Joe and Biddy as soon as they become incompatible with his new self-image. Pip's is a less intense version of Miss Havisham's manipulation. Pip neglects his loved ones, whereas Miss Havisham actively punishes her adopted daughter. Pip's identification with Miss Havisham is underlined by their strange embrace during Pip's rescue: "we were on the ground struggling like desperate enemies ... the closer I covered her, the more wildly she shrieked and tried to free herself" (402). As she staggered toward him, her garments ablaze, she was both the demon who had ruined his dream of love *and* a reminder of his own internal devil whose temptations he fought "like [a] desperate enemy." In the struggle, Pip vanquishes his demon.

Great Expectations is often praised for its meticulous structure. The repetition of scenes about Pip's guilt and redemption are a careful accumulation of progressive steps that lend credibility to Pip's final transformation so that his self-improvement appears neither coincidental nor sentimental. Thus, Pip's near-death at the fiery limekiln reinforces the scene of his mortal struggle with flaming Miss Havisham—a struggle for their souls against the devilish temptation of pride.

The limekiln scene is even more infernal than the one at Satis House. Dickens may have had Dante's *Inferno* in mind when comparing Orlick to a tiger and Pip to a wolf. In Canto I, Dante finds himself in a dark wood symbolic of his sinfulness. At the brink of the forest, he encounters three beasts, which represent three categories of sin: the wolf (representing immoderation and greed), the lion (pride and violence), and the leopard (fraud and betrayal). In the limekiln, Orlick addresses Pip as "wolf" no fewer than eight times, threatening to kill him "like any other beast" (425). Orlick doesn't reveal why he chooses this particular epithet for Pip, but Pip's sins do belong to the wolf. Greed and ambition drove Pip from home and caused him to neglect loved ones. Orlick is an ironic choice of someone to preach to Pip, being guilty of far worse sins than his antagonist. In Dante's hierarchy, sinners of the wolf variety inhabit the top third of Hell, sins-of-the-lion the middle third, and sins-of-the-leopard the bottom, being the most egregious (Judas is bottommost). Orlick belongs in the bottom segment; he snarls like a tiger, his mouth waters for his kill, and he hugs himself with "a malignancy that made [Pip] tremble" (424). Orlick's sin is betrayal; in attempting to murder Mrs. Joe and Pip, he betrays his own benefactors—the Gargerys having provided him with a job. His other sins—stalking Biddy and blaming his own crimes on Pip—have the fraudulent characteristics of the sinners in Hell's lowest circles.

Like Dante's *Inferno*, the limekiln scene is a classic rendering of the trope of self-evaluation on the point of death. Some people believe that our sins pass before our eyes at the time of our death. Scenes of recent life flash through Pip's mind as Orlick accuses him of murdering his sister. Pip imagines Magwitch lying in wait for his deliverance at Mill Bank Pond, and Herbert, Joe, and Biddy's hurt expressions when they learn of his disappearance. Pip is terrified that Magwitch and Herbert will think he deserted them, while Joe and Biddy will never know how sorry he was if he dies before having had a chance to explain himself: "The death close before me was terrible, but far more terrible than death was the dread of being misremembered after death…. I saw myself despised by unborn generations while the wretch's words were yet on his lips" (425). Pip shares the fear of being misremembered with the souls in *The Inferno*. When Dante makes his journey through Hell, he talks to sinners in every circle. Most of them complain of their pain even though they realize that their punishment, or *contrapasso*, is tailored exactly to the nature of their sin. Many of them want Dante to be more than a listener; they ask him to clear their name back on earth. For them, the horror of being misremembered forms a great part of their suffering because it hurts their pride. Unlike Dante's infernal souls, Pip dreads misunderstanding due to a genuine remorse for the way he treated his loved ones.

In addition to the "tiger" of fraud and betrayal, Orlick is closely aligned with the Christian devil. When Pip was young, Orlick identified himself with the devil in order to scare him: "He gave me to understand that the Devil lived in a black corner of the forge, and that he knew the fiend very well: also, that it was necessary to make up the fire, once in seven years, with a live boy, and that I might consider myself fuel" (112–13). Orlick resented Pip's status as favored "son" of Joe and began planning his revenge even before Pip had started working alongside him at the forge.

While holding Pip captive before the kiln fire, Orlick heightens the danger by flaring the candle in his face: "Ah! The burnt child dreads the fire!" he cackles, like the Wicked Witch of the West taunting the Scarecrow with flaming torches (428). The third time that Orlick thrusts the candle at him, Pip is momentarily blinded by the flame—adding another injury to the burnt hands he received when rescuing Miss Havisham. In this moment, Orlick is a laughing devil who thrives on inflicting pain and inspiring terror. Devils are often represented in popular culture as beings who laugh while threatening their victim in front of a roaring fire, pitchfork in hand. This is an image straight out of Dante's eighth circle, in which grafters swim in a vat of boiling tar while black devils re-submerge them with pitchforks each time they rise to the surface. Orlick's method of torture by fire recalls the earlier scene when Miss Havisham "flares" at him, her own garments the weapon that threatens his safety. Pip's injuries from that first devilish encounter—his burnt hands—return to haunt him when Orlick ties him, for Orlick intentionally binds Pip tightly at the site of the burns in order to increase his pain. Orlick's intoxication adds suspense to the scene, as Pip realizes that Orlick will feed him to the fire as soon as the bottle of liquor is drained. Pip refuses to cry out for mercy, but fortunately, he shouts for help once Orlick finally raises the hammer to kill him.

Just as Miss Havisham's remorse provides an object lesson to Pip—he must repent his own arrogance or burn in hellish fire—so too does Orlick's accusation contribute to Pip's full repentance. Orlick's assertion that Pip caused him to kill Mrs. Joe is ridiculous, but at the moment of death, Pip may see some truth in the accusation, which is perhaps an explicit statement of an unconscious death wish that he harbored toward his sister. He did abandon his family, and his sister died thereafter. Pip's conscience may tell him that his abandonment caused her death.

The shock of the limekiln encounter, added to Magwitch's capture and death, causes Pip to succumb to a serious fever. He spends weeks in delirium, imagining horrific men who visit the bedchamber, some of them real and others imagined. Actual creditors come to demand payment for jewelry purchased on credit, and Joe takes care of them. Pip's fevered imagination also revisits the traumatic moments of his last eventful months: "a closed iron furnace in a dark corner of the room, and a voice had called out over and over again that Miss Havisham was consuming within it" (461). This hallucination combines the hellish vision of a burning Miss Havisham with the limekiln fire that Orlick intended for Pip: "the vapour of a limekiln would come between me and them [the figures in his vision]" (461). The fear that Miss Havisham is burning in hell is thus a mirror image of Pip himself, as his unconscious mind works through his issues during the long weeks of illness. Weeks later, Pip's vision finally clears and he's able to recognize Joe at his bedside. At this point, Pip reaches a full redemption, as though resurrected from near-death. Reminiscent of Miss Havisham's repentance ("What have I done! What have I done!") is Pip's repetition of the phrase, "O God bless him! O God bless this gentle Christian man!" (463). Pip's unconscious psychic work has burned away his pride and embarrassment over his simple relative, leaving an immense gratitude for Joe's kindness.

With this sentiment—which will last until the end of the book, eleven years later—Pip redeems himself. But his dark doppelgängers, Orlick and Havisham, don't fare as well. Miss Havisham's deathbed repentance should see her to heaven, but Orlick, who will hang or be transported for the aggravated burglary he committed on Pumblechook's house, is unlikely to repent. He is not a round character. Pip has shared guilt with his devilish doppelgängers, but, unlike them, has been refined in the purgatorial fires that they thrust at him. Losing his arrogance and selfishness, he is able to enjoy a good life with Clara and Herbert. He remains close to Joe and Biddy through regular correspondence. Whereas Havisham and Orlick are associated with the iron furnace—an image of hellfire—Pip's burnt hands and blinded eyes are relics of purgatorial fires that refine his sins out of him. The fiery encounters in which he received his wounds lead him to full repentance, humility, and reform.

Works Cited

Alighieri, Dante. *The Divine Comedy*. Trans. John Ciardi. Penguin, 2003.

Dickens, Charles. *Great Expectations*. Penguin, 1996.

Tautges, Paul. "The Refiner's Fire." https://biblicalcounseling.com/resource-library/articles/the-refiners-fire/.

15

Anti-Semitism, Casual Racism, and Pedagogy

"There was a red-eyed little Jew...."

"a Jewish man with an unnaturally heavy smear of eyebrow"

Question:

Dickens consistently refers to Jewish characters with accompanying racial epithets. While *Great Expectations* is not the most anti–Semitic of Dickens's novels, Jewish characters lurk around the city's alleys like a perceived threat to gentile solvency and English national character. *Casual racism* is defined as epithets that are not central or related to the plot or main characters (Betensky). The term "casual" does not mean "trivial" or that the racism shouldn't be taken seriously; it is, instead, a term that denotes the speaker's or author's gratuitous addition of the epithet. How should we read Dickens's casual racism regarding Jews, and more broadly, how should English teachers cover the subject of Victorian racism in literature?

Analysis:

England, like most other countries in the world, has a long history of anti–Semitism. In 1066, William the Conqueror brought a contingent of Jews from Normandy to England. They were considered desirable members of the new kingdom because they could pay fees in cash rather than kind. In return, William provided Jews protection and free access to the king's highways in order to ply their trades, such as moneylending and coin dealing. Many non–Jews resented Jews' privileges and spread anti–Semitic canards such as blood libel (that Jews use Christian blood in religious rites) and the poisoned-well theory (that Jews caused the Black Death). In the 1190s, anti–Semitic mobs exterminated whole settlements of Jews in York, Norwich, and London. In 1290, King Edward I signed an edict called the Expulsion of the Jews. Jews were no longer allowed to live within British territory. From 1290 until 1656, when Oliver Cromwell unofficially readmitted Jewish residents, many crypto–Jewish families remained in England (*crypto* meaning practicing their own religion under cover). Due to a relatively low incidence of anti–Jewish violence in Britain during the eighteenth and nineteenth centuries, many Jews immigrated to England from Europe and Russia.

The Victorian age saw the gradual removal of civil and political disabilities for Jews. Centuries of struggle by Catholics culminated in the passing of the Catholic Emancipation Act in 1829 and Jews hoped to ride the liberal tide to arrive at full equality under the law. It would take another sixty years of struggle. In 1828, Jews were excluded from Crown offices, corporations, parliament, and most of the professions. By 1833, the first Jew had been admitted to the British bar. In 1837, Queen Victoria knighted the first Jew, Moses Montefiore, and Jewish-born Benjamin Disraeli became a Member of Parliament in the House of Commons; he was made eligible by a declaration of Anglican faith. In 1841, Isaac Lyon Goldsmid was the first Jew to receive a hereditary title (baronet). In 1858, the Jews Relief Act allowed Jews to become Members of Parliament by omitting the declaration of Christian faith. In 1868, again because of his Anglican faith, Disraeli was able to become Prime Minister, thereby becoming the only Jewish-born Prime Minister in the history of Great Britain. By these incremental measures, complete *de jure* equality was finally gained by Jews in 1890, though *de facto* discrimination continued. Starting from the late 1880s, immigration to England of persecuted Jews from Russia increased dramatically, which began to pose a perceived threat to English security. In 1905, the Aliens Act was enacted to control Jewish immigration to Britain, and anti–Semitism was once again on the rise.

Turning our attention to Dickens, we note that he shared the attitudes of the British gentile intellectual class, that is, a reluctant admiration for Jewish achievements in business, government, science, and the arts, combined with a distrust of the very qualities that made such achievements possible. Oxford historian U.R.Q. Henriques breaks down Victorians' arguments against Jewish emancipation into three categories: the argument from religion, the argument from nationality, and the argument from moral character. It is worthwhile to review these arguments, as they would have been the basis for Dickens's Jewish caricatures:

1. The argument from religion claims that being Christian is "part and parcel" of the English constitution, and therefore Jews cannot be citizens of England. The religious argument gains its emotional strength from the age-old prejudice that the Jews had crucified Christ and considered him an imposter. Allowing Jews into British government would incur the wrath of God, who had dispersed the Jews in a worldwide diaspora as punishment for their crimes, intending that they should never be rulers anywhere (Henriques 131). The assumption is that British people are Christian by definition, and that only Christians can be good and moral.

2. The argument from nationality is similarly flawed; it supposes that Jews are so confident of returning one day to the land of their ancestors that they would be unpatriotic toward England. Simultaneously, an opposite fear was that Jews *would* stay in England, buying seats in Parliament in order to seize political power and taking control of the nation (Henriques 133).

3. The argument from morality is the most egregious; it assumes that Jews love money more than gentiles do, and more than anything else. Henriques calls it the "Shylock and Fagan [*sic*] money-bags stereotype" (140). Other moral stereotypes about Jews are easily refuted, such as their lack of charity, or their lack of interest in art and literature. These claims are demonstrably false: some of the greatest philanthropists are Jewish, and their contributions to the arts are immense. But English people were famously xenophobic, and their sense of Jewish difference resulted in a myriad of myths and stereotypes.

Dickens may have absorbed these stereotypes in part because he was ashamed of his own lower-class family and determined to rise above his origins to become a gentleman. Offhand stereotypical remarks were not only acceptable but *de rigueur* in his intellectual milieu, though Dickens did face resistance from Jewish readers, which I'll discuss in a moment. The epigraphs to this lecture are two instances of anti–Semitism in *Great Expectations*. The first, "there was a red-eyed little Jew," is a description from Pip's point of view when, in the alley behind Mr. Jaggers's office, he sees several clients waiting for Jaggers and worrying out loud about their law cases (166). After describing two or three groups of people who are trying to reassure one another that they've hired the best lawyer, Dickens ends the paragraph with a more detailed sketch of one particularly anxious client: the red-eyed little Jew who does a jig and sings a ditty with a lisp. Dickens seems to be saying that, of all the anxious clients, the Jew is the most exaggerated in his response. Dickens makes fun of a Jewish tendency to worry, and to make strong, physical expression of emotions. The second example, "a Jewish man with an unnaturally heavy smear of eyebrow," comes as Pip and Herbert try to sneak away after Mr. Wopsle's performance of *Hamlet* but are waylaid by a Jewish man with big eyebrows who turns out to be Wopsle's dresser (255). The dresser admonishes the actor because during key speeches he hadn't shown off the stockings that the dresser had made. The dresser advises Wopsle to give the audience a full-frontal view in order to display the stockings. The dresser's anxiety, bossiness, and attention seeking are stereotypical of a Jewish garment maker. This dresser steps outside the bounds of his job description, provoking a fear that Jews don't know their social place.

"Casual racism," as defined by Carolyn Betensky, is that which is off-hand—in other words, not central to the plot or main characters of the story. Neither Jaggers's client nor Wopsle's dresser is central to the plot in any way. How should we read casual racism in *Great Expectations*? It certainly isn't Dickens's only or most famous example of anti–Semitism. Fagin, the Jewish crime boss in *Oliver Twist* (1837), earns that distinction. Fagin is almost always described in the text with the epithet "the Jew," and he sports stereotypical Jewish characteristics such as a big nose, a stoop, and miserliness. A stoop is the physical manifestation of the stereotypically Jewish activity of perpetually counting money or doing fine-detail work such as sewing or reading the Torah. Jews were thought to be frail of physique, opposite to the stereotype of the strong, manly English or "Aryan" male. Though he makes a good profit off the boys' thefts, Fagin is still close with his money. He beats his wards and provides only meager lodgings and food. Fagin would rather put aside money than nurture his band of ragtag orphans. Dickens created several gentile villains with similar selfish traits, but it's Fagin's shameless money-loving aspect that makes him unique among them. In this aspect, Fagin is akin to Shylock among stereotypical Jews in literature.

We tend to think of the Victorians as being far less sensitive to racism than we are. Yet, in his time, Dickens received so much negative feedback for his racist portrayal of Fagin that he decided to excise 180 instances of the word "Jew" from the text. He publicly announced that he was not anti–Semitic.[*] He also toned down the racial caricatures of Fagin in his public readings of *Oliver Twist*, losing the "nasal intonation and shoulder-shrug," according to a contemporary report.[†]

Victorian fiction is scattered with casual racist references, which

---

[*] Geoffrey Nunberg. *The Way We Talk Now: Commentaries on Language and Culture.* Houghton Mifflin, 2001, p. 126.

[†] Edgar Johnson. "Intimations of Mortality." *Charles Dickens: His Tragedy and Triumph.* Simon & Schuster, 1952.

today's readers readily pick up on. In the contemporary climate of heightened awareness about institutional racism, Americans are reckoning with our own national traditions of racism. We are thus in a position to reconsider the ways in which we teach Victorian literature. Some British literature scholars skirt the issue of race by shifting the focus to imperialism. Some instructors explain casual racism in Victorian texts by noting that Victorians lacked the benefit of critical race theory to educate them about the wrongs they were committing. But that may not be an entirely accurate picture of nineteenth-century awareness. Obviously, since he received feedback, Dickens did know that readers perceived and were hurt by his racism, so there must have been a clear concept of the ills of racism at the time of *Oliver Twist*'s publication in 1837. In the nineteenth century, however, the problem was not couched as institutional or structural racism—these terms were coined in the late 1960s—though interpersonal racism was easily identifiable. Nor did the word "race" have the meaning we associate it with today. In early Victorian times, the term *race* designated either (a) a group of people, a nation or tribe, with a common cultural or linguistic inheritance, or (b) a category of humans who shared a particular trait (Betensky 728). To prepare my lecture on race and color in *Jane Eyre* (1847), I traced the use of the word "race" in the novel, and found it referred variously to Rochester's ancestors, or the fairies and sprites that Jane resembled, or the "human race" which St. John aims to save by missionary work. After 1860, racism against Black people grew stronger when race-based discrimination was fed by popular theories of scientific racism. Skin color, skull shape, size and proportion of facial features, hair texture and hair color were some of the exterior features that theorists used to categorize people. Moral and intellectual capabilities and debilities were some of the character traits that scientific racists assigned to these respective categories. Especially damaging was the theory that Black people had less capacity for intelligence than whites.

According to Professor Carol Betensky, casual racism is so pervasive in Victorian fiction that readers become inured—the more Victorian literature we read, the more we expect it, until eventually it passes by, noticed but unexamined. To right this wrong, Betensky proposes a strategic intervention in Victorian studies. She would like us to examine casual racism not only in the context of history, but also with regard to the present moment. Betensky believes it's dangerous to portray Victorian sensibilities as being far different from our own because it blinds us to the fact that we are still a racist culture. "Claiming the speaker's benefit"—pretending we've transcended racism because of our ability to identify and disparage it in earlier cultures—leaves us no more enlightened than before the discussion (734). I'm not sure she's claiming we *aren't* more evolved than the

Victorians, but that we need to admit our own racism whenever we discuss that of other people.

To rectify this situation, Betensky introduces the topic of America's structural racism into her classroom discussions of Victorian fiction. She specifically refers to teaching Dickens novels. Betensky avoids making the statement that Dickens didn't have the benefit of knowing critical race theory, because that sends the message that "our intentions are more significant than our actions" (735). Although today's readers know the language of racism and may intend to combat it, she asserts that "racism functions without the knowledge or intention of the racist subject" (735). It is not enough to identify Dickens's racism. We need to go a step further.

To solve the problem of unintentional racism in the classroom, Betensky recommends that we "foreground historical continuities between past and present" (736). Recognizing, however, the danger of focusing on current events in a Victorian literature class, Betensky names and addresses this risk. "Presentism" is the practice of always interpreting the past in terms of present concerns. Betensky recognizes the risk of presentism, which is "exaggerating our present problems out of all proportion to those that have previously existed" (737). Nonetheless, Betensky advises a "strategic presentism," wherein the focus on the present is justified by the political gains that can be achieved by it (739). Talking about current events in tandem with studying Victorian literature, she says, will further the aims of social justice.

To illustrate what she means by the continuum of past and present, Betensky offers an example from Wilkie Collins's popular 1868 novel, *The Moonstone*. In one scene, Mr. Bruff makes casual reference to "some of those strolling Indians who infest the streets" of London (740). He is referring to immigrants and visitors from Victorian Britain's most important colony, India. It is obviously racist to say that Indians *infest* the streets as though their different looks and habits were a disease that Englishmen could catch. The word *infest* is toxic and disturbing in this context; we associate it with rats and viruses. Betensky points out that our then–President, Donald Trump, used the same word in 2019 with reference to illegal immigrants to the U.S. He tweeted, "Democrats want illegal immigrants to infest our country" (741).

This is a convincing example used to illustrate Betensky's point that (some) Americans are no less racist in 2019 than Victorians were in 1868. Our ex-president, for instance, is defiantly racist, and proud of his constitutional right to speak his views. Acknowledging the structural racism in the United States means that even if we (individually) may not approve of Trump's tweet nor share his view, we are still implicated in racism because we partake in our racist institutions. Critical race theory demands a radical reformation of the structure of government, education, medicine, banking, law, and all other institutions in order to transcend racial injustice.

I agree with Betensky's intentions to maintain respect in the classroom for the struggle to achieve social justice. On the other hand, I have not experienced the phenomenon she describes of students being "inured" to Victorian racism. Instead, my students write about racism and critical race theory in passionate and accurate ways. I believe that readers of literature instinctively compare the settings of the texts with their own world. It is useful for professors to raise issues of Victorian racism and to invite comparisons to racist actions and statements occurring in our own time and place. Based on my experience, however, I would suggest two caveats to this practice. First, take care that discussion of current events does not overtake discussions of the Victorians. Analogies and contextualization are important pedagogical tools for explaining concepts and making learning relevant. But the finite amount of time that classroom teaching affords (two and a half hours per week) requires careful planning. I don't mean to imply that racism in Victorian literature should not be taught. On the contrary, race, gender, and class issues are the bulk of what I do teach in literature classes. I am referring instead to Betensky's presentist approach. A shift in focus from Victorian to American twenty-first-century racial attitudes may impede the achievement of learning outcomes in a class on Victorian literature or a survey course of British fiction. On the other hand, if the class is an upper-division seminar called "Race in Victorian Fiction," or "Race, Gender, and Class in Victorian Fiction," then present-day analogies are integral to the teaching of the subject and should occupy a more substantial portion of class time.

My second caveat is the danger of failing to historicize the issue, both in neglecting to recognize gains made in civil rights since the Victorian era and in failing to study English history in favor of making American historical analogies. Britain didn't have plantations within its national borders as the U.S. did, but slavery was the modus operandi of her colonies, and the source of her phenomenal wealth. Victorian racism didn't end with the dawn of the twentieth century and the change of monarch. Modernist literature abounds with racist references too, some of them more coded than those of the Victorians, but nonetheless present. But Britain had a strong civil rights movement in the mid- and late twentieth century. Britain's first civil rights law was the Race Relations Act of 1965. It prohibited discrimination on public grounds on the basis of color, race, ethnicity, or national origin. A 2010 amendment extended jurisdiction to include private services and added other categories: age, disability, gender reassignment, marriage, maternity, race, religion, sex, or sexual orientation. Despite this protective legislation, *de facto* racial discrimination remains. As in America, so too in Britain there is health inequality, disparity in educational levels, and over-representation of Black people in jails and prisons. Since the turn of the century, hate speech and hate crimes have increased as immigration rates rise. The Brexit issue (2016–2020) polarized English racial attitudes. The problems of race discrimination and immigration are as important to current politics in England as they are to the United States.

Analogies of British history to various American civil rights movements are certainly appropriate within context. Being clear about the different, more nuanced, and unintentional ways in which racism continues to manifest itself today is an important pedagogical strategy, both for teaching the Victorian period and raising awareness about social justice. If, however, professors suggest to students that we are just as racist today as the Victorians were in the 1860s, they risk undervaluing several decades' worth of civil rights activism. I believe it's important to point out progress in any discussion of the history of race relations. One instance of our progress is the existence of exacting language standards in the academy and the publishing industry. In thirty years of academic experience at both northern and southern universities, I have not heard white professors or students utter racist statements, either in the classroom or outside. There are at least two reasons for this: first, we genuinely believe that racism is wrong, and we understand that our language reflects our values, so we construct our utterances with due care. Second, the harassment policies adopted by most institutions of higher education, Title VI legal protections, and the progressive climates on most campuses effectually deter racist speech in the classroom. If we deny that we have made any collective progress in fighting racism since Victoria's time, I fear we are courting a sense of helplessness, which tends to deplete the courage we need for the ongoing fight for racial justice.

Betensky's essay is a springboard into classroom discussion about racism today and in Dickens's time. I do not mean to suggest that we have wiped out racism in the thoughts and utterances of all English literature students or professors; this will never happen. Nor do I want to curtail comparison of Victorians to twenty-first-century Americans. As Betensky points out, all human beings are (at least) unintentionally racist. "Race" is a construct fully embedded in our language and culture. Classrooms are one of the few places in which people can have a well-regulated conversation about racism because classroom discourse has certain implied and expressed parameters. A competent professor curtails violent or prejudiced speech and lets every voice be heard. A literature class is a setting in which social justice is an implied (and sometimes stated) topic, practice, and goal.

Works Cited

Betensky, Carol. "Casual Racism in Victorian Literature." *Victorian Literature and Culture* 47:4 (2019). 723–51.

Dickens, Charles. *Great Expectations*. Penguin, 1996.

Henriques, U.R.Q. "The Jewish Emancipation Controversy in Nineteenth-Century Britain." *Past & Present* 40 (1968). 126–146.

Ragussis, Michael. "The 'Secret' of English Anti-Semitism: Anglo-Jewish Studies and Victorian Studies." *Victorian Studies* 40:2 (1997). 295–307.

"United Kingdom Virtual Jewish History Tour." https://www.jewishvirtuallibrary. org/united-kingdom-virtual-jewish-history-tour.

16

Angel of Destruction
or Spacious Mind?

Question:

In "George Eliot as the Angel of Destruction," Sandra Gilbert and Susan Gubar assert that George Eliot invests her heroines with destructive urges: they either self-destruct or destroy others due to their anger at the confinement which patriarchy imposes upon them. I think that Gilbert and Gubar's thesis accurately describes Eliot's earlier novels, such as *Scenes of Clerical Life, Adam Bede, Romola,* and *The Mill on the Floss.* But Eliot may have worked through her feminist anger by the time of writing *Middlemarch* in 1871. Is Dorothea Brooke a bona fide Angel of Destruction? Does she destroy others, or does she destroy herself by performing the role of Angel in the House?

Synopsis:

Nineteen-year-old Dorothea Brooke is an intelligent woman who puts her talents to use planning improvements to tenant cottages on her uncle's estate. She turns down the marriage proposal of age-appropriate, handsome, wealthy Sir James Chettam, preferring the much older Reverend Edward Casaubon. She admires his high seriousness, moral probity, and book project, *The Key to All Mythologies.* Edward turns out to be a scholarly fraud; his research is out of date and his writing lacks a compelling voice. The more insight his young wife gains into his character, the more he condescends to her. Edward's young cousin, Will Ladislaw, is a dashing Polish journalist who is attracted to Dorothea but keeps a gentlemanly distance. Will assists

Dorothea's flighty uncle (Arthur Brooke) to run his political campaign for Parliament on a reform platform. Brooke doesn't actually believe in reform; he's only interested in the status he could achieve by holding political office.

Tertius Lydgate is an attractive young doctor who brings innovative medical practices to Middlemarch and carries on research "to discover the primitive tissue of all life." His ambitious plans are waylaid by his shallow wife, Rosamond Vincy, who wants more money and more status than marriage to a research physician can provide. Finally, she convinces him to move to Bath, where he joins a practice that treats wealthy gout patients. Being so far removed from

George Eliot, by Sir Frederick Burton, 1864 (frontispiece, J.W. Cross's *The Life of George Eliot*, reproduced in *The Works of George Eliot in Twenty Volumes* [New York, 1910]).

his youthful ambition to make a monumental discovery, Lydgate loses faith in himself and dies. Meanwhile, Rosamond's brother, Fred Vincy, has loved Mary Garth since childhood. Fred is lazy and doesn't plan for a career because he expects a large inheritance from his uncle, Peter Featherstone. He quits university, borrows from Mary's father, gambles the money, and is unable to pay back his debt. He offers to study for the priesthood, but Mary knows he has no vocation and will marry him only if he enters a profession for which he is qualified. Mary's father employs Fred as a land agent (estate manager), enabling the couple to marry and have a good life.

Nicholas Bulstrode is a wealthy, pious banker/philanthropist who is starting to build a fever hospital with Lydgate's help. He's anxious to hide his sordid past. He had married a wealthy widow whose daughter ran away. Bulstrode found the daughter but kept her whereabouts hidden from her mother so that he would inherit his wife's fortune instead of her daughter. When he learns that Will Ladislaw is the son of his wife's daughter, he is consumed with guilt and offers Ladislaw a substantial income. Ladislaw knows that the money is somehow tainted and turns it down. An unsavory itinerant, John Raffles, knows the exact details of Bulstrode's past, and uses his knowledge to blackmail Bulstrode into leaving him the majority of his estate. While alcoholic Raffles malingers at Bulstrode's country home, the banker speeds his death by giving him brandy against Lydgate's orders. As attending physician, Lydgate becomes a murder suspect. Eventually, town gossip forces him to leave Middlemarch. Casaubon dies a few years after marriage, leaving his estate to Dorothea upon the condition that she doesn't marry Ladislaw. Dorothea marries Ladislaw, who engages in a political career. Somewhat disappointed by the lack of an outlet for her intellectual talents, Dorothea determines to let family love be enough.

Analysis:

Angel in the House is a role prescribed for Victorian women that requires them to control their negative emotions and nurture their family members. The mother and wife of a Victorian household is the repository of goodness, a well from which husband and children can draw inspiration and nurturance. The Angel's role is to tend to others' spiritual and emotional lives; the presumption is that she attains her own fulfillment in directing her emotional energy toward fulfilling other people's needs.

Gilbert and Gubar posit two ways in which Eliot's female protagonists express rage against this role: (1) as destructiveness to another (usually the husband), and (2) as self-destruction. In *Mill on the Floss*, both Maggie Tulliver and her brother drown when Maggie attempts to rescue him. Eliot's destruction of her suffering characters is not usually so melodramatic. Typically, she situates them in a death-in-life situation, such as Dorothea's marriage to Edward Casaubon. Dorothea persistently struggles to repress her anger toward the dried-up bookworm. Yet Dorothea neither self-destructs nor kills him—though the result might have been different had Casaubon not died after two years of marriage. During this time, Dorothea chooses to acquiesce to his demands because she finds it easier than the alternative—speaking out and risking his anger. She stifles her anger to ward off his certain retaliation. If she were to speak her feelings, she fears he would stop speaking to her, leading to a rupture that would encumber her with guilt. If Casaubon had not died, Dorothea might have begun to dry up too. In this novel, George Eliot is not the angel of destruction but rather the angel of liberation, killing the deadening husband to liberate the vital wife.

Eliot is not alone in creating for her female protagonists a strong, difficult emotional life. In many woman-authored novels of the nineteenth and early twentieth century, the author kills off the female character who asks too much of society—though she is only asking things that many women now take for granted, such as the right to work or to remain single. Today, many women have the choice to refuse marriage and motherhood, and all their attendant duties. In the nineteenth century, if a woman character rebelled against patriarchy, the author would rarely reward her (*Jane Eyre* aside). Instead, she suffers death, insanity, or isolation—some form of the Madwoman's Attic—in compensation for her hubris. Such a fate befalls the protagonists of Olive Schreiner's *The Story of an African Farm*, Elizabeth Bowen's *To the North*, Doris Lessing's *The Golden Notebook*, Virginia Woolf's *Mrs. Dalloway*, and Charlotte Perkins Gilman's "The Yellow Wallpaper." By liberating Dorothea from Casaubon, is Eliot breaking the mold of destructive or destroyed female characters? Or are Dorothea's second marriage, and Rosamond and Mary's marriages, only a variation on the death-in-life theme? The novel's "Finale" attempts to answer this question. In this chapter, the narrator describes Dorothea's marriage to Ladislaw as a limiting, though safe, outcome. It is a middle ground, somewhere on a spectrum between the full angel role (of marriage to Casaubon) and full liberation from that role, which would entail being able to follow her own charitable and professional interests.

According to Gilbert and Gubar, Eliot's ambivalence about female rage creates an interesting tension in her work: "Eliot does not countenance female renunciation because she believes it to be appropriately feminine, but because she is intensely aware of the destructive potential of female rage. Thus, she simultaneously demonstrates the necessity of renouncing anger and the absolute impossibility of genuinely doing so" (513). When Dorothea begins to argue with Casaubon in Rome, and once again at Lowick, she quickly suppresses her objections to his behavior because they arouse attitudes in her husband that she cannot abide. He becomes "stupidly undiscerning and odiously unjust" (282). Readers have noticed these traits of Casaubon's far earlier—in fact, upon first encountering him. But Dorothea's idealism initially blinds her to two truths about her husband that will eventually alter her good impression: (1) he is not a good scholar, and (2) he is a selfish husband, despite his customary politeness of manner, which he wields as a cold-war weapon.

If Dorothea were unable to grant her husband a certain "spaciousness of mind" (i.e., non-judgment of his faults), her anger might kill her (Ashton *xi*). Fortunately, as early as the honeymoon, Dorothea begins to appreciate the otherness of her husband, which enables her to accept him on his own terms. She had "a presentiment that there might be a sad consciousness in his life which made as great a need on his side as on her own" (211). This is the first time she has truly understood that he is unstable, self-loathing, and vulnerable. She now sees him as distinctly other, having "an equivalent centre of self, whence the lights and shadows must always fall with a certain difference" (211). This revelation is particularly important for Dorothea because hitherto she has been, in her sister's opinion, too inclined to become angry at people for saying things contrary to her own values. With her recognition of Casaubon's otherness, she might be able to forgive him.

If an open mind and heart like Dorothea's are the only panacea for the ills of patriarchy, then many of us will never be healed of our anger. Dorothea is a rarity. It takes a very special temperament to accept the selfishness of another and yet continue loving them. A more common reaction to a partner's selfishness is annoyance or anger. Many marriages do work, however, on this principle of radical forgiveness or cultivated indifference, and of course it is not always the husband who is more selfish.

In her introduction to the Penguin edition of *Middlemarch*, Rosemary Ashton claims that Eliot possesses a "spaciousness of mind" that enables her to delineate flawed characters without judgment. The accepting tone of Ashton's essay contrasts sharply with the critical voices of Gilbert and Gubar. The authors of *Madwoman in the Attic* rout out examples of astonishing violence in the novel, while Ashton instead finds a positive, moderate tone in the narration. Eliot's characterizations are not black-and-white but nuanced, just as people are nuanced in real life. Quoting Henry James, Ashton agrees that "Eliot was the best English novelist for psychological realism" (*x*). She eschews the feminist approach of second-wave critics Gilbert and Gubar (who published *Madwoman* in 1979) in favor of gender studies and narratology. Perhaps this is why Ashton finds some of the male characters if not sympathetic then at least relatable, as presented by Eliot, the expert psychological realist.

Despite her emphasis, Ashton does not ignore the cost of separate spheres ideology—the relegation of women to the home and men to public life. Instead, she leaves open the question of whether the character or her environment is more to blame for marital difficulty. Ashton describes how Eliot softens the reader's impression of Rosamond by providing "many frank expressions of opinion on marriage, men's expectations of it and women's fitness or unfitness for the married state. Rosamond is a victim, sometimes pitied and sometimes not, who does not rise above her risible preparation for adult life" (xv). Eliot places the blame for Rosamond's selfishness on her upbringing rather than on her innate temperament. This is a prime example of Eliot's spaciousness of mind.

Instead of focusing on the "violent interior life" of the main characters, as Gilbert and Gubar do, Ashton appreciates the lighter aspects of Eliot's humor and wit, admiring particularly her elegant control of dialogue and narrative structure. Ashton praises the following aspects of Eliot's style:

- Eliot has a supreme command of dialogue. (xv)
- She integrates the themes of the large novel by presenting parallel cases. (xii)
- All her characters possess "inner space." Like the "spaciousness of mind" mentioned earlier, this phrase means that Eliot's analyses of characters' motives result in our sympathy for even the most difficult behavior. Her tolerance for difference gives the reader "human fellowship with the characters in *Middlemarch*." (xi)
- The central metaphor of the novel is the scratched pier glass metaphor, in which human self-centered consciousness is compared to the way that scratches on a mirror all seem to center around a certain point when you shine a light on it. The metaphor applies to every character. Its reveals the egocentrism not only of characters, but also of readers—you, *hypocrite lecteur*! (x)
- The large-minded narrator is compassionate and wise. (ix)
- Eliot adopts a traditionally male mode of writing, in which historical events are woven into Middlemarch affairs so that an "individual's lot is seen to be affected by historical changes as they happen" (viii). Historical examples are thoroughly integrated with plot and character. (ix)
- Her narrative voice is flexible and powerful, enabling her (and the reader) to accommodate conflicting opinions. She has extraordinary command of "narrative irony, wit, and intellectual surprise." (xix)

Ashton agrees with Gilbert and Gubar that there is an interesting tension between the characters' righteous anger against patriarchy and the narrator's calm, moderating tone of diplomacy. The narrator's omniscience creates a container for emotions which all characters feel and are unable to renounce. Anger is not the exclusive preserve of men; there is a special kind of anger in women who rage against the constraints of Victorian customs such as the separate spheres doctrine. Ashton recognizes Eliot's anger while refusing to make it the central theme of the novel: "There is nothing feminist or progressive about her [Dorothea's] action or the narrator's presentation of it, in contrast to the more radical moments in the novel in which George Eliot airs a deeply felt anger at the limitation of possibilities for women" (xix). Such tension is what makes the novel, despite its seriousness, surprisingly entertaining. Isn't it true to life that we can perceive injustices and feel anger without actually destroying the structures in which we live? Probably Dorothea attained the best arrangement she could within the limits of her time and place, and Eliot refuses to either denigrate or celebrate her situation.

Works Cited

Ashton, Rosemary. Introduction. *Middlemarch*. Penguin, 1994. vii–xxii.
Eliot, George. *Middlemarch*. Penguin, 1994.
Gilbert, Sandra and Susan Gubar. "George Eliot as the Angel of Destruction." *The Madwoman in the Attic: The Woman Writer and the Nineteenth-Century Imagination*. Yale, 2000. 478–535.

17

Mrs. Cadwallader, Busybody

Question:

Emily Dickinson wrote, "What do I think of Middlemarch? What do I think of glory?" *Middlemarch*'s glory depends on many things, but one of the most delightful is its colorful minor characters. Their dialogues and interior monologues infuse wit and humor into a narrative concerned with serious social issues. I asked my students to write a short essay on the question, "Who is your favorite minor character in *Middlemarch*, and how does Eliot characterize him or her?"

Analysis:

For my own essay, I chose Mrs. Cadwallader because she is clever and funny. She has the free tongue that we all wish we possessed but which most of us lack the courage to try. Her epigrams are reminiscent of Oscar Wilde—an odd, gender-bending anachronism, since Eliot is a woman who is writing in an age of comparative conservatism. Cadwallader has many negative qualities—she is stingy, meddling, and so frank that it would be painful to be the object of her analysis. What I like about her are her hilarious remarks—though it is not her that I like but Eliot's witty characterization. I like her as a character; I wouldn't like her as a person. If I met a Mrs. Cadwallader, I would cringe at her shameless criticisms.

In addition to her wit, her intelligence shows in her many spoken metaphors, which have a complexity akin to that of the metaphysical poets. In the narrator's initial figurative description of Mrs. Cadwallader, we find one of the layered metaphors that make the text deeply thoughtful. Chapter VI is dedicated to developing Mrs. Cadwallader's unusual character (she is a gossip with a literary knack). It begins with an epigraph about her:

> My lady's tongue is like the meadow blades,
> That cut you stroking them with idle hand.
> Nice cutting is her function: she divides
> With spiritual edge the millet-seed
> And makes intangible savings [52].

The blade-of-grass metaphor works in two ways: it's akin to the sharpness of her tongue and denotes the stinginess with which she "divides" things. Nice cutting is her function; she not only cuts "nicely" or neatly, but also under the guise of manners. She pretends to care for fellow parishioners as a rector's wife should, but she is really dividing them with spiritual edge, putting them in their places. Her "savings" are "intangible" because she's a penny pincher, but also because she fails to save the souls or reputations of her neighbors with her "spiritual" divisions. Given her miserliness, it's surprising that she married the poor rector and that they have four children. Theirs may, however, be a good match of opposites: Mrs. Cadwallader is as judgmental as her husband, Humphrey, is tolerant. The exaggeration of personal characteristics and matching of opposites recalls Dickens's caricatures and odd unions, such as violent Jerry Cruncher and his pious, submissive wife in *A Tale of Two Cities*.

At the beginning of the chapter, Mrs. Cadwallader goes to Tipton Grange to visit Mr. Brooke, arriving just as the Reverend Casaubon is leaving. This encounter gives her the opportunity to formulate a figurative putdown of the scholar, which she will share with Celia at the end of her visit. Despite Mrs. Cadwallader's harsh judgments of everyone, she is well liked in Middlemarch, precisely because she brings a much-needed piquancy to town gossip. She next encounters the lodge keeper's wife, Mrs. Fitchett, with whom she enjoys a humorous exchange about fowls that eat their own eggs. The narrator comments on the servant's delight: "Mrs. Fitchett would have found the countryside somewhat duller if the rector's lady had been less free-spoken and less of a skinflint. Indeed, both the farmers and laborers in the parishes of Freshitt and Tipton would have felt a sad lack of conversation but for the stories about what Mrs. Cadwallader had said and done" (53). So Mrs. Cadwallader not only spreads gossip, but is the subject of it, and entertains the townsfolk by her extroverted personality.

The reader sees through Mrs. Cadwallader's social pretensions. Do the Middlemarchers likewise doubt her claims of noble provenance? Mrs. Cadwallader exaggerates her ancestry: "A lady of immeasurably high birth, descended, as it were, from unknown earls, dim as the crowd of heroic shades—who pleaded poverty, pared down prices, and cut jokes in the most companionable manner, though with a turn of tongue that let you know who she was" (53). Mr. Brooke's servants, such as Mrs. Fitchett, seem to believe her assertions, and if this is the case, the narrator may be making fun of their gullibility. Alternatively, they may see through her tall tales yet admire her for having the courage to dissemble. Perhaps they simply believe that a rector's wife would not lie. Also, since she proclaims that she is poor, the neighbors feel better about their own hardships: "Such a lady gave a neighborliness to both rank and religion and mitigated the bitterness of uncommuted tithe. A much more exemplary character with an infusion of sour dignity would not have furthered their comprehension of the Thirty-nine Articles, and would have been less socially uniting" (53). Here, Eliot utilizes paradox to delightful, if somewhat confusing effect. A good rector's wife would have made the congregation regret their tithes (the ten percent of income owed to their church), whereas a gossipy skinflint is relatable and on their level. Apparently, the working-class parishioners feel less intimidated because the "lady" has faults. Those of higher classes, such as Mr. Brooke, are cowed by her rampant tongue; he "winced when her name was announced" (53). For years, it had been her habit to "scold him with the friendliest frankness and let him know in confidence that she thought him a poor creature" (61).

Once seated in the library, Mrs. Cadwallader begins on Mr. Brooke. She chides him about standing for Parliament on the Whig platform, knowing that he and members of his class are fundamentally conservative. She teases him about turning into a Papist: "Who was it sold his land to the Papists of Middlemarch? I believe you bought it on purpose. You are a perfect Guy Faux [*sic*]. See if you are not burned in effigy this 5th of November coming." (53). Guy Fawkes was a famous revolutionary, member of a Catholic conspiracy to overthrow the throne. In 1605 the traitors stored gunpowder underneath the houses of Parliament, planning to set it on fire and kill the King. The attempt failed. British people still celebrate Guy Fawkes Day on November 5 with fireworks, bonfires, and burning effigies. By comparing Brooke to Fawkes, Cadwallader exaggerates so colorfully that we begin to see why Fitchett and the townsfolk appreciate her. Having Mrs. Cadwallader in the neighborhood is like having a travelling music hall performance come to their doors. Like Oscar Wilde, she likes to say the opposite of what's true, for the sake of its absurd effect.

Cadwallader is adamant in her view that Mr. Brooke is unfit for parliament, saying, "Now do not let them lure you to the hustings my dear Mr. Brooke. A man always makes a fool of himself speechifying…. You will make a Saturday pie of all parties' opinions and be pelted by everybody" (54). Her tone is unusually aggressive for a lady speaking to a gentleman.

We do not expect the rector's wife to undermine a landholder's masculine pride. Clearly, Mrs. Cadwallader should run for Parliament herself. In the Houses of Lords and Commons, the MPs regularly cut one another to the bone.

Nor does she spare that other gentleman who is soon to become part of Brooke's family. When Celia tells her of Dorothea's engagement to Casaubon, she ejaculates: "This is frightful. How long has it been going on?" She laments, "We're all disappointed, my dear. Young people should think of their families in marrying," as though Dorothea's choice will hurt her family more than herself. The next comment has a double edge, as do nearly all of her utterances. She seems to be humbling herself, when in fact she's setting herself above her husband: "I set a bad example—married a poor clergyman and made myself a pitiable object among the De Bracys—obliged to get my coals by stratagem and pray to heaven for my salad oil" (56). If it were not for her colorful metaphors, Mrs. Cadwallader might be scorned for her lack of discretion. It is not honorable for a lady to cast aspersions on her husband's earning power or family origins.

But it is not poverty that disqualifies Casaubon from marriage to Dorothea; in Mrs. Cadwallader's opinion, it is his failure to have a career more manly than scholarship: "Casaubon has money enough. I must do him that justice. As to his blood, I suppose the quarterings are three cuttlefish sable, and a commentator rampant" (56). It would be easy to pass over this difficult metaphor of heraldry without catching its emasculating thrust against the nonproductive scholar. Her quip cuts deeply, speculating that his coat of arms consists of three black octopuses (who spout black ink) with a commentator rearing on his hind legs ("rampant") as if to intimidate. Mr. Casaubon does spill a lot of ink but commentating on the common origin of all mythologies is, in Mrs. Cadwallader's judgment, not a very intimidating, or manly, occupation.

Energized by the horrid thought of Dorothea ruining herself in marriage to a nerd, Mrs. Cadwallader rushes to the Chettams' house to spread the painful news. Sir James Chettam is sorry to hear it since he is in love with Dorothea too. Thus, his insult may be forgiven: "It is horrible! He is no more than a mummy!" But Mrs. Cadwallader's comeback trumps Sir James's epithet: "She says he is a great soul.—A great bladder for dried peas to rattle in!" (58). Her image captures many of the scholar's attributes: his spiritual vacuity, his dry ideas, the sense that they rattle around rather than making sense. A feeling of the man's irrelevance or vulgarity is conveyed by comparing him to the (malfunctioning) organ of elimination. Bladders are wet and filled with liquid; Casaubon is dry and empty. Eliot's genius in portraying Mrs. Cadwallader is the unexpectedness of her frankness, the incongruity of a social-climbing parson's wife in a nineteenth-century English town shamelessly putting her neighbors down. Readers may wonder why no one stops her or cuts her socially, but Mrs. Fitchett provides the clue—she's entertainment.

Part of Mrs. Cadwallader's cruelty may derive from a sense of inferiority to her own good-natured husband. Apparently, he never thinks a bad thought of anyone. Mrs. Cadwallader's defense mechanism against a comparison in which she loses is to pretend that Mr. Cadwallader's goodness is unnatural. When Chettam suggests that Mr. Cadwallader may be able to persuade Mr. Brooke to talk Dorothea out of the marriage, Mrs. Cadwallader replies: "Not he! Humphrey finds everybody charming. I never can get him to abuse Casaubon. He will even speak well of the bishop although I tell him it is unnatural in a beneficed clergyman; what can one do with a husband who tends so little to the decencies? I hide it as well as I can by abusing everyone myself" (58–9). Like Oscar Wilde, Mrs. Cadwallader turns the situation on its head. We expect clergymen to be nonjudgmental about other people. Because they're men of the cloth, we desire them to be Christlike. Mrs. Cadwallader, on the other hand, finds her husband's kindness "unnatural" and claims that it would be "decent" if her husband hated the bishop. The punchline is that she has to abuse everyone because her husband won't do it, as though it were a clergyman's job to gossip about his parishioners. Mrs. Cadwallader's is an example of British humor which can be shocking and unfamiliar to American readers, yet we love her for it because she gets away with expressions of opinion that would put most of us into a social deep freeze. Mrs. Cadwallader speaks the unfiltered thoughts and feelings which the majority of her neighbors probably share, and she has gained either their respect or tolerance for doing so.

On the other hand, perhaps Mrs. Cadwallader's acceptance stems more from the narrator's affection than that of her actual neighbors. As we see in the famous pier glass metaphor, the narrator knows that people are more complex than they seem and that we all share a common inability to be objective about any set of circumstances or people (264). Just as the scratches on a mirror appear to circle around the reflection of a candle placed near it, so does the world circle around the individual egos of every person, since we inevitably see events in a way most favorable to our own vanity and needs. People's psyches are their own "centres," as Dorothea articulates in her epiphany, and each person is as much the center of their own universe as the next is of theirs. Dorothea is stating the need to accept the radical otherness of the other, if one is to be happy in marriage and other relationships. Applying this philosophical view to Mrs. Cadwallader, the narrator cautions the reader not to judge the town's busybody too harshly: "Let any lady who is inclined to be hard on Mrs.

Cadwallader inquire into the comprehensiveness of her own beautiful views and be quite sure that they afford accommodation for all the lives which have been honored to exist with hers" (60). The dripping sarcasm of "beautiful views" and "honored to exist" captures exactly the propensity of all minds to judge the behaviors of one's neighbors and to hold oneself above them.

As to her interference in other people's affairs, Mrs. Cadwallader's habit is made less heinous by comparison to, of all things, an amoeba. A microscope metaphor conveys the human need to see better, to get closer to the minutiae that make up our world: "What might seem under a weaker lens to be a creature exhibiting an active voracity into which other small creatures actively play … a stronger lens reveals to you certain tiniest hairlets which make vortices for these victims while the swallower waits passively at his receipt of custom" (60). In the corrective view of the metaphor, Mrs. Cadwallader is not actually exerting herself to meddle in others' lives, only waiting patiently while smaller creatures wander into her orbit. The implied distinction between active voracity and patient waiting is so fine that the narrator helpfully explains: "In this way, metaphorically speaking, a strong lens applied to Mrs Cadwallader's matchmaking will show a play of minute causes producing what may be called thought and speech vortices to bring her the sort of food she needed" (60). Apparently, Mrs. Cadwallader's thoughts and speech are so compelling that people want to gossip to her and provide her the food she rather desperately needs. Eliot hints that meddlesomeness may not be strictly Mrs. Cadwallader's fault; it's somewhat out of her control. Idleness and a greater intelligence than can be satiated by women's work cause voraciousness in a woman whose mind is "active as phosphorus, biting everything that came near into the form that suited it" (60).

Looked at through this lens, Mrs. Cadwallader's wit and sarcasm are by-products of the separate spheres practice that keeps women domesticated and barred from outside employment or involvement in public affairs. Her intellectual power equals Dorothea's, though they put their energies into vastly different enterprises, Dorothea into cottage-building and assisting Casaubon's scholarship, Mrs. Cadwallader into influencing the marriages and political careers of her neighbors. The novel's great achievement is the construction of multiple characters who inhabit every level of the social scale and whose lives are intimately interconnected. The town of Middlemarch is a great social web in which people are interdependent and mutually influencing. Even such a busybody as Mrs. Cadwallader has her place in the scheme, if only to entertain neighbors with her prodigious wit and satire. I wouldn't want to meet her, for fear of what she'd think of me, but I like her as a character who gives piquancy to neighborly chats. She serves to express opinions that other people are afraid to voice. As such, there is a liberating quality to Mrs. Cadwallader.

Works Cited

Dickinson, Emily. Letter to Frances and Louise Norcross, April 1873. http://archive.emilydickinson.org/correspondence/norcross/l389.html.
Eliot, George. *Middlemarch*. Penguin, 1994.

18

What Is a Gentleman?

Question:

So far, we have discussed the term "gentleman" in the works of Emily Brontë, William Thackeray, and Elizabeth Gaskell. In the Victorian era, it meant different things to different people. To be a gentleman, did a man have to be born to gentry, or could stellar manly behavior grant one such a status regardless of class? Upwardly mobile or "new money" people yearned for the status that the term carried yet met with resistance from the aristocracy. What is George Eliot's working definition of the term "gentleman" and to which characters does this term apply? Can we tell from Eliot's discussions of the term whether she is critical of class distinctions in English society?

Analysis:

In English culture, one's class rank is essential to one's sense of self and one's role in society. English writers through the ages have satirized this class consciousness. In 1400, Chaucer was no less riveted by its importance in English society than Jane Austen in 1800. The Victorians avidly pursued ideals of progress and tried to ameliorate social ills. In Victorian literature, then, we might expect to see a solid critique of the class system, but this is surprisingly rare—perhaps because most writers were middle class and determined to maintain their positions. Some of the male writers even desired to attain the status of gentleman for themselves, Dickens being a prime example. In her novel of 1830s Midlands morals and manners, Eliot gently satirizes, but does nothing to ameliorate, the class hierarchy of Middlemarch society.

165

At the heart of the distinction between middle and upper classes is the concept of a gentleman. With its combination of social and moral components, the concept has an elasticity and complexity that make it a natural subject for fictional development. Does it mean that one has money and property? No, because it is not synonymous with gentry. Does it mean that one has good manners and helps other people? Yes, a good gentleman is like that. But not every good person is a gentleman and not every gentleman is a good person. According to Robin Gilmour and David Cody, literature was the arena in which the debate of what constituted a gentleman most frequently took place: "Just as in society at large the gentlemanly idea exercised its fascination because it was neither a socially exclusive nor an entirely moralized concept, so too the novelists move naturally and easily between the moral and social attributes of gentlemanliness" (Gilmour 12). As industry and trade flourished in the nineteenth century and wealth poured into English coffers from the enterprises of empire, new elements of society were eager to become gentlemen. Traditionally a term reserved for aristocrats and members of certain professions (Church of England clergy, military officers, and members of Parliament), the gentleman category opened up by the end of the century to include the well-educated: "By the latter part of the century it was almost universally accepted that the recipient of a traditional liberal education based largely on Latin at one of the elite public schools—Eton, Harrow, Rugby, and so on—would be recognized as a gentleman, no matter what his origins had been" (Cody). But such liberality is not shared by the conservative residents of Middlemarch in the years 1829–32. From the following discussion it should be clear that, in Eliot's fictional world, one is born, but cannot become, a gentleman.

One of the gentlemen in *Middlemarch*, Sir James Chettam, is self-conscious about his status. He is the character who most frequently introduces the term "gentleman" as a category of value and exclusion. Born a baronet—the lowest rank of the peerage—Sir James enjoys the outdoorsman's life associated with "county people": he rides, hunts, makes social visits to members of his class, discusses the merits of parliamentary candidates, and executes the cottage-building plan of his neighbor, Dorothea, in order to get close to her. In gentlemanly fashion, he continues to respect and work with Dorothea even after she turns down his marriage proposal. As a gentleman, he strives to protect her from the "low born" Will Ladislaw, who "has some foreign blood in him" (379). Chettam subscribes to the traditional notion that British gentry must marry other members of the British gentry. On the other hand, compared to Mr. Brooke, Chettam is progressive in his views of improving his land and managing his tenants. Chettam wants to improve the tenants' quality of life, whereas Brooke is content to let their cottages go to ruin.

As a proud gentleman, Chettam polices the boundaries of the category, making sure to keep out the people whose birth does not qualify them for admittance. He tries to keep English gentry pure by denigrating upstarts such as Will Ladislaw and dishonorable gentry such as Casaubon. As soon as Casaubon has coupled Dorothea with Ladislaw in his will, Chettam ejects him from gentleman status because of the rule that a gentleman does not tarnish a lady's reputation (485).

Because Eliot makes fun of the pomposity of traditional gentlemen such as Chettam, we should consider whether men outside that category actually fit its requirements better, at least in a moral sense. Like many Victorian novelists, Eliot portrays a distinction between gentlemen-in-behavior and gentlemen-by-birth. Ladislaw makes the best example of a man who follows the gentleman's code of behavior but whose family roots are suspect. Though Ladislaw has gentry in his family (Casaubon is his cousin), his ancestors have gradually de-classed themselves over the past two generations. His grandmother married a poor Polish musician and was disinherited. His father was a poor artist and his mother an actress who ran away from her family of pawnbrokers. Since Casaubon has hidden information about Will's inheritance, Middlemarchers (and Will himself) don't know how to place him. (To "place someone" in British society means to identify the class to which they belong.) Once the news about Casaubon's will gets out—Dorothea will forfeit the legacy if she marries Ladislaw—the townspeople have reason to suspect Ladislaw's integrity. In their view, if he isn't of pure birth, he can't possibly be a gentleman. The townspeople exchange the phrase, "Young Ladislaw, the grandson of a thieving Jew pawnbroker" (772). British anti–Semitism was overt and shameless. The English imagined that only Jews practiced pawnbroking because it was a form of moneylending, a vocation traditionally associated with Jewish people from at least the time of the Bible. Racism is added to classism and nationalism in the stew of English class snobbery.

Yet it is Ladislaw who exhibits the most intrinsically gentlemanly traits of any male character in the novel. When he learns of Casaubon's will, he stops visiting Dorothea (the only person who respects him) so as to protect her reputation. Nor will he accept Bulstrode's money, since the "ill-gotten gains" are tainted by their unknown but suspicious provenance. Never does he flirt with Dorothea or lead her on with false expectations of his intentions. He does not tell lies, and he does not try to use his cousin Casaubon—a man whom he dislikes—to attain social advantages.

From the above comparisons, it appears that the following are traits of a gentleman that are agreed upon by most characters in the novel. The list contains more social than moral components. Several items, such as "Chastity" and "Chivalry" belong to both social and moral components because the moral duty is differentially applied depending on class: for instance, a gentleman must be chaste and chivalrous to a lady, but the same obligation is not owed to a peasant woman.

1. Honor. A gentleman neither lies nor breaks a promise.
2. Integrity. A gentleman does not gossip or seek to damage other people.
3. Origins. A gentleman is either born to gentry or enters it by marriage.
4. Chivalry. A gentleman protects ladies' reputations and shields them from harm.
5. Money. A gentleman does not deal in shady financial business.
6. Civic duty. A gentleman participates in the civic activities of his district.
7. Religion. A gentleman belongs to the Church of England and participates in the religious activities of his district.
8. Chastity. A gentleman respects the purity of womanhood (though this is qualified by class). If he impregnates an upper- or middle-class woman, he marries her.
9. Education and Military Service. A gentleman attends Oxford or Cambridge or serves as a military officer.
10. Noblesse Oblige. A gentleman offers charity to those less fortunate than himself, especially those he knows or is responsible for (i.e., tenants).

Since she is a woman of strong character, we might wish that George Eliot's views on social class distinctions were more radical. It would be pleasing to see a gentlemanly character who was not to the manor born. The most liberal thing she does in this direction, however, is to give Will a "queer genealogy," as Farebrother puts it. The genealogy may be queer, but it is nonetheless gentry, ensuring that Dorothea doesn't end by de-classing herself in marriage to Will. Eliot's conservatism requires that her heroine maintain her class status. The full array of Eliot's gentlemen, middle-class men, and working men display nuanced behaviors without actually transgressing class barriers by moving to a different class than the one into which they were born. Caleb Garth is a working-class man who exhibits noble traits, but he lacks the education to constitute true gentlemanliness. Although Eliot is a strong moralist and appreciates nobility of character— Dorothea's being the epitome—she is also a realist who is writing about a conservative community. Therefore, the idea of a *gentleman*, in *Middlemarch*, has closer ties to social class than to innate goodness.

We have discussed what constitutes a gentleman, but gentlewomen are a different class of people with different moral attributes. They share some, but not all, characteristics of gentlemen. First and foremost, they must be of good birth. They must have good manners, practice charity, and receive an education in the feminine disciplines of languages, letter writing, music, sewing, and drawing. They must have honor and integrity (remember Margaret Hale's extreme guilt about telling a lie to the police in *North and South*). They must guard the chastity of their thoughts, speech, and action. Yet they should not fulfill other requirements that pertain to their male counterparts, such as "civic duty," "education and military service," or "chivalry." The most interesting distinction between male and female members of this elite is that, typically, the standards of honor and integrity to which ladies are held are lower than those for gentlemen. Female gossiping prevaricators frequent the pages of Victorian novels, receiving only minor censure. Despite their moral weakness, these characters are still classed as "ladies." So, to our definition of gentleman, we might consider adding an additional feature:

11. Gender. A gentleman is not female.

In other words, the highest moral status within any social category within patriarchy will always be granted to the male members of that category. To be female was to be considered inherently less capable of developing one's nobility of character. One of the most compelling aspects of certain woman-authored Victorian novels is, however, their implicit challenge to this notion insofar as their heroines have more of the gentlemanly qualities than do several male characters. Dorothea is the epitome of a noble character in *Middlemarch*: self-sacrificing, tolerant, charitable, self-critical, and respectful, Dorothea grows through experience and becomes more altruistic. Jane Eyre and Margaret Hale also belong to this category of noble women, regardless of their class at birth.

Works Cited

Cody, David. "The Gentleman." http://www.victorianweb.org/history/gentleman.html.
Eliot, George. *Middlemarch: A Study of Provincial Life*. Penguin, 1994.
Gilmour, Robin. *The Idea of the Gentleman in the Victorian Novel*. Allen & Unwin, 1981.
Terci, Mahmut. "Images of the Gentleman in Victorian Fiction." *European Journal of Language and Literature Studies* 1:3 (2015). 7–20.

19

Dorothea and Lydgate's Unrealized Potential

Questions:

In early April 2020, I was teaching *Middlemarch* while we were just beginning to learn about the seriousness and magnitude of the coronavirus pandemic. Like many others, I became curious about the history of epidemics and pandemics in the world. In 1830, cholera and influenza were about to strike the region of the fictional Middlemarch (based on the actual town Coventry, in Warwickshire, the West Midlands). Lydgate would have been positioned to fight the cholera epidemic had his personal problems not interfered. What would have happened if an epidemic or pandemic had infected the town of Middlemarch in 1830? What roles might Lydgate and Dorothea have played in fighting it?

Analysis:

In this lecture, I indulge in some speculation which I hope will not seem idle. The first question arises from acute concern regarding the Covid pandemic that we are experiencing, while the second question addresses the marital couplings that Eliot made and the reasons why she may have chosen them and not others.

Dr. Lydgate is an interesting character who reveals Eliot's interest in the medical issues of her day. His research topic indicates that he was on the cutting edge of contemporary medical research, which was about to discover germ theory. The fact that the town drove out this capable scientist due to scandalous gossip is disappointing. His life, and that of most other townspeople, would have gone far differently if he'd stayed, built the hospital, and carried out the research he planned. Not only would he be professionally fulfilled, but England and the world might have bene-fited from his breakthroughs in cellular research and epidemiology as they faced the cholera and influenza epidemics of those years. His medical and public health instincts were ahead of his time and he could possibly have put Middlemarch on the map. Let's consider what the medical commu-nity believed about contagious diseases at the time when Lydgate practiced medicine in Middlemarch.

In 1830, the miasma theory of disease was prevalent; it had not yet given way to germ theory, which says that disease spreads by germs passed through air, feces, or skin-to-skin contact. Even if Middlemarch had let Lydgate stay and manage the New Fever Hospital, he might not have been able to save enough lives to convince them of his abilities. Let's say that a virus as serious as Covid had struck the town. He may not have known that he should quarantine the sufferers to prevent the spread of disease. On the other hand, his close observations of flu virus—its symptoms, expo-nential spread, deaths, and recovery rates—may have led him to discover germ theory or cell theory, or both.

Miasma theory states that disease is caused by bad-smelling air; this was the Western world's understanding of the etiology of disease from the Middle Ages till the mid–1800s. Literally, the bad smells caused by parti-cles of rotted organic matter were believed to infect people through the air that they breathed. Early Victorians didn't know how germs pass from person to person. In order to stem the tide of diseases like cholera, they would simply flee their villages to get away from the "bad smell." Since they continued to use poor sewage systems, they were inevitably rein-fected. Cholera is caused by a bacterium, *vibrio cholerae*, that people ingest when drinking water and eating food contaminated by human feces. In 1854, Dr. John Snow discovered that a particular water pump on Broad Street in London was contaminated by a sewage pipe from a nearby dwell-ing. From this observation, he went on to hypothesize that cholera was spread by drinking water contaminated by feces, and his data served to prove his theory. Germ theory was born.

Cholera was sometimes lethal, but it was never as fatal as influenza; its symptoms included diarrhea and dehydration. England had a chol-era pandemic in 1830, and a flu pandemic at the same time, from 1830 to 1833. Originating in China, this flu reappeared twice during its three-year span, exhibiting the same kind of spikes that we are experiencing with the coronavirus. Cholera affected a quarter of the world's population. At this point, Middlemarch badly needed the Fever Hospital, and Lydgate was the man to manage it.

172 VII. *Middlemarch* (1871)

Lydgate's special value as a medical man is his unusual combination of a reforming passion (for public health) and an intellectual passion (to discover the primitive tissue of all life). George Eliot was a polymath, and must have known, while writing the novel in 1871, that cell theory was discovered in 1839 by a pair of German scientists called Theodor Schwann and Matthias Schleiden. Although the word "cell" was coined as early as 1665, when cork cells were microscopically examined by British physicist Robert Hooke, the discovery that cells were the building blocks of all life didn't occur until 1839. A basic tenet of the new theory was that the cell is the most basic unit of life. In 1832, this is exactly the line of research that Lydgate was interested in. With the retrospect of 1871, George Eliot creates a likable character who seems on the verge of discovering the cell's functions but, instead of giving him this accomplishment, leads him through scandal, marital difficulty, displacement, and a routine practice of medicine for rich people. Lydgate's disenchantment with this life results in his early death. The social conditions of Middlemarch life interfered with the conditions needed for scientific discovery. Given the right working conditions, Lydgate might have been the one to discover that "the primitive tissue that underlies all life" was the cell.

Besides having a passionate interest in biological research, Lydgate's other idiosyncrasy (from the local doctors' point of view) is his refusal to dispense drugs. Once again, Eliot applies her knowledge of legislative history to build tension around her forward-thinking character. The Apothecaries Act of 1815 began the regulation of the medical profession to eliminate the quackery that was the standard medical practice of the time. Middlemarch's doctors prescribed elixirs, panaceas, and tonics that Lydgate knew to be ineffective. His unwillingness to dispense drugs made Lydgate unpopular with fellow doctors, seeming "to cast imputations on those who did" (182). Lydgate explains his rationale to a grocer: "It must lower the character of practitioners, and be a constant injury to the public, if their only mode of getting paid for their work was by their making out long bills for draughts, boluses, and mixtures" (444). The implied imputation of wrongdoing to his fellow doctors, added to his arrogance, causes a gradual boycott of his practice. The killing blow is his association with Bulstrode in the suspicious medical case of John Raffles. When Bulstrode leaves town, Dorothea steps into his shoes as principal contributor to the hospital. It appears for a short time that the project will continue despite Bulstrode's withdrawal. Lydgate has the opportunity to direct the New Fever Hospital but his wife blocks his way. Rosamond's wish to leave Middlemarch clinches the decision for the doomed pair. Lydgate's career change depletes his *élan vital* and he dies young, feeling himself a failure. The narrator implies that his dissatisfaction with his new practice—a gout doctor for rich patients—shortened his life.

Building the Fever Hospital with Lydgate would have changed Dorothea's life too. In my opinion, the novel's "Finale" chapter fails to convince us that her role as Ladislaw's wife is only a *small* sacrifice of Dorothea's talents. Rather, it is a contradiction of her essential creative nature. She serves her new family as a helpmate: "Her full nature … spent itself in channels which had no great name on the earth" (838). In other words, she helped Will and their son to lead full, contented lives. What would happen if we hypothetically diverted that river channel, so that Dorothea never remarried, and instead lived on her inheritance from Casaubon? As a single woman (respectable, since widowed), she might have made a great contribution to the Fever Hospital, rather than a "small sacrifice" of her life. Before marrying Will, she was willing to pledge to the hospital the same amount of money that Bulstrode had given. Moreover, she was glad to help Lydgate reach his potential and save people's lives. During her first tour of the New Hospital grounds, Dorothea says: "I have some money and don't know what to do with it—that is often an uncomfortable thought to me. I am sure I can spare two hundred a year for a grand purpose like this. How happy you must be, to know things that you feel sure will do great good! I wish I could awake with that knowledge every morning" (440). Dorothea could have served her *grand purpose* if she had not married, if Lydgate had stayed, run the hospital, and taken her on as an equal partner. She has the qualities to become such a partner, helping Lydgate to reform the hospital and discover germ theory. She is his spiritual and moral equal.

If cholera and flu had stormed Middlemarch before Lydgate left, and the townspeople had subscribed to the New Fever Hospital, the combination of Lydgate and Dorothea working together might have made Middlemarch a healthier place. Dorothea could have contributed not only her finances but also her considerable intellectual talent in helping Lydgate organize the hospital with a research focus. In her first marriage, she had proven the nature of her intelligence and the extent of her work ethic by remarking that Casaubon's thesis had been superannuated by German scholarship. She was nonetheless willing to help him organize it. How much more fruitful it would have been for her to work on "the primitive tissue of life" with Tertius Lydgate than "the syncretism of all ancient mythologies" with Edward Casaubon.

It is interesting to speculate why Eliot chose not to pair Dorothea and Lydgate romantically, instead of Dorothea with Casaubon and Lydgate with Rosamond. Dorothea at least has the opportunity to learn, from the pain of her first marriage, the kind of men that she's suited to partner, but Lydgate never recovers from the mistake of his marital choice. Dorothea and Lydgate are spiritually suited; they share the belief that, to live fully, one must do great things for humankind. For his own part, Lydgate is much in need of the maturing and refining effect of Dorothea, whom he "doesn't think of as a woman," but rather as a great person. Partnering her would help break down the separate spheres doctrine which he has assimilated. Just by being near him, Dorothea would refine his coarse understanding of women, and he in turn would afford her a respectful entry into the male realm of work.

Perhaps it is Eliot's chosen genre, her psychological and social realism, that requires her characters to fail to see their proper mates, as people so often do. Maybe Dorothea was not of sufficiently feminine appearance to interest Lydgate sexually—and if Eliot sees much of herself in Dorothea, then the plain appearance would be an issue. The physical descriptions of Dorothea are general; lacking are the detailed colorings and facial structures given by a Charlotte Brontë or a William Thackeray. Instead, hers is the kind of beauty "which seems to be thrown in relief by poor dress," her finely formed hands and wrists being her most attractive features (7). Or maybe it is a conservative or depressive strain in the author that determines the heroine's destiny of succumbing to the separate spheres ideology that kept her away from work. This attitude, however, is inconsistent with Eliot's own life, for she was unconventional in her professional and marital choices. She cohabited with George Henry Lewes for twenty-four years, calling him "husband" though he was still married to Agnes Jervis. Eliot had no children; she was an atheist, editor of the *Westminster Review*, writer of seven popular novels, translator of the difficult philosophical text Spinoza's *Ethics*, and the list goes on—by all accounts a woman who fully realized her potential and was, in this sense, unlike Dorothea Brooke.

Works Cited

"Death and Miasma in Victorian London: An Obstinate Belief." www.ncbi.nlm.nih. gov>pmc>articles>PMC1121911.
Eliot, George. *Middlemarch*. London: Penguin, 1994.

20

Bathsheba's Feminism

Question:

An anomaly of her time, Bathsheba Everdene is a self-supporting female farmer who manages her estate for many years before marrying. She likes to flirt but doesn't take men's courtship seriously. Once she feels lustful attraction of her own, however, she quickly falls victim to the first cad who pursues her. Finally liberated from a terrible marriage, she succumbs to another man whose proposal she had earlier refused. Does Hardy support Bathsheba's independence? Does he admire her feminism? Does the narrator?

Synopsis:

Gabriel Oak is a shepherd who has just leased a farm when he meets neighbor Bathsheba Everdene and asks her to marry him. She scorns the idea of marriage, saying she's too independent to be the property of a man. One night, Gabriel falls asleep in a shepherd's hut with the fire still blazing. Bathsheba sees the building smoking and saves his life. Gabriel's overzealous sheepdog herds his flock over a steep cliff, and Gabriel must give up the farm and seek work. On his way to Casterbridge Fair, he comes across a burning hayrick. He organizes laborers to put out the fire and save the farm. Before identifying him as her former suitor, Bathsheba hires him as shepherd, for it is her newly inherited farm that went up in flames.

In jest, Bathsheba sends a valentine asking prosperous landowner William Boldwood to marry her. He takes her seriously and begins a lifelong quest to earn her love. She toys with him by delaying her response. When Gabriel hears of it, he chides her for leading Boldwood on, and

Bathsheba promptly fires him for insubordination. Sometime later, Bathsheba's flock is dying from a disease that bloats their stomachs. Since Gabriel is the only farmer who knows how to treat this disease, Bathsheba reluctantly agrees to call for him. After he saves her flock, she rehires him. She begins a flirtation with Sergeant Frank Troy, who's on leave from the army. Initially, she distrusts his flattery, but after he performs a sword show, she succumbs to his masculine charisma and becomes jealous when he says he also likes another woman. She begs him to marry her. Unbeknownst to her, Troy has been sleeping with Bathsheba's former servant, Fanny Robin, who is pregnant with his child.

Thomas Hardy, by Herbert Rose Barraud (1889).

Not even a month into the marriage, Troy reveals his gambling addiction, his insolvency, and his inability to love Bathsheba. Coming across an impoverished, pregnant Fanny on the road to Casterbridge, Troy is guilt-stricken and offers to support her. She returns to the workhouse that night and dies in childbirth. Bathsheba learns that Fanny was Troy's lover, and Troy takes a swim far out into the ocean. Later, townsmen find his clothes and presume he's dead, but actually he's been rescued by a ship and resumes life as a carnival worker. A year later, Bathsheba has given in to Boldwood's insistence that they become engaged. At a Christmas party, Troy reappears and demands his marital rights. Boldwood shoots him and tries to kill himself. He is committed to an insane asylum and pardoned for murder on grounds of insanity. Gabriel plans to leave the farm because of the rumors that he's going to propose to Bathsheba again. She insinuates that she wouldn't mind being married to him. He proposes, and this time she accepts. The rustics celebrate the union, but they also utter sobering comments about the transience of all love and romance.

Analysis:

Charles Dickens, William Thackeray, and George Eliot's best work came out in the middle Victorian period, when Britain was enjoying economic prosperity and a growing middle class that avidly consumed their novels. Thomas Hardy is a late Victorian whose novels express a very different sensibility. From 1873 to 1896, a slump known as the Great Depression curtailed Britain's economy. The manufacturing sector declined, railway construction slowed, and the agricultural sector suffered terribly (Steinbach 93–96). In addition to economic ills, people felt anxious about social changes as the shibboleths of class privilege and gender inequality began very gradually to erode. Hardy's famously dark tone is a foreshadowing of the modernist angst that will pervade the literature of the coming era.

Far from the Madding Crowd describes an agricultural community in rural Dorsetshire whose inhabitants are affected by both economic stagnation and social change. As Steinbach writes, "Agriculture went into a decline [after 1860] that never reversed.... Those who remained in farming found it difficult to make a living as farm work mechanized and food prices dropped" (92). The farmers, shepherds, and day laborers of Hardy's novel all struggle to earn a living and keep their jobs. What makes the novel unusual is that the protagonist is an unmarried female landowner who decides to manage the farm on her own. She fires the bailiff as soon as she inherits the property. Such a decision is uncommon for a woman of her time and place, and consequently it brings derision and distrust upon Bathsheba Everdene.

Hardy is known as a protomodernist, not only for his dark tone, but also because he questions Victorian mores. Specifically, he interrogates the gender roles inherent in separate spheres ideology. His position on the true equality of men and women is, however, complex. In this novel, he does not unequivocally accept the gender role known as the New Woman—she who would earn her living and find fulfillment without marriage. He is aware that the Wessex farmers oppose Bathsheba's assertion of a woman's right to be independent. Although Hardy's narrator provides the perspectives of male and female characters alike, he understands only too well the male characters' personal resentment of Bathsheba's vanity and position. My conclusion is that Hardy (and his narrator) champions the idea of independent womanhood but is too much of an economic and biological determinist to believe in its plausibility.

Too frequently to ignore, Hardy's narrator asserts stereotypes about women that reflect the community's sexist views, suggesting that the narrator's views are not different from those of the male Wessexers. After

Bathsheba saves Gabriel's life by evacuating him from his smoky hut, the narrator describes her "speaking in a tone which showed her to be that novelty among women—one who finished a thought before beginning the sentence which was to convey it" (19). This harsh judgment jangles in our contemporary ears. It proclaims that women are impulsive and unable to think logically or speak authoritatively. Chapter IV opens with a similarly sexist stereotype: "The only superiority tolerable in women, as a rule, is that of the unconscious kind, but a superiority which recognizes itself may sometimes please by suggesting at the same time possibilities of impropriation to the subordinated man" (21). [*impropriate*: to take over and make one's own] This sentence claims that men might actually enjoy witnessing a woman's self-confidence because they imagine that they (men) can change it to subordination by the exercise of their own natural superiority and the rights and privileges of their gender. In other words, the "chase" is fun for men, who are certain—by virtue of patriarchal ideology—that they can conquer their prey. In this case, the chase is not only the marriage conquest, but the challenge of besting Bathsheba in her business dealings.

Bathsheba is not such a pushover as her fellow farmers suppose. In two key scenes, she demonstrates her determination to master the men's resistance to her unusual position, that of being employer of men and business dealer among them—on payday and market day, respectively. After paying wages she makes a small speech that warns her laborers not to underestimate her: "Don't any unfair ones among you (if there are any such, but I hope not) suppose that because I'm a woman I don't understand the difference between bad goings-on and good" (73). In 1588, Queen Elizabeth I spoke in a similar vein to her troops before they went into battle against Spain, likewise asserting her power and understanding as a woman leader: "I know I have the body of a weak, feeble woman, but I have the heart and stomach of a king.... [R]ather than any dishonor shall grow by me, I myself will take up arms" ("Elizabeth"). In maintaining their authority, both Bathsheba and the Queen of England found it essential to refer outright to their gender in order to acknowledge its supposed weakness and then to defy the presumption so that their men might proceed with confidence in their leaders. Hardy's narrator approves of Bathsheba's tactics and presents her on her first payday as a figure of dignity and generosity.

His presentation of Bathsheba on market day at the Casterbridge Corn Exchange is, however, satirical:

> This Saturday's debut in the forum, whatever it may have been to Bathsheba as the buying and selling farmer, was unquestionably a triumph to her as a maiden. Indeed, the sensation was so pronounced that her instinct on two or three occasions was to merely walk as a queen among these gods of the

fallow, like a little sister of a little Jove, and to neglect closing prices altogether [80–81].

It is clear that, in the narrator's view, women are apt to become distracted from business by flattery about their feminine charms. Bathsheba neglects business while enjoying male attention. Like men who love the chase of a woman, Bathsheba also likes to initiate the hunt for male attention, but she does not intend to deliver the goods if confronted. She admires Farmer Boldwood precisely because he does not appear to notice her, and this causes her to investigate his personality with the intent of changing his perceptions. Inasmuch as the quoted passage demonstrates a generalized male distrust of female vanity, there is an even deeper threat to male superiority deriving from Bathsheba's business capability and self-esteem. As one farmer says, "'[T]is a pity she's so headstrong … 'tis a handsome maid, however, and she'll soon get picked up" (80). Women's self-assurance is pitiable, but it can be ended by marriage, after which her property will be handled by a man and her authority properly curtailed.

In the same scene, the narrator gives away some of his own presumptions about gender when he describes the male and female attributes combined in Bathsheba. She has the male traits of aggression, courage, and willingness to exploit a situation for her benefit, but the "softness" of a woman is in her gaze. During her market negotiations, the narrator observes:

> Something in the exact arch of her upper unbroken row of teeth, and in the keenly pointed corners of her red mouth when, with parted lips, she somewhat defiantly turned up her face to argue a point with a tall man, suggested that there was depth enough in that lithe piece of humanity for alarming potentialities of exploit, and daring enough to carry them out [80].

This description of her sharp teeth, open red mouth, and defiance of tall men suggests the *vagina dentata*—a classic male fantasy of a vagina ringed with teeth meant for devouring men. In other words, Hardy is painting Bathsheba as a *femme fatale* who must be guarded against rather than admired. The use of the words "alarming," "exploit," and "daring" convey the impression that she is like a man in her approach to courtship and love. Indeed, her next exploit is to toy with Farmer Boldwood's affections by sending him a request to marry her. By the standards of her time, Bathsheba is an outrageous flirt, but attractive enough to drive at least one of her victims to madness.

The end of Chapter XII, "A Pleasant Time: A Second Declaration," leaves us with the distinct impression that Bathsheba is a hypocrite. She is either unaware of or indifferent to the effects of her own flirtations. When Liddy says a woman jilted Boltwood, Bathsheba corrects her: "People always say that—and we know very well women scarcely ever jilt men; 'tis the men who jilt us" (82–83). Yet Bathsheba has recently jilted Gabriel Oak and is about to do the same to Farmer Boldwood. Even though she knows and appreciates her own sexual power—the charisma that magnetizes men—she regularly denies or diminishes its importance. Only momentarily affected by Oak's disappointment, she blithely moves on, able to forget about his feelings while he is still suffering.

To answer the question at the start of the lecture, whether Hardy admires Bathsheba's feminism, it is instructive to consider his body of work. Although it is his fifth novel, *Far from the Madding Crowd* is nonetheless an early work. In 1874, he is still working out his craft. In the same year, he marries Emma Gifford; his mature views about the respective roles of men and women in marriage and in society, are yet unformed. By 1891, when he writes his other Wessex novel about female (dis)empowerment, *Tess of the D'Urbervilles*, Hardy has become emotionally estranged from Emma. He has gained a far greater appreciation of the challenges that women face within the restrictive conditions of Victorian patriarchy. Unlike middle-class Bathsheba, working-class Tess is not economically empowered. Her life opportunities are severely limited by class and gender restrictions. Hoping to save her parents from eviction, she falls prey to a Sergeant Troy–like rake. After a long period of fighting to remain independent, Tess finally succumbs to D'Urberville and in doing so, destroys her own chance for happiness.

Hardy was well aware that gender and class oppressions were intersectional. Any straying from her expected gender role was more damaging to working-class Tess than to land-owning Bathsheba. Gender and class oppressions operated in an inverse relationship. As Rosemarie Morgan writes in her introduction to the Penguin edition, "Victorian women did not of course lack sexual power. But in contrast to men, social codes and practices gave recognition either to their sexual power or to their class power but very rarely both in tandem" (xx–xxi). In other words, Bathsheba could be a successful single farmer as long as she ignored her devastating sexual effect on men but would lose that status if she wielded sexual power and took a husband. "Culturally speaking the one was doomed to arrest the other," continues Morgan. The power of Bathsheba's land-owning, farm-managing status arrested the power of her sexuality, for it was not acceptable to flirt if one also exerted economic power over men. The power of her sexuality "arrested" the power of her class status, because if she flaunted her sexuality, she would attract both flirtation and distrust from her workers. She could be either a leader or a woman, but not both. In 1874, Hardy understands this behavioral bind, but expresses male distrust of powerful women in ways that suggest he's complicit in the agenda of restricting women's choice. By 1891, with *Tess*, Hardy has matured to a point of empathizing with his female protagonist far more than he does with the male character who some readers say is his alter ego, Angel Clare. So does Hardy support Bathsheba's feminism? Apparently neither he nor his narrator do; the narrator mocks it, and Hardy tames her with marriage at the end of the novel. On the final page, however, the question again arises—whether marriage can ever be totally fulfilling. The rustics make dubious statements about the possible success of Bathsheba and Gabriel's union, or of any marriage at all. This leaves open the question: if marriage can't make women happy, what can?

Works Cited

"Elizabeth's Tilbury Speech—The British Library." www.bl.uk/learning/timeline/item102878.html.

Hardy, Thomas. *Far from the Madding Crowd*. London: Penguin, 2000.

Morgan, Rosemarie. Introduction. *Far from the Madding Crowd*. Penguin, 2000. xvii–xxxii.

Steinbach, Susie. "Wealth and Poverty, Growth and Slumps: The Economy." *Understanding the Victorians: Politics, Culture and Society in Nineteenth-Century Britain*. Routledge, 2012. 77–97.

21

The Role of the Rustics

Question:

The rustics are farmworkers who populate the crowd scenes and social events of Hardy's Wessex novels. They know the main characters fairly well because they have lived in the same village, drunk in the same pubs, and worked the same farms for many years prior to the action of the novels. They generally, but not always, belong to a lower class than the protagonists, and consequently, they bring a different perspective to their affairs. In each of Hardy's novels, the rustics play a slightly different role. In *Far from the Madding Crowd*, the rustics are the workers who shear and graze sheep, cultivate land, and attend markets, weddings, fairs, and other social functions. What is the role of the rustics in *Far from the Madding Crowd*?

Analysis:

Hardy's cast of minor characters seasons the novel with dialect, opinions, and folk customs. The rustics comment upon the main action like the chorus in a Greek tragedy. They also provide a framework in which to understand Gabriel's rise and fall in class status as he gains, loses, and regains positions and property. Rosemary Jann claims that the rustics' role is to justify the rise of the rustic protagonist to what she calls middling status. Since his virtues, language, and behavior are demonstrably more genteel than theirs, it proves that he deserves to enter the middle class. Jann identifies Thomas Hardy's class insecurity—his father a mason, his mother a servant—as the root of his ambivalent portrait of rustics who are both virtuous and laughable. Gabriel Oak is both superior to and similar to the rustics.

Another possibility is that they are simply there for comic relief. Critic Shuchita Mital believes that the rustics' most important role is comic relief from the serious trials of protagonists Bathsheba, Oak, and Boldwood. The rustics don't take themselves as seriously as this trio; they even know how to make fun of themselves. They are practical rather than tragic, commenting on the main action with a stoicism absent from the main characters. A second function of the rustics, according to Mital, is that their activities and beliefs reveal centuries-old agricultural traditions of the Wessex region. The rustics engage in farming and shepherding rituals such as the birthing, washing, and shearing of sheep. Their superstitions include the ability of women to find a husband by playing the old Bible and Key game. Their songs and dances are traditional folk arts of the region.

Mital's and Jann's arguments complement each other, providing both traditional genre analysis and poststructuralist social commentary. Jann's insight—that the rustics provide a foil to the genteel characteristics of the class-rising Gabriel—assists our understanding of the many ways in which class issues dominate this text. For my analysis, I'll focus on the introduction of the rustics in Chapter 8, "The Malthouse," contrasting their personalities with Gabriel's and discussing their comic and social roles.

Hardy depicts the malt house as an inviting haven for men. Steam from the malting process "mists out" from the roof-top lantern, and the kiln's "red comfortable rays stretch out upon the ivied wall in front" (46). Inside, the kiln fire throws a ruddy glow upon the drinkers' faces and the sweet smell of new malt pervades the atmosphere. On the other hand, there's a quality of grotesquerie to the rustics. Their clothing, utensils, and food are dirty. The dark, cave-like structure of the malt house and the shadows of "facial irregularities" thrown upon the wall by the firelight might allude to Plato's *Allegory of the Cave*, which I describe at length in Chapter V, "*A Tale of Two Cities*: Allegory and Personification." Might these shadows be illusions, and the rustics akin to the blind ignoramuses of Plato's cave? Newcomer Gabriel would then be their liberator, the prisoner who sees the light. They squint at him "as if he had been a light too strong for their sight," just as Plato's freed philosopher was at first blinded by the light of truth (47). When we meet them one by one, however, we perceive that the rustics have their own wisdom, and their own role in teaching Gabriel the history of the neighborhood that he's about to join.

The men speak a colorful, figurative dialect, which Hardy keenly appreciates. When the old maltster exclaims that Gabriel is "never Gable Oak's grandson over at Norcombe—never!" the narrator describes it as "a formula expressive of surprise, which nobody was supposed for a moment to take literally" (47). The maltster is understood to be a teller of tall tales.

When he is asked his age, he responds circuitously by giving an account of his life. The quiet observer in the corner tallies these years and the age of the maltster comes out to 117 years. (I once came across a tombstone for "the oldest man in England," who was 169.) Hardy begins describing the individual rustics' grotesque and supernatural characteristics, reminding me of the hobbits and trolls of Middle Earth. The maltster had "frosty white hair and [a] beard overgrowing his gnarled figure like the grey moss and lichen upon an old appletree." His eyes were "vermilion red and bleared" from gazing into the fire for so many years (46, 48).

Each character is both minor and, at the same time, larger than life. They are characterized by their most noticeable external traits of physical appearance and behavior, but we don't get to know their inner life beyond what they share at the malt house, hayfield, or shearing barn. On the other hand, they each represent some droll or admirable characteristic of Dorset farmworkers culled from Hardy's experience.

The men exaggerate one another's defects to create a feeling of bonhomie. Mark Clark is a leech, who always lets others buy him drinks. He's a cynic of a smarter order than Henery Fray, who's a cynical simpleton, who "laid it down that the world is bad." Henery is characterized by his frustrated ambition to be a bailiff (49). Laban Tall is bland and timid, with "no individuality worth mentioning"; he's so afraid of his wife that he's earned the nickname "Susan Tall's husband" (58). Jan Coggan is a respected worker, the appointed master of ceremonies at communal gatherings, a spokesperson for the crew, an upholder of tradition, a man who instinctively plays the diplomat. When courting his first wife, he would eat salt to make himself thirsty before visiting her farm, as her master promised him as much ale as he could drink, and Coggan aimed to please. Joseph Poorgrass is known for his piety, simplicity, and shyness. Although he is debilitatingly shy with women, he begins to boast about his shyness when supported by the all-male crowd of the malt house.

In this pub-like atmosphere, we don't know which stories are true, which embellished, and which straight-out apocryphal, such as the one about Bathsheba's father. During courtship, Levi Everdene had been attracted to his wife, but once wed, the state of marriage felt confining and he feared he would stray. In order to keep himself on the straight and narrow, Levi asked his wife to remove her ring during sex and called her by her maiden name in an effort to feel like he was committing adultery—the fantasy fueled his desire. Although it might not be true, this story piques the reader's and the rustics' interest, in part because Bathsheba too is a fickle lover who has three love interests in the course of the novel.

Gabriel plays a different role than the rustics in this scene, being consistently more reserved and non-judgmental. He is both newcomer and soon-to-be leader. When the rustics' gossip turns negative, he changes the subject, curtailing Henery Fray's criticism of Bailiff Pennyways (57). He treats the elderly maltster with respect, showing admiration for his age when others tease him about it (58). Instead of boasting like the others do, Gabriel displays the modesty required by good manners when complimented on his looks (59). He shows that he knows how to fit in when he accepts a drink from the communal, germ-ridden, dirt-encrusted God-forgive-me cup (48). He shows restraint when he carefully considers whether it is the proper time and place to say "damn" instead of "dang" (51).

The malt house chapter shows in microcosm what Rosemary Jann argues for the entire novel: that the rustics act collectively as a foil to Gabriel. They exhibit lower-class behavior and language, which highlight Gabriel's greater finesse and thereby justify his rise up the social ladder. The malt house scene also illustrates Shuchita Mital's conviction that Hardy's writing is most humorous when addressing the speech and beliefs of the rustics. When Hardy writes about the common folk, he eschews the occasionally ponderous syntax and distracting classical allusions that characterize his serious mode. The lightly ironic tone in which he presents the rustics provides much-needed comic relief from the tragedy of Bathsheba's mistakes, Boldwood's obsession, Fanny's degradation, and Gabriel's serial misfortunes.

Works Cited

Hardy, Thomas. *Far from the Madding Crowd*. Penguin, 2000.

Jann, Rosemary. "Hardy's Rustics and the Construction of Class." *Victorian Literature and Culture* 28:2 (2000). 411–425.

Mital, Shuchita. "Role of Rustic Characters in the Early Novels of Thomas Hardy." Dissertation submitted to the Aligarh Muslim University, India. 1991. https://core.ac.uk/download/pdf/144517872.pdf.

22

Hardy's Life and Loves

Question:

Marriage is always a troublesome issue in Thomas Hardy's novels, which is perhaps unsurprising given his pessimistic outlook about the potential for human happiness. The author's life is an interesting subject for many reasons: the early promise of his art, the strong attachment to his native Dorsetshire, his construction of the imaginary world of Wessex, the interlinking of his novels, and his less-than-satisfactory marriages. What light can a close reading of his biography shine on the relationship problems of Hardy's men and women characters?

Analysis:

I formulated my answer to the Question based on a reading of Claire Tomalin's 2007 biography, *Thomas Hardy*. Tomalin addresses Hardy's upbringing and marriages in a detailed manner, bringing insight to bear on his notorious pessimism. Hardy was a very private man, who rewrote his diaries before giving them to his memoirist (his second wife, Florence). Even though the evidence is thus limited by a reticent subject, Tomalin found quite enough material to make his life story interesting. The battle between competing drives within his psyche makes Hardy a fascinating biographical subject as well as an emblem of conflicting late Victorian ideologies. I will focus on the influences of his troubled marriages and of his mother on his personal development and his fiction.

Hardy's mother, *née* Jemima Hand, warned all four of her children never to marry, though without giving them any reasons for this unusual advice. The eldest son (Thomas) was the only one who disobeyed his mother's recommendation. At about the time of his own marriage, Hardy learned that Jemima had been three months pregnant with him when she married and that neither his father nor his mother had wanted the marriage or the child. Tomalin speculates that this information may have caused a sense of unwantedness in the adult Hardy and contributed to his recurring depression.

Before her wedding, Jemima was happily employed as a cook at Stinsford House for a well-connected Dorset clergyman, the Rev. Edward Murray. During her tenure with the Murrays, Jemima spent the London season (April to August) at their city home, giving her a taste for urban life and an opportunity for vicarious enjoyment of the gentry's social affairs, such as debutante balls, flower shows, dinner parties, regattas, and polo matches. The influence of her employer's scholarly interests filtered below stairs; Jemima liked to read sophisticated literature such as Dante's *Divine Comedy* and Dr. Johnson's *Rasselas*, the historical novels of Sir Walter Scott, and the poetry of radical Lord Byron. Young Thomas could read by the time he could walk, and his mother supported his intellectual development. She carefully planned and paid for the best education that the region offered. Hardy acquired his love of books from his mother.

From his father, he inherited a sense of rhythm and the foundations of an architectural career. Thomas Hardy Sr. played violin for the hymn singing at Stinsford Church and played jigs, hornpipes, reels, and waltzes at home for the family's pleasure. Hardy Jr. recollects spinning like a dervish to his father's music, elated beyond his capacity to express. Hardy Sr. was a respected building mason with a clientele large enough for him to employ apprentices. He earned enough to be able to turn down business opportunities in other counties because he did not want to leave his childhood home, which he inherited upon his parents' death. Thomas Hardy Sr. allotted plenty of time for leisure activities such as birdwatching, moor walking, and violin playing for weddings and other celebrations, often accompanied by young Tommy.

The author inherited aspects of his mother's stoic pessimism and his father's optimism, or at least the father's ability to release his tensions in healthy recreation. Thomas Hardy Jr. was not physically hardy—the kinds of recreation and work he could do were lighter than those of his father. The son instead escaped stress through his imagination—in writing and reading—and became an apprentice to an architect rather than following his father's more demanding trade of builder.

Thomas Hardy Jr. was a physically and romantically amorous person. He records many crushes on women and girls. When he was eight years old, he fell in love with his teacher, Julia Martin, who sat him upon her lap, to kiss and cosset. The "frou frou" sound of her rustling skirts was an erotic stimulus, and those sensations of young love were never forgotten. When Hardy traded architecture for a writing career, he aspired to the companionship of genteel ladies instead of working-class girls. On a work trip to repair a church in St. Juliot, north Cornwall, Hardy met Emma Gifford, the younger daughter of a solicitor. Emma's family was of the in-between, or shabby-genteel class, living in straitened circumstances after her father had given up the practice of law. Mr. Gifford preferred to lead a life of leisure paid for by an allowance from his mother—thus explaining their residence in a remote Cornwall village, where life was relatively inexpensive.

Emma's attempt to be a governess failed after six months. Her father's example of quitting law might have been an influence on her decision. Like him, she enjoyed the pastimes typical of "county people." She loved to ride her mare over the cliffs and moors of Cornwall's rugged coast. Hardy was quite impressed with her personality, including her enthusiasm for nature and literature, her genteel accomplishments, and her horsemanship. This last feature went into the character Bathsheba of *Far from the Madding Crowd*, who fearlessly rides on a man's saddle and balances supine upon her horse's back. The lovers courted for four years while he saved money to lease a house. When they did marry, it was over the objections of Thomas's mother and both Emma's parents. Emma's father rejected Hardy on their first visit because of disdain for his working-class background; the two men never spoke again. Fortunately, the couple was welcomed into the home of Emma's sister and brother-in-law, so Emma did not have to completely give up her family.

Judging from diaries and letters, the marriage quickly cooled Hardy's admiration for Emma. Tomalin speculates that there are at least three reasons: he acquired a taste for a higher level of literary discourse than Emma was capable of providing, he tired of her frivolity, and he suspected her of having inherited the family's insanity gene. As his books gained in popularity, Hardy was accepted in London literary society; meeting men and women of the educated classes changed his taste in companionship. His editor for *Far from the Madding Crowd* was the renowned biographer Leslie Stephen (father of Virginia Woolf and founding editor of the *Dictionary of National Biography*). At the time that *Cornhill* magazine serialized Hardy's novel, it was the most widely read and respected magazine in England. Meeting literary people made Emma's company less appealing.

Upon marriage, Hardy quickly learned that Emma's literary aspirations were unfounded; she was a poor poet and her contributions to his writing were more in the manner of muse than editor. Muse is a good role for some women, and every good novelist needs a model of the opposite sex for insights into character. But Emma wanted more of a partnership.

For decades, she pretended that she had written certain passages of Hardy's novels. When Hardy stopped sharing his work with her, she felt rejected and began to boast of her class superiority. She would have to "win" at something—if he was a better writer, she was of better birth. Over time, Emma's pretenses eventually developed into delusions. We have no medical proof that she suffered from mental illness, yet guests found her talk disjointed, irrelevant, and uninteresting. She lost her youthful good looks and some of her resilience. Hardy's wife had ample reason to become depressed as she watched several young ladies try to attach themselves to him, hoping to find a mentor for their writing and to be loved for their intellectual and feminine charms.

When Emma died at seventy-two, one of these young aspirants had been courting Hardy for seven years right under Emma's nose. Florence Dugdale, twenty-six when she met sixty-five-year-old Hardy, latched onto her best chance for patronage. Hardy was in love with her, and she was in love with his literary stature. Rather than expend energy on hiding their relationship, Florence decided to befriend Emma too. Perhaps it was Emma's increasing religious piety or her alleged madness that caused her to regard Florence as Thomas's platonic literary friend. And perhaps it was Emma and Thomas's physical estrangement that enabled his long trips with Florence—often accompanied by members of his or her extended family—to pass without causing Emma concern. Emma and Florence took their own holidays together too; it's likely that Emma was in such great need of a friend that she suppressed her awareness of the romantic bond between Florence and her husband. She might have "known without knowing" of the love affair between her best friend and her husband.

This state of affairs led to the next bizarre paradox of Hardy's life. Two years after Emma's death, Hardy married Florence Dugdale. Upon doing so, he was suddenly overcome with immense guilt for having neglected Emma. He felt that he had lacked empathy and gratitude during the marriage. Thenceforth the majority of his verses were tributes to Emma or inspired by his recollection of their early love. Understandably, Florence was displeased by her new husband's preference for his dead wife, but there was nothing she could do to change his subject matter. By that time, he was far too beloved by the world to be moved by the exhortations of a mediocre woman writer, even if that writer happened to be his wife. In other words, the same pattern emerged in his second marriage as in his first: the couple was first attracted by each other's literary enthusiasms and skills and later, partially estranged by the power imbalance in the relationship, a disparity that was based on different skill levels as well as Victorian separate sphere ideologies.

As much as Emma and Florence played muse to Hardy, it is his mother, Jemima, whom Hardy credits as his strongest influence. Her condition of unwed motherhood inspired the character Tess Durbeyfield, whose fate was much worse than Jemima's. At least Thomas Hardy Sr. was a good and mild-tempered husband, whereas the father of Tess's child was a narcissistic cad. Jemima's independence and self-esteem also appear in Bathsheba Everdene of *Far from the Madding Crowd*. Bathsheba's strong personality and feminism cause her to repulse her first suitor with the explanation that she "hates to be thought of as a man's property." This line could have come straight out of Jemima's mouth; it was certainly her attitude toward men and marriage. Lucetta Templeman of *Mayor of Casterbridge* is also headstrong; she pursues Michael Henchard without much encouragement from him. The first time she meets Donald Farfrae, she doesn't bother to hide her sexual attraction to him. Once she decides she will have a man, she uses all her charm and strategies to close the deal but is ready to change course in the event that her libido leads elsewhere.

Hardy's own difficult marriages recall his mother's famous advice to her children: do not marry; you will be happier alone. Hardy lived that painful paradox common to writers and other sensitives: that female companionship can have a double edge. In the initial phases of courtship, it's comforting to vanquish one's loneliness. On the other hand, it's wretched to be bound to a partner whose skills, expectations, and outlook are contrary to one's own. Victorian rising-class male writers faced a particularly hard road. They felt the need to satisfy their powerful sexual desires by engaging in sexual relations, but the only way to do so in respectable society was by marrying. If they were raising themselves above the working class through a writing profession, they would often learn too late that the literary companionship of equals was a greater pleasure than sexual fulfillment in a marriage of unequal partners. Divorce laws and middle-class propriety forced them to remain in their marital prisons. This condition could, however, have a positive effect on their writing when they translated their emotional trauma into powerful art that spoke to readers with similar troubles.

Works Cited

Hardy, Thomas. *Far from the Madding Crowd*. Penguin, 2000.
Tomalin, Claire. *Thomas Hardy*. Penguin, 2007.

23

Jekyll's Downfall—
Sadism or Repression?

Question:

Dr. Jekyll is a weak-willed man who cannot control his desire for pleasures of an indeterminate kind. In addition to the protagonist's temperament, the narrator also alludes to weaknesses in the social structure of
the doctor's time and place, 1890s London, that pave the way for his plum-
met into moral degradation. To what extent do Victorian moral and social
requirements of genteel respectability determine the doctor's downfall?

Synopsis:

Dr. Henry Jekyll once had a respectable medical practice, which fal-
tered as he became increasingly obsessed with scientific experiments.
A deep thinker, Jekyll notes that man's nature is painfully dualistic; the
good side prohibits the bad side from fulfilling its desires, and the bad side
suffers from being shut down. Jekyll wonders whether man's evil aspect
could be chemically separated from his honorable side, thus allowing
each aspect to satisfy itself in its own manner. One day, he creates a potion
which changes him into a monstrous human who fulfills all his instinctual
desires, which the narrator implies are of a violent and/or sexual nature.
He trammels a young girl in the street simply because she's in his way, and
later, he kills Sir Danvers Carew, Member of Parliament, simply because
he asked directions. Jekyll creates a name and identity for the monstrous
aspect of himself—Mr. Edward Hyde—and orders the servants to allow his
"guest" access to the house and laboratory.

Robert Louis Stevenson, by Henry Walter Barnett (1893).

Jekyll's legal counsel, Mr. Utterson, becomes concerned when Jekyll bequeaths all of his assets to the suspicious Mr. Hyde. Another friend, Dr. Lanyon, has long distrusted Jekyll's obsessions and fanciful ideas about the medical profession. After murdering Carew, Hyde realizes he's been identified as the murderer by Jekyll's maidservant, and that police are on the lookout. He needs to transform back to Jekyll before returning home. He calls for Lanyon to bring him the chemicals from his laboratory in order to switch personalities. Lanyon watches Hyde drink the potion and become Jekyll. The sight shocks him to the point of illness and death. Upset by his master's prolonged illness and seclusion, servant Poole seeks Utterson's help. Utterson and Poole break into the laboratory to find Jekyll already dead. Letters from Jekyll and Lanyon describe Jekyll's experiment and its failure. Once the transformations from Jekyll into Hyde had become automatic, and the potion stopped working, Jekyll no longer had control over his personalities. Jekyll killed himself before he became forever Hyde.

Analysis:

The 2002 Penguin cover displays a head-and-torso daguerreotype of a Victorian gentleman in shirt, collar, necktie, and coat looking directly at the camera. He has average features and a complacent expression, but a strange blur around his head suggests that he is more or other than he seems. This image conveys the message of the novel—that people are made up of composite parts, with one sometimes coming to the fore. "Composite portraiture" is a technique by which several exposures are made on the same photographic plate. In the 1880s, Sir Francis Galton developed the technique to create what he called a "photographic average" of many portraits. He applied this technique to the project of defining a "criminal type." After averaging several criminals' faces, Galton became so disgusted by looking at them that he suffered a gag reflex similar to what Dr. Lanyon experienced when seeing Mr. Hyde. I suggest that this aversion to looking upon degraded humans is due to our refusal to admit that we have some primal link to psychopaths through that fearful but universal component of all human psyches—the id. Our ability to accommodate the id's desires with the needs of the superego determines how integrated and healthy a human we can be.

Dr. Jekyll and Mr. Hyde is an apt introduction to the late Victorian period, for it is steeped in contemporary influences from the fields of criminology (Cesare Lombroso), sexology (Richard von Krafft-Ebing), and psychiatry (Sigmund Freud). Cesare Lombroso was an Italian criminologist who believed that criminals were of a lesser "race" than so-called normal people. This inferior race shared both the physical and behavioral traits of apes (though I doubt that apes are as malicious). Criminals, according to Lombroso, had ample body hair, sloping foreheads, protruding jaws, large ears, asymmetrical faces, long arms, acute vision, and a lack of moral sense that made them remorseless, vindictive, vain, impulsive, and cruel. Criminals are more bloodthirsty than any nonhuman animal: "The criminal desires not only to extinguish life in the victim but to mutilate the corpse, tear its flesh and drink its blood" (Lombroso-Ferrero).

The late nineteenth-century imagination produced many subhuman types in literature, including Robert Louis Stevenson's Mr. Hyde, Bram Stoker's Dracula, and Oscar Wilde's Dorian Gray (whose portrait mutated to reflect the progressive corruption of his soul as he committed unspeakable acts of sex and murder). It is interesting to watch the terror genre morph throughout the nineteenth century, incorporating new psychological discoveries as they are made. The typical setting of late eighteenth-century gothic romance (in novels by Ann Radcliffe, Horace Walpole, and Charles Maturin) was the wilds of Spain or Italy—never England, since Protestantism elevated it above the supposed barbarism of Catholic countries. But in the late nineteenth century, Stevenson and Wilde brought terror to the London metropolis—the geographical center of British identity. These writers created a new sub-genre, the urban gothic, relocating the monster from outside the self to inside of the human mind, thus shifting the blame from other creatures onto humans themselves. Later writers would explicitly acknowledge this projection: Simon proclaimed in Golding's 1954 novel, *Lord of the Flies*, "Maybe it's only us," referring to "the Beast" that the boys had fantasized. The late Victorians' realization of humanity's dual nature reflects the end of an era and lays the foundation for modernism. Meantime, Sigmund Freud is working at his own laboratory—the psychiatric couch—plumbing the depths of the unconscious, which he compared to a pit of writhing snakes. Among other works, Freud's *Interpretation of Dreams* (1899) demonstrates that all human psyches are divided, not just those of literary aberrations such as Dr. Jekyll.

Since Stevenson is vague on details, critics love to speculate about the true nature of Jekyll/Hyde's pleasures. Just what does he get up to in the evenings, other than the assaults and murder that are explicitly described? Are Mr. Hyde's sins a more extreme enactment of Dr. Jekyll's trivial pleasures? Or are his monstrous propensities completely distinct from civilized people's private behaviors? Robert Mighall's "Diagnosing Jekyll" helps us to answer these questions. Researching the linguistic codes of nineteenth-century literature, Mighall argues that the "disgraceful pleasures" of Jekyll's youth "could have meant only one thing to his original readers"—masturbation (155). Krafft-Ebing's 1892 *Psychopathia sexualis* was daring in its subject matter but shared the unenlightened view of his fellow Victorians that masturbation was a slippery slope leading to ever more vile sins. Because masturbation was so reviled in polite society, the upwardly mobile Jekyll experienced immense shame over his habit and consequently repressed his desire to self-stimulate. This repression led inexorably to the creation of a monster within. As Freud famously said, there is always a return of the repressed material, unless one brings it to light (in psychoanalysis) and understands its proper place in one's moral life. A thinker ahead of his time, Stevenson reveals a fundamental Freudian paradox—that the superego is crueler than the id. Jekyll's repression of the harmless activity of masturbation perverts his desires and turns him into a sadist who delights in sexually assaulting and killing other people.

In the novella's final chapter, "Henry Jekyll's Full Statement of the Case," the doctor reveals that originally, his Jekyll persona was worse than his Hyde persona. He criticizes his own indiscretions but also reveals a severe problem caused by Victorian codes of behavior, in which "gentlemanly" meant utterly chaste until marriage (and after marriage, using sex only for procreation).* Jekyll believes he is *not* a hypocrite, because his "bestial" self and his professional self are equally "in dead earnest," and are separate beings (55). In the beginning, it is Jekyll, not Hyde, who is the

---

* Susie Steinbach (author of *Understanding the Victorians*) says this was the prescriptive vision of gentlemen's sexual behavior, "but we really do not know, and cannot assume, that this was actually typical behavior. Some masturbation and sex with sex workers was probably typical" (letter to the author, July 1, 2021).

problem: "It was thus rather the exacting nature of my aspirations [the desire to succeed as gentleman doctor] than any particular degradation in my faults, that made me what I was and, with even a deeper trench than in the majority of men, severed in me those provinces of good and ill which divide and compound man's dual nature" (55). It is the severance of the two parts—not the fact that they both exist—which constitutes the true problem.

Jekyll's mistake was to separate rather than integrate the parts. "Integration" is a key therapeutic concept in both Freudian and Jungian psychoanalytic theory. Freud claims that the superego, ego, and id make up the psyche, performing discrete functions that ensure the healthy function of the whole. The superego holds the internalized moral standards of a person's parents and society; its role is to control the id's impulses, especially those which society forbids, such as nonmarital sex and aggression. The ego operates on the reality principle, mediating between superego and id to make sure that the id's impulses are expressed in acceptable ways. The id operates on the pleasure principle, aiming for immediate gratification of urges, needs, and desires.

Jekyll's fear of the conflict between superego and id leads him to try to separate them completely, forming two entities, neither of which is whole or wholesome: "I was driven to reflect deeply and inveterately on that hard law of life, which lies at the root of religion and is one of the most plentiful springs of distress … man's dual nature" (55). By equating the root of all religion with the source of man's worst pain, Jekyll is not exactly condemning religion. But his statement makes clear that division between the parts (good and evil; superego and id)—and even their absolute severance, in his experiment—is the cause of human unhappiness, *not* the existence of the parts in and of themselves.

So how do we integrate our good and evil, our superego and id? W.H. Auden has an answer in the poem "In Memory of Sigmund Freud." The poet speaks reverentially of Freud's wisdom regarding psychic health. The psychoanalyst's goal was to "unite the unequal moieties" of superego and id. In Auden's explicit language, psychoanalysis frees people from shame over their impulses and lets their urges have expression in the light of day, rather than the darkness of guilt and shame where they fester and cause harm. Here are a few of the relevant stanzas of Auden's poem (the "He" in the first line is Freud), with my *comments* in the right-hand column:

… He would unite
the unequal moieties* fractured
by our own well-meaning sense of
    justice,
	*moieties *are parts into which a thing
	   is divided*

would restore to the larger* the wit
and will
the smaller possesses but can only use
for arid disputes, would give back to
the son the mother's richness of
feeling*:

    *The larger is the id; the smaller,
      the superego.*

    Oedipal love isn't an evil; shame is.

but he would have us remember
   most of all
to be enthusiastic over the night,
not only for the sense of wonder*
it alone has to offer, but also

    *Let us befriend our impulses; they
      start out benign. They start as love.*

because it needs our love. With large
   sad eyes
its delectable creatures* look up and
   beg
us dumbly to ask them to follow:
they are exiles* who long for the future

    These creatures are the id's impulses.

    *They've been exiled by strict Victorian
      morals.*

that lives in our power, they too would
   rejoice
if allowed to serve enlightenment like
   him*,
even to bear our cry of 'Judas,'*
as he did and all must bear who serve
   it.

    him=Freud, possibly likened to Christ
    *healed analysands will be reviled by
      the majority because they "betray"
      Christianity*

Auden's "delectable creatures" are the urges and needs of the id, and his "night" is our unconscious, where they abide. "The mother's richness of feeling" is the child's Oedipal love for the mother and for life; such love is not evil, and not genitally sexual, but erotic in the broadest sense, where eros is equivalent to the life force. The superego can use its wit and will only for arid disputes, whereas the id can use its rich feeling for wonderment and love. Auden, Freud, and Stevenson embrace these creatures. Jekyll says of Hyde: "This, too, was myself. It seemed natural and human. In my eyes, it bore a livelier image of the spirit, it seemed more expressive and single, than the imperfect and divided countenance I had been hitherto accustomed to call mine" (58). Stevenson spoke directly to the moral allegory of his tale when writing to his friend John Paul Babcock in 1887:

> There is no harm in a voluptuary.... The harm was in Jekyll, because he was a hypocrite—not because he was fond of women; he says so himself; but people are so filled full of folly and inverted lust, that they can think of nothing but sexuality. The hypocrite let out the beast Hyde—who is no more sensual than

another, but who is the essence of cruelty and malice, and selfishness and cowardice; and these are the diabolic in man—not the poor wish to have a woman, that they make such a cry about. I know, and I dare to say, you know as well as I, that good and bad, even to our human eyes, has no more connection with what is called dissipation than it has with flying kites [quoted in Bell, 179].

In the final chapter of the novella, Jekyll says that it is his shame, *not* his "irregularities," that is the author of his evil doings: "Many a man would have even blazoned such irregularities as I was guilty of; but from the high views that I had set before me, I regarded and hid them with an almost morbid sense of shame" (55). With his "irregularities" which other men might "blazon," I think that Jekyll may be referring, not to masturbation, but to something more general, such as his strong eros or erotic energy—his "impatient gaiety of disposition"—that is not strictly of a sexual nature but is a life force that can assist in one's work if integrated with the principles of one's discipline. As Mighall writes, "It is his overdeveloped sense of sinfulness that constructs Hyde. The more Jekyll sought to do and appear to be 'good,' the more 'evil' he made Hyde" (xxii). So Jekyll's apparent goodness is in direct proportion to the wickedness he cultivates when hiding and being ashamed of his "gaiety of disposition." His overdeveloped superego is a killjoy that causes great damage to self and others. The superego is the internalized voice of external authorities and institutions. Dr. Jekyll wanted to be such a perfect gentleman doctor that he thought he had to repress all pleasurable impulses. Especially when we regard Dr. Jekyll as an aspirant to professional-class status, we appreciate that the rigid sexual and social codes of Victorian society would be more demanding for him than for aristocracy or gentry. (It's interesting to note Jekyll's difference from Mary Shelley's Dr. Frankenstein, who created his monster out of scientific hubris. In contrast, Dr. Jekyll creates his monster out of his desire to attain and maintain social status.) The middle class had stricter sexual codes than the upper class. His drive for social betterment and attempted obedience to rising middle-class standards caused Jekyll to split himself into a beast and a gentleman, neither of them happy. To answer the question that I raised at the beginning of the lecture, Dr. Jekyll's insane experiment was a result of one man's attempt to meet the moral requirements of a Victorian upper-middle-class identity.

Works Cited

Auden, W.H. "In Memory of Sigmund Freud." 1939. https://poets.org/poem/memory-|sigmund-freud.

Bell, Ian. *Dreams of Exile: Robert Louis Stevenson.* Macmillan, 2015.

Lombroso-Ferrero, Gina. *Criminal Man (According to the Classification of Cesare Lombroso).* Patterson Smith, 1972.

Mighall, Robert. "Diagnosing Jekyll: The Scientific Context to Dr. Jekyll's Experiment and Mr. Hyde's Embodiment." *The Strange Case of Dr. Jekyll and Mr. Hyde*. Penguin, 2002. 143–161.
Stevenson, Robert Louis. *The Strange Case of Dr. Jekyll and Mr. Hyde and Other Tales of Terror*. Penguin, 2002.

24

Dr. Jekyll and *Mary Reilly*: Abuse, Trauma, and Gender

Question:

A hundred years after Stevenson's publication of *The Strange Case of Dr. Jekyll and Mr. Hyde*, novelist Valerie Martin brings contemporary cultural awareness about issues of childhood sexual abuse to her reworking of Stevenson's "case" from the viewpoint of Jekyll's maid (*Mary Reilly*, 1990). Martin's neo–Victorian novel raises questions about different ways in which men and women, and upper- and lower-class people, might respond to sexual trauma and attempt to resolve inner conflict. What is the bond between Mary Reilly and Dr. Jekyll, and why is Mary's love insufficient to cure him of his affliction?

Synopsis:

Ten-year-old Mary Reilly cowers in a small cupboard under the stairs where her father has locked her while he's in a drunken rage. Intensifying her terror, he introduces a rat in a hopsack bag, which gnaws its way out and bites Mary in the leg and neck. She faints and wakes up two weeks later in a hospital. Twelve years pass, and Mary is now employed as Dr. Jekyll's housemaid. One day as she is blacking the grate, the doctor notices scars from the rat bites on her hands and neck. He asks her permission to examine them. She first goes to scrub herself clean "as a bride" for the examination. When Dr. Jekyll places his soft, cool hands on her skin, Mary becomes aroused, and is immediately ashamed by her fantasies. Jekyll asks her to write down the story of her experience in the closet. From this point on, Jekyll and Mary develop a mutual fondness. Jekyll is impressed by her intelligence and sense of propriety, while Mary reads kindness and sadness in his looks and manner and longs to help him overcome his obsession.

For a week at a time, Jekyll secludes himself in his "cabinet," presumably doing his scientific work. The servants are concerned when he emerges, pale, emaciated, and troubled, after a particularly long seclusion. Jekyll informs them that he's hired an assistant, Mr. Edward Hyde, who should be given free rein of house and laboratory. The servants hate this hairy, short, evil-looking person. One day Hyde entices Mary into the study by laying a book open upon a table. When he catches her reading his filthy marginalia, he accuses her of understanding them. In a lustful rage, he cracks the teacup he's holding and smears his bloodied hand across her lips. Hyde is consciously replicating the scene of Mary's trauma because the mistake for which her father punished her was the breaking of a teacup. Mary has an inkling that Hyde is Jekyll but suppresses the knowledge. When she senses Hyde in the house, she confuses him with her father, feeling the same terror of both men.

Jekyll commands Mary to deliver a letter and a check to Mrs. Farraday, a Soho brothel keeper. She is a terrifying harridan who ridicules Mary and implies that Mary is Jekyll's whore. Mrs. Farraday brings Mary to an upstairs room where the walls and bed linens are smeared with blood. Mary overhears from other girls in the house that "they've taken her an hour since." She surmises that Mr. Hyde has killed a woman in this room and that Dr. Jekyll is paying hush money out of compassion for his friend. News that Hyde has killed Sir Danvers Carew gets out; the servants' suspicions that "something is not right" about Hyde are confirmed. Jekyll stops being Hyde, reverts to being the kind master of earlier times and resumes charitable works, such as running a school for the poor.

Mary receives news of her mother's death and walks the long road to Shoreditch to arrange a funeral. Her mother's landlord tells Mary of her father's visits to her mother. Her father had asked the landlord for Mary's address and said only that there was "bad feeling" between them which he'd like to mend. Mary is shocked that her father could trivialize her abuse as only "bad feeling," and makes the landlord swear not to give him her address.

Dr. Jekyll's condition worsens. He secludes himself for weeks at a time, allowing only the butler, Poole, to enter the medical theater and leave food. Finally, Poole and Mr. Utterson break down the door to find Hyde gasping his last breath after taking poison. While they are out seeking assistance, Mary steals across the courtyard to visit her friend and master one last time. His corpse has a hybrid appearance of both Jekyll and Hyde. Mary remembers that Jekyll had said he no longer cared for the world's opinion. In tribute to the dead man, she decides to sacrifice her own reputation. The maid lies down and embraces the corpse of her master as footsteps sound on the stair.

Analysis:

Valerie Martin's revision of the story suggests that Mary Reilly and Dr. Jekyll share an affinity based on their experience of sexual abuse (I am suggesting that Jekyll is experiencing Hyde's abuses of his victims). Martin plants clues about the nature of Mary's closet experience that lead the reader to the conclusion that she was raped by her father. Upon hiring her as maidservant, Jekyll immediately detects the true nature of the closet incident. He tries to elicit Mary's awareness of the rape while simultaneously admiring her ability to keep it repressed. There are good reasons for Martin to avoid stating outright the nature of Mary's childhood abuse. The story is told through Mary Reilly's journals; if Mary never realized that she was sexually violated by her father, or repressed such knowledge, she wouldn't have stated it as such in the diary. Or, perhaps knowing, she was nonetheless conditioned by Victorian standards of respectability not to record such a transgression explicitly in writing.

Psychological parallels between the two main characters suggest that Mary's trauma is sexual, like her master's. Regarding Mary's closet experience, Martin adopts the same art of suggestion, rather than assertion, that Stevenson used in *Dr. Jekyll and Mr. Hyde* to adumbrate Hyde's nefarious activities. The nebulous nature of Mary's abuse jibes with the unspoken nature of Hyde's crimes in Stevenson's novel, where we know only that Hyde indulges in abject sensual pleasures, including beating and murdering those who get in his way. The previous lecture investigates the nature of his crimes and entertains Robert Mighall's thesis that the necessity of repressing Jekyll's masturbation and lustful desire led to Hyde becoming a rapist/murderer who frequented seedy neighborhoods to find victims. Valerie Martin's reimagining of the novel adds details such as Mrs. Faraday's brothel and Mr. Hyde's murder of a prostitute, bringing the nature of Hyde's nighttime crimes to light. Differences in the ways in which Mary and Jekyll work out their trauma reveal the relative privileges, constraints, and customs of their respective gender and class.

The novel opens with Mary's journal entry about the closet punishment. Initially, the reader is misled into thinking that her abuser is Edward Hyde because we know that Stevenson's *Jekyll and Hyde* is the inspiration for this adaptation, and we recognize his monstrosity in this character. Mary doesn't identify him as her father until much later in the text. Her written report of the incident contains imagery, lacunae, and reactions that suggest a scene of incest. The rat—in size, shape, and persistence—is a symbol for her father's penis, but since Mary has never seen male genitals, she's confused by what could be in the "bag" (her father's trousers): "I knew at once there was something in the bag, that it was meant to harm me, but what it was my childhood imagination couldn't conjure" (5). The rat crawls up her body, from thigh to neck, biting all the way, like a man accosting a woman: "I'd only a thin skirt on, which I had pulled over my knees as best I could, so it wasn't long before the creature began to work its way through the two thin layers separating us in that narrow, breathless space" (5).

Although she describes it as cramped, the closet may have been large enough to hold the father and daughter. The rape that took place there was repressed and turned into a screen memory—a recollection of early childhood that masks another memory of deep emotional significance. To block the sexual element from memory, Mary turns her father into a rat—considered a dirty, diseased, and despised animal. Similarly, Jekyll's sexual aspect—Hyde—is seen by others as an ape-like creature, not quite human. Mary depicts the growing terror of her encounter: "I felt a claw sink into my thigh and I pulled myself up rigid ... the rat was gnawing at the cloth and I knew in no time the bag would give out and my own skin would be next.... I could feel the animal's snout against my leg, but of course I could see nothing and scarcely move, so I was helpless" (7). She could see nothing because it was dark, and she didn't know what was in the father's hopsack bag, as she had never seen a penis.

Aware that she has substituted rat for penis in the story and in her memory, Jekyll smiles. He reiterates the fact that she could not see the rat and asks her how she knew what the object was. Her defense mechanism of displacement amuses him because he knows the truth that she has repressed. He's aware that her father is a sexual pervert like Hyde, and the Hyde part of him is sadistically amused to hear a victim's account of the kind of sex that Hyde regularly engages in when he assaults girls. On the other hand, the Jekyll part of the doctor identifies with Mary's trauma and her attempts to overcome it. In my reading of both Stevenson and Martin's versions of the doctor, I am assuming that Jekyll, like Mary, has been traumatized by his nighttime crimes, even though he was the one to instigate the behavior. His splitting off makes him suffer the crimes that Hyde commits. He also might have been sexually abused as a child, leading to the creation of his alter ego, Hyde, as a rapist/murderer of prostitutes. What is done to us we do to others, even though we suffer from our own aggressions. Jekyll has dissociated himself from his perverted desires to such an extent that the Hyde part violates him each time it kills a prostitute.

Mary's reaction to her father's assault is paralysis, a feeling that she could scarcely move. This is a typical response to rape. The victim shuts down the body's motor reflexes and wills herself out of her body. Mary's psyche may have created the cupboard setting for the rape as a symbolic representation of what paralysis felt like—the inability to move because one is hemmed in on all sides. She screams and tries to protect herself, but before penetration, she goes numb: "or that is how I imagine it must have happened for I did not know at the time, nor did I know anything or anyone for some time to come" (7). Her trauma is so severe that she remains in a coma at the hospital for two weeks. In addition to physical paralysis, the mind tries to numb itself as a defense against events too shocking to process. Dissociation or fainting will achieve this numbing effect. Another clue to the sexual nature of her father's attacks is that afterwards, Mary avoids contact with men and eschews sensual pleasures. In her previous job, coworkers had asked Mary to go out evenings and meet men, but Mary refused. She has no interest in sex and is afraid of reviving feelings of shame and terror related to her father.

To cope with a dangerous world, a rape victim will often create a strict set of rules to abide by—hoping to impose a sense of superficial order over an abyss of chaos. Mary has what Jekyll calls a "profound view of the social order and propriety," which amuses Jekyll—perhaps because he too obeys the rules religiously as Jekyll but gleefully breaks them when cruising in the guise of Hyde (21). Mary tries to respect the hierarchy of the staff and its chain of command but is challenged when Poole becomes jealous of her conversations with Jekyll. When Poole and Jekyll's orders conflict, Mary doesn't know whether to obey the butler or the master of the house, both of whom are her bosses. Jekyll only laughs when she tells him that Poole wants to be the intermediary for Jekyll's orders to Mary. She fervently desires to comply perfectly with the highest house standards. The sense of order this affords is the only thing that stands between her and the sadness and darkness which she constantly feels: "So I feel that my father made me thus, or left me thus, with this sadness which has been hard to bear and will likely never leave me no matter what fortune I have, and it sets me apart from my fellows who seem never to know it" (36). One of her favorite outlets from the stress and sadness of her trauma is scrubbing things. Her avid housecleaning is an effort to cleanse herself of sin, to rid herself of the shameful taint of incest. Mary recognizes the link between her maniacal cleaning and her depression, noting that she and Cook take on extra projects—usually deep cleaning of floors, cupboards, and draperies—when they are feeling depressed.

As trauma sufferers, Mary and Jekyll recognize each other's inner demons as well as their struggles to overcome the darkness they carry.

This identification makes it difficult for them to resist each other, though prohibitions are strong on both sides. Jekyll, if he cares for her, must keep her safe from Hyde, while Mary needs to observe the proprieties required of members of her subordinate gender and class. Several scenes portray Mary almost merging her own identity with the good aspect of Jekyll. But when she sees Hyde, her imagination merges his image with that of her sadistic father. When she hears Hyde's uneven footsteps on the stairs, for instance, it reminds her of the "halting way about her father's walk" (40). On the edge of sleep, she realizes that her master's kindness "has brought him [father] back to life for me" (41). This is a curious linking of Master Jekyll's kindness with memories of her vicious father, because it is Hyde, not the master, with whom she associates her father. This confusing blend of good and bad parental imagos (internalized images) evokes the most tragic aspect of father/daughter incest: the mixture of benevolence and sadism in the single figure. The child might remember times when her father was kind and gentle, along with the (repressed) memories of the sexual abuse. This causes a desire to trust which is constantly thwarted by a wariness of all men. Mary is sometimes fleetingly aware that her deepening relationship with Jekyll represents a journey—an attempt to recover memories in order to work them out. Their relationship functions in the novel as an opportunity to heal from trauma. Although fraught with danger (because Hyde could emerge at any moment), I would like to suggest that the affectionate relationship between Mary and Jekyll is what begins to heal her trauma, or at least reduce its effects. The fact that their bond does not, and cannot, heal Jekyll's trauma is linked to his different gender and class, and thus to the different ways in which he is wounded.

Since the novel is primarily Mary's story, Valerie Martin doesn't reiterate Jekyll's explanation for how and why he began taking the transformative potion. *The Strange Case of Dr. Jekyll and Mr. Hyde* provides Jekyll's back story: he strove to be an excellent gentleman doctor, but he couldn't resist indulging in sensuous pleasures of which he was greatly ashamed. He theorized that the sensual part of himself could be separated from the "good," dutiful, gentlemanly part, resulting in the creation of two happy beings instead of one that was divided and guilty. The result was catastrophic. The more that Hyde indulged his desires, the more stimulation he wanted—he became addicted to his violent sexual behaviors. Soon, he became stronger than Jekyll and threatened to take over Jekyll's whole personality.

Jekyll's trauma is poignantly of his own making—quite unlike Mary's. Jekyll's hubris led him to manipulate human psychology in ways that were decidedly unhealthy and illegal. Because of the privileges of his profession, class, and gender, Jekyll was able to conduct such an abominable experiment without check. He was able to support himself without seeing patients, to attain chemicals for the making of the potion, to house Hyde at his own home despite the unease of the servants, and to retain the goodwill of his professional friends even when his sickness became apparent. It is clear that Jekyll brings on his own traumatic experience singlehandedly. No one else causes any harm to him; on the contrary, everyone in his social circle tries to help. Jekyll aims to brook all social constraints and find absolute freedom to pursue his basest instincts.

The stark differences in Jekyll's and Mary's goals and behavior can be elucidated further with reference to feminist scholarship on the social construction of gender. In 1982, psychologist Carol Gilligan (*In a Different Voice*) performed research regarding different ways in which men and women conceive of ethical responsibility toward others. Correcting Sigmund Freud's infamous dictum that men's morals are more highly developed than women's, Gilligan proposes that women and men cultivate a different set of ethics based on their different social conditioning in patriarchy. While men develop an ethics of rights, women develop an ethics of responsibility. Men ask of themselves: as a free man, what is the highest degree of freedom I can enjoy without violating the rights of others? In contrast, women ask: what responsibilities do I owe to other people as a duty of being human? In other words, women feel an affirmative duty to care for others, whereas men obey a law-based prohibition against harming others. Applying Gilligan's theory to Valerie Martin's book, we can see that Jekyll's problem is one of overreaching his rights. When he dissects himself into two parts (a bizarre birthing of another individual), he doesn't accept responsibility for the harm that the second part will cause. He doesn't meet even the minimal standard of an ethics of rights. Mary, on the other hand, constructs an ethics of responsibility, regardless of her damaged ability to trust that resulted from childhood abuse. Mary feels obliged to serve her master and help him through his deepest existential battle. Unlike Jekyll, Mary does not visit her rage upon other innocent victims.

In contrast to Henry Jekyll, Mary Reilly does nothing to create or exacerbate her horrific circumstances. As maidservant at Jekyll's establishment, her only desire is to be safe and keep her demons at bay. She does nothing to attract violence; she strives to be kind and good and refrains from any attention-seeking behavior. She doesn't seek to educate herself above her class but reads history and poetry to satisfy her active mind, while Jekyll, on the other hand, is consuming alchemy texts and Hyde is looking at pornography—both genres indicating their hubristic and monstrous desires to infringe on other people's wellbeing. As a woman and a servant, Mary is a foil to Jekyll's privileged status as a man and gentleman.

206 IX. *The Strange Case of Dr. Jekyll and Mr. Hyde* (1886)

Many abuse victims seek to work out their trauma through further unsavory encounters. Mary, though, is different. She is innocent and tries to be pure—perhaps this is why her relationship with Jekyll results in her working through her trauma while he careens toward an inevitably violent early death. Their relationship is symbiotic, but not equal. She needs him because their relationship prompts her to work through her repressed memories of abuse. Through this identification, she finds a way to move on. At the end of the novel, her fear is gone, replaced by anger against her father: "[T]hough I do not hate him I do not forgive him" (204). Mary is conscious that her writing is a way of working out the trauma. She keeps it up because it eases her mind and serves as a record of her abuse so that she will never deny "the long horror that was [her] childhood" (204).

Valerie Martin avoids the temptation to make the Mary/Jekyll relationship exactly parallel. We might feel emotional relief and aesthetic symmetry if love had also cured Jekyll of the desire to let his Hyde out. Mary's love for Jekyll assisted her to bring out her own demon and kill him. But Jekyll's illness is self-inflicted and has progressed too far to be cured by Mary. Moreover, his class status would have prevented him from marrying a servant; his desire to live up to bourgeois standards of respectability and establish a gentleman's reputation are made clear in the original text. Valerie Martin does a better job than turning a popular horror story into a romance. She rewards Mary, a pure-hearted woman, for her persistent efforts to contain, understand, and accept her sorrow. Despite the abuse she sustained from a sick father, Mary has the capacity to love and see the good in others, even in a man whose class status allows him to condescend and to tempt her. Because of this capacity to love, and through loving Jekyll, Mary is able—not to forgive, nor even understand—but to minimize her father's dark shadow over her life. After her mother's death, her father loses the power to terrorize her. She sees his plea for forgiveness in old age to be the pitiable gesture it is, not the abominable wish of a predator. As Cathy Caruth and other trauma specialists attest, in order to *begin to heal*, trauma victims need to tell their story, to give witness to their own emotional damage and to share it with responsible others. Through her writing and her identification with Jekyll, Mary begins to move on. We see this in the release of terror toward her father, in her ability to see him as a man.

In the end, Mary is lying with her head on the dead Jekyll's chest and her arms around his neck. This is the tableau that Poole, Utterson, and the police will see when they climb the stairs to the laboratory. This shocking scene will certainly cost her the job reference needed to obtain her next position. Has Mary destroyed her own chance for a successful post–Jekyll life? The narrator doesn't think so. She believes that Mary is resourceful, honest, and "a better than average servant" who will "land on her feet in some less fantastic household" (260). Mary's journey—from abuse victim to faithful servant to lover of a madman—was a way to confront the fantastic aspect of her screen memory and begin to heal from trauma.

Works Cited

Caruth, Cathy. *Unclaimed Experience: Trauma, Narrative, and History.* Johns Hopkins UP, 1996.
Gilligan, Carol. *In a Different Voice: Psychological Theory and Women's Development.* Harvard UP, 1982.
Martin, Valerie. *Mary Reilly.* Doubleday, 1990.
Stevenson, Robert Louis. *The Strange Case of Dr. Jekyll and Mr. Hyde.* Penguin, 2002.

25

Hardy's Modernity and Cosmic Irony

Question:

Hardy is a proto-modernist in the sense that his work of the 1880s and '90s contains a tone of cosmic irony that anticipates the modernist mood of the early twentieth century. The introduction of machines into pastoral Wessex is a harbinger of industrialism and mass production that threaten the ancient agricultural economy and the united community. A sense of godlessness or an indifferent God makes characters vulnerable to chains of events over which they have no control, often resulting in tragedy. Cosmic irony is Hardy's characteristic way of conceptualizing events in his fictional world of Wessex. How does Hardy use cosmic irony to dramatize Tess's downfall?

Synopsis:

In the farming district of Wessex during the Great Depression of the 1870s, Tess Durbeyfield is the daughter of a poor peddler. Her father learns that he is related to a noble family, the D'Urbervilles, that came over to England with William the Conqueror. Tess is studious and plans to become a schoolteacher. When the family's horse dies, Tess's mother, Joan, asks her to introduce herself to Mrs. D'Urberville, a rich widow whom Joan erroneously presumes is a relative. Tess becomes poultry keeper for Mrs. D'Urberville, whose son, Alec, begins to court her. Tess dislikes him but can't escape his advances. One night she agrees to ride away from the village with him when he saves her from the attack of a jealous woman.

Pretending to be lost, he takes her to a forest, where he drugs and rapes her. She has his child, who dies in infancy. The incident brings shame on Tess and her family. Two years later she is working at Talbothay's Dairy, where no one knows of her past. Angel Clare, son of a clergyman, comes to study farm management. They fall in love and become engaged. Tess tries to inform him of her past "transgressions" via letter, but the letter doesn't reach him, so her confession has to wait until their wedding night. Though Angel confesses he's had another lover, he can't accept Tess's past. He leaves for Brazil to seek his fortune, saying he'll contact Tess if he ever manages to forgive her transgressions.

Unhappy at her parents' home, Tess finds work in the rutabaga fields of Flintcomb-Ash, a starve-acre farm with a harsh master, Farmer Groby, who knows Tess's secret. Alec finds her and recommences his stalking, trying to convince her that Angel will never come back, and that she should ease her struggles by accepting his support. When her father dies, her mother and siblings are evicted from their cottage. They decide to move to Kingsbere because it's the family home of the D'Urbervilles. Alec comes on the scene once again to offer assistance at this time of great vulnerability. Tess begins to weaken: Angel has not relented, the family is destitute, outdoor labor is very hard. Finally, she submits to Alec, who immediately sets up her family in a comfortable cottage and takes her to Sandbourne, a seaside resort, for a "honeymoon." Meanwhile, Tess's fellow milkmaids from Talbothay's Dairy write to Angel, informing him of Tess's dilemma and asking him to rescue her. He arrives too late—tracking her down to the Sandbourne rooming house, he finds that she's already the mistress of Alec D'Urberville. Ashamed, she begs him to leave her alone, and he departs. She argues with Alec and murders him. Tess follows Angel and tells him of her deed, hoping it will redeem her in his mind. They flee from Sandbourne and hide in a vacated mansion for five days. On their way to the coast, they stop at Stonehenge to rest. Tess senses she will be apprehended and asks Angel to marry her sister, Liza Lu, when she is hanged. The police arrest Tess and take her to prison. At her execution, Angel and Liza Lu watch hand-in-hand, indicating that they will marry, as Tess wished.

Analysis:

Thomas Hardy's cosmic irony conveys his impression that the world is unjust. People lack control over their own destinies. *Irony* is the contrast between what a person expects and what actually happens to them. Most authors use irony, since it's a useful way to introduce their commentary on events and characters. Jane Austen is famous for social irony that pokes fun at the mores of lower-middle-class country people who try to raise their status by marrying their daughters into a higher class. The opening sentence of *Pride and Prejudice* establishes her satirical voice: "It is a truth universally acknowledged that a single man in possession of a good fortune must be in want of a wife."

Cosmic irony, on the other hand, is more philosophical. External forces, such as gods or fate, intervene in a person's life to create an outcome that is indifferent to that person's merit. Perfectly virtuous people undergo trying or disastrous ordeals. Tess Durbeyfield starts out innocent and good: she hopes to become a schoolteacher and help support her family. In trying to rescue her parents from their foolish choices, however, she descends step by step from shame to degradation to murder to death. The novel's subtitle, *A Pure Woman Faithfully Presented,* signals that Tess did not give consent to sexual intercourse with Alec, nor accede to his proposal out of selfishness, but rather from the real necessity of saving her family. Despite her good traits (generosity, conscience, rationality), Tess is driven to insanity by Alec's cruelty and by fate. The fact that Angel just missed saving her by a matter of days, due to delayed mail, miscommunications, and faulty assumptions—factors beyond either's control—is one example of Hardy's cosmic irony.

This ironic mode reflects the author's internal conflict about the nature of God. Like Angel, Hardy is more attracted by the religious beliefs of the ancient Greeks than the evangelical Anglicanism of Wessex preachers. The Greeks more fully appreciated the role of fate and the intervention of jealous gods in human affairs. Free will was not a strong concept in ancient theology. Odysseus, hero of Homer's *Odyssey,* could brave the elements and fight superhuman monsters, but his ultimate fate was determined by Athena's love and protection rather than his own courage or cleverness. As a late Victorian and early modern, Hardy is not alone in believing that a dark fate controls our lives. American modernist Robert Frost (1874–1963), for one, shared his bleak, agnostic view of God's indifference. British modernist D.H. Lawrence went even further by attempting to become a pagan, although his Nonconformist religious upbringing shackled him with a load of guilt and prudery that he strenuously fought to conquer.

In addition to cosmic irony, Hardy employs lighter forms, such as situational irony, which provide a measure of comic relief from the heavier kind. The Wessex community is obsessed with the value of noble ancestry when in actual fact, having good blood doesn't necessarily help families survive in a depressed economy. There is situational irony in Durbeyfield's belief that his ancestry would help him and his family, when in fact it hurt them. John Durbeyfield felt that his link to the noble D'Urbervilles would necessarily ensure a fortune and he could quit working. Instead, his poverty led to his daughter's needing to work for the D'Urbervilles, whose "noble lineage" turned out to be a fraud. There is also situational irony in Angel Clare's problematic attitude to "good blood." Angel scorns his community's obsession with lineage, saying that he hates "old families." Nevertheless he feels that Tess's old family is her one selling point when he presents her to his parents. For all his attempts to defy convention, Angel Clare is, ironically, one of the more conventional characters in the book. One way that authors can dramatize the limited perspectives of their characters is to show the difference between their self-perception and the external perception that others (including the reader) formulate upon observation of their words and deeds.

Hardy's brand of cosmic irony is distinguished by its tone of melancholia and nostalgia for a simpler past era. This tone eloquently expresses his sadness at humans' inability to stop time, turn back the clock, maintain the innocence of childhood, prevent death, or slow the effects of industrialization upon rural communities. I've selected several passages in which Hardy reflects on the anxieties of the modern age, while noting the ironies of the human condition:

1. We happen to live on this planet, rather than another, possibly better one. Tess tells her younger brother, Abraham, that stars are other worlds, "most of them splendid and sound—a few blighted," and that ours is one of the blighted (31). The child's reply is cosmically ironic: "'Tis very unlucky that we didn't pitch on a sound one, when there were so many more of 'em!" Abraham is right: our fate is so arbitrary that we seem "pitched" randomly on planets by an unknown entity. The comment also regretfully records the blighting of childhood innocence. Young Abraham believes that most planets are good, but that fate happened to deliver him to a bad one. Such knowledge must have the effect of burdening a child's conscience with a sense of guilt and doom.

2. Hardy muses that romance is based on chance encounters over which we have no control. Wandering the earth separately are soul mates who have little chance of coincidentally meeting each other: "In the present case, as in millions, the two halves of an approximately perfect whole did not confront each other at the perfect moment; part and counterpart wandered independently about the earth in the stupidest manner for a while" (43–44). Instead of their soul mates, people will meet and marry partners who are wrong for them and live unhappily ever after. Angel and Tess would have been "perfect" for each other at one time, but Alec got there first and spoiled their opportunity. Adding to the irony of Tess and Angel's fate is the fact that they narrowly missed meeting at the May Day

dance. Tess "loved Angel at first sight," but he unwittingly chose another dance partner.

3. Why do bad things happen to good people? The narrator is sincerely disturbed by the fact that Alec chose Tess as his rape victim, as Tess is the type of person who won't recover from the ordeal: "Why it was that upon this beautiful feminine tissue, sensitive as gossamer, and practically blank as snow as yet, there should have been traced such a coarse pattern as it was doomed to receive; why so often the coarse appropriates the finer thus, many thousand years of analytical philosophy have failed to explain" (74). If one coarse nature would only wed another coarse nature, all would be (comparatively) well in the world. Instead, coarseness is inexorably attracted to fineness, whether in the desire to corrupt it, or in the hope of being redeemed by it.

4. The simplicity of farm life offers some respite from the modern tendency to intellectualize experience and thereby cause unhappiness. Living a simple country life may delay the inevitable decline in religious faith. Angel consciously tries to avoid modernity's mental diseases—anxiety, anomie, melancholia—by choosing to work with simple peasants: "Considering his position he became wonderfully free from the chronic melancholy which is taking hold of the civilized races with the decline in belief in a beneficent Power" (118). Hardy clearly believes that loss of religious faith leads to melancholia.

5. The "ache" of modernism is transmitted inexorably through education and culture; it cannot be avoided. When Tess first reveals to Angel her sorrowful outlook on life, Angel is startled to see such melancholy in one so young: "He was surprised to find this young woman … shaping such sad imaginings…. She was expressing in her own native phrases—assisted a little by her Sixth Standard training—feelings which might almost have been called those of the age—the ache of modernism" (124). Modernism can be felt as an ache because the age has lost faith in God but has found no meaningful substitute of equal value. Technology is the engine of progress, but machines symbolize alienation on the Wessex farms. "Progress" is inevitable, but it takes a toll on human happiness.

6. We are our own worst enemies. Momentarily, Alec was redeemed, and Tess was safe from his advances, when the Reverend Clare successfully converted Alec into a pious Christian. Ironically, it is Tess's repetition of Angel's heresies that dismantle Alec's newfound faith. With this complex chain of events, Hardy shows that we are easily our own worst enemies. Tess preaches Angel's pagan creed to Alec; Alec loses religion and reverts to the seducer he used to be. Only Alec appreciates the irony of the situation: "He said to himself, as he pondered again and again over the crystallized phrases that she had handed on to him, 'That clever fellow

little thought that, by telling her those things, he might be paving my way back to her!'" (324). By sharing Angel's teachings, Tess inadvertently contributes to her own downfall.

7. The nature of existence is change. Noble families die out over time, losing their land, and even their leases. The high are brought low. When John Durbeyfield dies, his family is evicted from their leased cottage, just as John's ancestors had evicted peasant farmers from their own lands: "Thus the Durbeyfields, once D'Urbervilles, saw descending upon them the destiny which, no doubt, when they were among the Olympians of the county, they had caused to descend many a time, and severely enough, upon the heads of such landless ones as they themselves were now. So do flux and reflux—the rhythm of change—alternate and persist in everything under the sky" (351). The irony is not only that the Durbeyfield name, derived from the noble Norman ancestor, no longer carries privilege. There is an added disappointment in the fact that most noblemen behave uncharitably; they evict tenants without concern for their plight. We can only hope that aristocrats will behave nobly, though history shows us this is seldom true. Social groups that hold power are always reluctant to relinquish it, and they retain it by protecting their own interests.

8. The final irony of the book is that Tess, the epitome of purity, is driven to one of the most impure acts—murder—by fate and circumstance. This irony is too monumental to be described in colloquial or contemporary terms. Hardy borrows words from Aeschylus, the "father of tragedy," to express the cosmic irony of her execution: "'Justice' was done, and the President of the Immortals (in Aeschylean phrase) had ended his sport with Tess" (397). In addition to the Greek tragedian, the narrator alludes to Shakespeare. *King Lear*'s Gloucester utilizes the same metaphor as Hardy does—humans are playthings for the gods: "As flies to wanton boys are we to the gods;/ They kill us for their sport."

Hardy repeatedly uses an animal metaphor to express Tess's entrapment in circumstances beyond her control: she is a bird caught in a "springe." Rigid gender roles ensnare women and men's predatory sexual desire captures them as prey. For Hardy, there is another springe even more encompassing than gender and hypocritical sexual standards: this is the fundamental human condition of being trapped, men and women alike, in a fate we cannot control.

Works Cited

Hardy, Thomas. *Tess of the D'Urbervilles*. Penguin, 1998.

26

Pagan versus Christian Values

Question:

In *Tess of the D'Urbervilles*, Hardy uses both Biblical scripture and pagan ideals as theological and ethical standards by which to assess the actions of the characters. What relative roles does he give to pagan and Christian values in framing the way we see Angel and Tess's moral characters and Tess's downfall?

Analysis:

By the time of the late Victorian era, many writers had become skeptical of the Christian faith, including Samuel Butler, Edmund Gosse, Thomas Hardy, George Gissing, Robert Louis Stevenson, and George Meredith. Almost all major Victorian authors experienced major crises of faith, some ending in agnosticism or idiosyncratic belief, though few authors became declared atheists (Landow). The social stakes of proclaiming atheism—especially for a writer—were high.

Although many people were able to reconcile religious faith with evolution, Darwin's theory of natural selection, published as *On the Origin of Species* in 1859, challenged the belief in creationism, planting seeds of doubt about the nature of God and the universe. If God didn't create the earth and heavens, then what did cause life and the planets to exist, and what basis for an ethical system remains once God is dead? In turning to the ancient Greeks for inspiration, Hardy shares a predisposition of the Romantic poets and anticipates a taste of the modernists. Twenty years after *Tess of the D'Urbervilles'* publication, D.H. Lawrence, E.M. Forster, Rupert Brooke, and other modernists would advocate a return to pre-Christian ethics, integrating classical ideas into their work and beliefs. Turning away from his non-Conformist religious upbringing, Lawrence proudly proclaimed his belief in the life force that is human sexuality. Hardy's (and Angel Clare's) projections of rural simplicity onto Tess Durbeyfield come close to D.H. Lawrence's model of living "in the rhythms of the cosmos."

Pagan ethics appealed to modernists who had lost faith in the Christian God, but for many (Hardy included), paganism was more an ideal of modern life than a focus of scholarly study. There is little evidence of Hardy's historical research into Greek culture except for his reading of John Mahaffy's *Social Life in Greece from Homer to Menander* (1874) and Matthew Arnold's essays on pagan ideals, including *Culture and Anarchy* (1869) and *Essays in Criticism* (1865) (Panter). From his readings in poetry and philosophy, Hardy presumed that the ancient Greeks practiced a religion that was more tolerant than Christianity with regard to sexuality. The emotional basis of the modernists' philhellenism is the longing for a way of life in which sexuality is considered a natural aspect of human life, a positive acceptance of the instinctive sex drive of men and women. In fiction and essays, the modernists (and some late Victorians) criticized the hypocritical moral code that had been derived from scripture. One aspect of this hypocrisy demonstrated in *Tess* is the censuring of female sexuality far more harshly than its male counterpart. Tess's rape ruins her for marriage, whereas Angel carried on an affair with an older woman, is forgiven instantly by his wife, and remains unhampered by societal judgments. What constitutes scandalous behavior in a woman is excusable, or even expected, in a man.

On its face, the looming question of *Tess of the D'Urbervilles* is rather like that of Thackeray's *Vanity Fair*: did she, or didn't she? Did Tess fight back against Alec's advances or did she succumb with pleasure? Did Becky Sharp sleep with Lord Steyne or did she only flirt to the point where he thought she would? These questions remain unanswered, as Victorians were not willing to write about female desire. Hardy's audience was sharply divided on the question of Tess's purity. He wrote that his work suffered from the misinterpretation of the "Grundys," who he felt had missed the point. Regardless of her intercourse with Alec, or of how hard she resisted him, Tess remained "pure" because she was innocent in spirit; she did not use her sexual appeal to manipulate men. This quality, of course, distinguishes her from the Becky Sharps of the world, who consciously wield their sexuality as a tool for financial gain.

In Victorian society, women were not supposed to enjoy sex. Accepting intercourse was their duty to their husband, God, and their country. "Close your eyes and think of England" was a Victorian saying that was supposed to help wives endure their marital duty. Sex would produce children who could serve their country in the offices of soldiers, sailors, or merchants. But Hardy portrays Tess as a woman who enjoys nature's sensations in her body, such as the first smells of spring and the feel of wind on her skin. Her sensuality is part of nature, and she has what the narrator considers a pagan enjoyment of the land, animals, seasons, sunsets, stars, and so on. When she is upset by scandal, she takes midnight walks during which she blends her consciousness into the landscape, when "her whimsical fancy would intensify natural processes around her till they seemed part of her own story" (85). After spending a chilly night on a bed of leaves during her journey to Flintcomb-Ash, she recovers from self-pity by comparing herself to earth's other creatures. She euthanizes the pheasants left half-dead by callous hunters, "feeling for kindred sufferers as much as for herself" (279). Angel is right to think her a "daughter of Nature," for this night in the woods reminds her that scandal is only "an arbitrary law of society which had no foundation in Nature," and she feels relieved and renewed by her communion with animals, plants, and the landscape (279).

Tess and the other milkmaids do know sexual desire, which Hardy is courageous enough to write about, though he uses euphemistic rather than graphic terms. After Angel has carried the girls across a wide puddle, their desire is stoked, which keeps them awake at night with longing: "the incident of the day had fanned the flame that was burning the inside of their hearts out" (147). Hardy depicts their sex drive as something impersonal, grounded in nature instead of personality: "The differences which distinguished them [the milkmaids] as individuals were abstracted by this passion, and each was but portion of one organism called sex" (147). The idea of sex as an organism is interesting in light of the different theology that neo-pagans such as Hardy were theorizing. If sex is an "organism," then it is part of nature, and thus, something larger than the individual rather than a personal sin or something shameful to think about—as Victorian social mores demanded. Everyone feels the sex drive, so nature must have placed it within us, as it is in other animals and plants. It is an instinct common to all life forms, engineered for the survival of the species. Darwinian sex is not mortal sin.

Because of her innocent naturalness, Angel thinks of Tess as a pagan goddess, as well as a Platonic archetype of perfect Beauty, "a whole sex condensed into one typical form"—his word choice, "condensed," alerts contemporary readers to his dangerous stereotyping. When they are alone together in the predawn light, he calls her "Artemis, Demeter, and other fanciful names" (130). Whether intentionally or not, he has chosen two goddesses who are *least* associated with sex and sexuality in the pantheon. Artemis, the Goddess of Chastity, obtained Zeus's promise that she could always remain a virgin, whereas Demeter, the Earth Goddess, was more identified with her love of her daughter and her role of fertilizing the land than by her relationships with male consorts (Zeus, Poseidon, and Iasion). In the next moment, Hardy juxtaposes Angel's ideal of Tess's purity with the reality of her sexual past (which Angel does not yet know). To represent this actual, as opposed to idealized, womanhood, Hardy uses a Christian symbolic figure, a prostitute: "He little thought that the Magdalen might be at his side" (130). The contrast between Artemis and Mary Magdalen illustrates the difference between Angel's pagan idealizations and the Christian interpretation he will put on the reality of Tess's past. The pagan archetype is one of female chastity, while the Christian figure is a fallen woman. On their wedding night, Angel's ideals disappear when he learns of Tess's nonvirginal state. Then he readily defaults to a Christian definition of the only kind of woman fit for marriage, a virgin. Angel fails to live up to his liberal ideals, which were borrowed from books and untested in real life. The hypocrisy of his supposedly pagan views becomes apparent. Despite his desire to be different, Angel is just as influenced by his moral upbringing as his conventional brothers are by theirs. Freethinking vanishes when actual womanhood stands in front of him.

In Brazil, Angel begins to suffer from illness, loneliness, and boredom, which causes him to self-reflect. His estrangement in a foreign land leads him to regret his harshness to Tess. He perceives the fact of his hypocrisy, realizing that if he truly lived by a pagan ethics, he wouldn't see Tess as a "fallen woman." Angel considers that "he had persistently elevated Hellenic Paganism at the expense of Christianity; yet in that civilization an illegal surrender was not certain disesteem" (341). "Illegal surrender" is Angel's euphemism for a word, *rape*, that might come with difficulty to his lips. Angel's Tess had been a fantasy of his own mind, created out of a desire to know and marry a being "more pagan" than himself.

Tess's mind also contains a mix of pagan and Christian values. When she composes her own hymn to God, Tess blends pagan and Christian elements, which the narrator describes as a "Fetichistic [*sic*] utterance in a Monotheistic falsetto" (104). The "falsity" implied by "falsetto" is Hardy's condemnation of Christian hypocrisy, and of Angel's unfair treatment of his wife. The following is the narrator's, rather than Tess's, opinion of the nature of her spirituality: "women whose chief companions are the forms and forces of outdoor Nature retain in their souls far more of the Pagan fantasy of their remote forefathers than of the systematized religion taught her race at later date" (104). Tess is happiest when out of doors and in communion with those "forms of Nature"—trees, cows, clouds, and stars—but she is blissfully ignorant of the forms of Plato, those Hellenic archetypes that her feminine presence conjures in Angel's mind.

Rather than resolving the tension, the ending of the novel raises questions about the conflict between pagan and Christian virtues. After the murder, the reconciliation with her husband, and their flight from the law, Tess gives herself up, lying on the sacrificial altar at Stonehenge. Tess's demise at the ancient pagan site might signal Hardy's relinquishment of hope that pagan ethics could ever take root in Victorian England. If she represents a true pagan ethics, then what does Tess's sacrifice on a Druidic altar mean for the future of English moral life? Her death may spell the impossibility of any healthy alternative to Victorian hypocrisy.

An opposite reading is also possible. Marie Panter, for one, claims that the marriage of Angel and Liza Lu signifies the beginning of a new civilization. She reads it as an instance of the Adamic myth—that human history is capable of a new spiritual beginning, when humans are given the chance to "do it over" and get it right the second time: "Hardy turns Stonehenge, a quintessentially English place, into the cradle of a renewed civilization, based on Greek pagan virtue" (¶ 21). But Margaret Higonnet points out that the last image and words of the novel resemble Adam and Eve's expulsion from Eden at the end of Milton's *Paradise Lost*. Hardy writes, "As soon as they had strength they arose, joined hands again, and went on" (398). Compare this to Milton's version: "They hand in hand with wandering steps and slow/Through Eden took their solitary way" (Higonnet, 461). Are "pure" Liza Lu and a chastened Angel about to live out the pagan idyll that Angel had mismanaged in his marriage to Tess? Such an outcome is hardly likely, if the last line likens them to the fallen Adam and Eve. In Milton, the original sinners are about to enter the Christian moral universe in which they and all their descendants will suffer because of their transgression. Or perhaps Hardy's reference to the Garden of Eden, if intended, was meant to satirize the human tendency to create utopias in our minds, as Angel does when constructing Tess as a *tabula rasa* which wasn't, after all, so blank.

Hardy wrote this about the mutability of literary genres: "If you look beneath the surface of any farce you see a tragedy, and if you blind yourself to the deeper issues of a tragedy you see a farce" (*Life*, 224). There is no farcical value in the final scenes of *Tess of the D'Urbervilles* unless we look at cosmic irony as *comic* irony. Humans—at least up until a certain age—tend to expect far better outcomes than they generally experience. We continue to attribute meaning to our lives and moral structures to the world even though we know, or suspect, that they don't exist. Yet we feel driven to order the universe in our idealized image. The literature of the absurd becomes, during the mid-twentieth century, a legitimate way to deal with the cruel and unpredictable nature of life. Absurdism is a compassionate stance toward the benighted human desire to continue creating meaning even when, or especially when, meanings elude or disappoint us. Humans need meaning in order to live worthwhile lives—and stay sane. Applying Hardy's statement about the comedy within tragedy, we might say, like Abraham, that most stars are splendid worlds, but we happened to "get pitched on a blighted one!" This idea is only comic insofar as it raises a small chuckle over humans' erroneous yet perhaps sanity-saving belief that we can control our own destinies.

Narrators of Hardy's novels sometimes zoom out from their scenes of *Sturm und Drang* to take the bird's eye perspective of their characters, reminding me of the seventeenth-century philosopher Baruch Spinoza (1632–1677), who felt happy only when he realized he was a speck in the universe, *sub specie aeternitatis*, "under the form of eternity." Pina Totaro has explained the famous philosophic concept as follows: "While love for transitory assets such as good fortune, honor, and wealth subjects us to every sort of sadness and conflicting passions, only the love of that which is eternal and infinite truly nourishes and fills the soul with joy and thus proves itself as the only worthwhile object of our desires." This thought might be consoling, except for the fact that a late Victorian such as Thomas Hardy no longer knows what, if anything, is eternal and infinite.

Works Cited

"Atheism in the Nineteenth Century and Today." https://conwayhall.org.uk/from-the-archives/victorian-blogging-atheism-in-the-nineteenth-century-and-today/.

Franks, Jill. *Revisionist Resurrection Mythologies: A Study of D.H. Lawrence's Italian Works*. Peter Lang, 1994.

Hardy, Thomas. *The Life and Work of Thomas Hardy*. Ed. Michael Millgate. Macmillan, 1984.

Hardy, Thomas. *Tess of the D'Urbervilles*. Penguin, 1998.

Higonnet, Margaret. Introduction and Notes. *Tess of the D'Urbervilles*. Penguin, 1998.

Landow, George P. "Atheism." https://victorianweb.org/religion/atheism.html.

Panter, Marie. "Paganism in *Tess of the D'Urbervilles* and *Jude the Obscure*: The Possibility of Faith and Ethics in a Darwinian World." *Cahiers victoriens et édouardiens* [online] 80 Autumn (2014).

Totaro, Pina. "Translating Sub Specie Aeternitatis in Spinoza : Problems and Interpretations." *Translatio Studiorum: Ancient, Medieval and Modern Bearers of Intellectual History*. Brill, 2012.

27

The Challenge of Writing a Novel of Ideas

Question:

The New Woman is a term coined in the 1890s to express emancipation of women from confining gender roles. The phrase referred to "a young woman of principle, middle-class, independent, and financially self-reliant, reflecting her class's increased opportunities for education, work, career, and feminist activism" (Steinbach 278). A related phrase, "the woman question," was coined even before Mary Wollstonecraft's time; it asks, what is the nature of woman? Is she equal to and/or similar to men? What is the proper role of women in society? The New Woman question adds a bolder angle to the age-old woman question: can a woman be happy, healthy, and financially secure without the patronage of men? A subsidiary question was whether patriarchy could survive the independence of women; if women didn't play their prescribed role in the domestic sphere, how would the family survive? If women entered the workforce and competed with men, how would men retain their power and privilege? *Far from the Madding Crowd* addresses the New Woman question obliquely when Bathsheba becomes financially independent and competes with neighboring farmers for trade. *The Odd Women* addresses it directly through the voices of its feminist characters, who establish a school for women. The explicit purpose of this school is to provide an alternative for women so that they are not dependent on marriage for survival. Reading these novels back-to-back raises questions about genre. How effective is the novel of ideas for making political statements while achieving an aesthetically pleasing narrative? Can a novel do both at the same time? What are the obstacles to achieving both objectives in the same novel?

Synopsis:

In rural Somer-
set, widowed Dr. Madden
brings up six daughters on
limited resources, making
insufficient plans for their
support after his death.
When he dies, the eldest
daughter, Alice, becomes
a governess; the second
daughter, Virginia, a lady's
companion; the third,
fourth, and fifth eventu-
ally die from accidents, illness, and suicide; and the
sixth, Monica, becomes
a draper's shop assistant.
Meanwhile, their feminist
friend Rhoda Nunn fares
better, becoming assistant
to Mary Barfoot, director
of a secretarial school in
London. The elder Mad-
den girls are too plain to

George Gissing, published by R.F. Fenno & Co.,
New York (1896).

interest suitors, but pretty Monica attracts Edmund Widdowson, a retired
clerk with a substantial inheritance. When they marry, he becomes pos-
sessive, and Monica loses respect for him. She engages in a love affair with
Mr. Bevis, who, out of fear of losing his own respectability, reneges on
their plans to live together in France.

Meantime, Mary's cousin, Everard Barfoot, courts Rhoda. He's
intrigued by her progressive ideas about gender equality, and proposes
his own version—will she join him in a free union, that is, romantic partnership without the benefit of marriage? Rhoda prefers marriage, but is
willing to negotiate: if Everard will clear his name of the scandal attached
to him and Monica Widdowson, she will enter the free union with him.
Prideful Everard refuses to do so. At length, Rhoda gets over him, only by
vowing never to love again. Everard marries Agnes Bressenden, a wealthy,
cultured young woman. Monica dies in childbirth, Alice becomes her
niece's guardian (paid by Edmund Widdowson), and Rhoda views the
newborn girl as a "poor little child."

Analysis:

The Odd Women belongs to the genre called "novel of ideas," and the main idea of this novel is women's emancipation. Gissing wants to show that Victorian women are tired of patriarchy, the marriage market, power imbalance within marriage, sexual double standards, and ill-paid, menial employment. He believes that women will be better served once they can support themselves. They shouldn't look to marriage for either material or emotional comfort. In contrast, *Far from the Madding Crowd*, written in the realist genre, shows the challenges for both men and women, both working- and middle-class residents of Wessex. Hardy's novel obliquely addresses the theme of the New Woman and specifically the issue of whether the self-employed woman can be happy without marriage, but this is not its main idea. Rather, Hardy takes care to show how passion can destroy men and women: Fanny, Troy, and Boldwood are each destroyed by their fateful love affairs. Whereas Gissing's Rhoda Nunn succeeds in evading marriage and making a fulfilling life, Hardy's Bathsheba Everdene relinquishes her adolescent credo of female independence and marries. Yet the ambiguous ending of Hardy's novel casts a doubt on whether this marriage will be happy. It is instructive to compare these two novels from the angle of their respective genres.

To drive home the message of the need for female emancipation, Gissing uses a plot device typical of Victorian novels. Two couples exist in parallel plots, serving as both similars and foils. One protagonist, Monica, develops a feminist consciousness but lacks the strength to disentangle from her marriage. The other, Rhoda, appears to come through her love affair unscathed. Unlike Hardy's rustics, who take center stage in a few chapters and provide background for many others, Gissing's minor characters function as repetitive instances of the two protagonists' problems. The experience of these characters mirrors the theme that marriage creates misery. Single women are happier—Mildred Vesper, Winifred Haven, Mrs. Cosgrave, Mary Barfoot, and the Miss Brissendens are some examples. No woman in *The Odd Women* is happily married except for Mrs. Micklethwaite, though we see her marriage only through her husband Thomas's eyes. Even Mrs. Widdowson, having finally reeled in her baronet, is dissatisfied with the marriage that she had sought for social status. The wealth and status of her husband are not enough to make her happy.

Gissing's message is lucid and well illustrated. Nevertheless, the novel of ideas is one of the most challenging genres to write. Too often, the characters become stick figures, mere spokespeople for the author's political ideas. For instance, George Bernard Shaw's social-problem plays are entertaining more because of their shock value (for a Victorian audience) than

for the believability of their characters. Fyodor Dostoyevsky is more successful with the genre. His characters live in settings replete with realistic
detail, which makes their material existence as interesting as their ideas.
Dostoyevsky lived in a time of political and religious turmoil which led to
the largest social and political revolution of all time—Russia's transformation to a communist state. Novels of ideas are more common in periods of social change, when political ideologies and their ramifications are
on everyone's mind. Late 1890s England is just such a period, since the
woman question (specifically women's suffrage) had been plaguing Victorians since at least the 1860s and turned into a militant campaign by the
1900s.

The challenge of writing a novel of ideas is to fully develop individual characters and their settings, making geographical and social environments as important as dialog and allegory. In my opinion, Gissing does not
quite clear the bar. Although he names several locations, such as the Chel-
sea Embankment and Victoria Station in London, and Boot, Seascale, and
Scawfell in Cumberland, he fails to give these places enough local color to
ground his characters in them. As for the characters, it is their ideas rather
than their physicality that monopolize these scenes. As readers, we inhabit
the characters' minds more than their locations, and their intellects more
than their emotions. One thing a writer should avoid is for a scene to be
capable of taking place anywhere else. Settings shouldn't be interchange-
able if a novel is to be immersive. In *The Odd Women*, Rhoda and Everard
might as well have broken up in Bournemouth as Scawfell, for what little
attention Gissing gives to scenery.

The Odd Woman is a talky novel, leaving the burden on the reader to
create images of its people and places. I'm left wanting to know more about
the characters' physical appearance. In addition to her ideas, I want to
know not only that Rhoda's eyes took on a brilliant light when she thought
of Everard Barfoot, but the color of her eyes, the shape of her face, the cut
and color of her outfit (other than the red silk blouse and black skirt that
signaled flirtation), and any coquetry that she may have unconsciously
practiced. In contrast, Hardy gives us many informative details about even
his minor characters. Consider, for instance, his introduction of Liddy
Smallbury:

> Liddy, the maltster's great-granddaughter, was about Bathsheba's equal in
> age, and her face was a prominent advertisement of the lighthearted English
> country-girl. The beauty her features might have lacked in form was amply
> compensated for by perfection of hue, which at this winter time was the soft-
> ened ruddiness on a surface of high rotundity that we meet within a Terburg
> or a Gerard Douw, and like their presentations, it was a face which always kept
> on the natural side of the boundary between itself and the ideal [64].

Hardy's description is detailed and figurative, illustrating why Liddy is a boon companion to Bathsheba. The comparison to the work of Dutch genre painters lends a visual specificity to Hardy's depiction of Liddy's beautiful English complexion.

Another difference between the realist novel and the novel of ideas is the relative development of the minor characters. In a realist novel like *Far from the Madding Crowd*, they merit their own chapters and play an essential role in the main action. In *The Odd Women*, the minor characters serve to repeat the main theme rather than adding depth to a background that contains and affects the protagonists. Virginia and Alice Madden are the unfortunate minor characters in *The Odd Women* whose education and attachment to gentility interfere with their ability to make a living, while Mildred Vesper and Winifred Haven are the lucky ones who don't depend on men for survival. Gissing has stereotyped the minor characters in order to show the various forms of damage facing women who leave home without training for independence. Alice develops an uncritical piety that makes her ridiculous, and Virginia becomes an alcoholic. The other Madden sisters are summarily dispatched in a sentence—Gertrude by tuberculosis, Martha in a boating accident, and Isabel by melancholia leading to her suicide. The most glaringly dangerous way for a woman to ruin herself is prostitution—here represented in the figure of Miss Eade. Single women Mildred and Winifred are said to be happy because they earn their own wages, but we are told rather than shown the nature of their contentment. Each of these characters is emblematic of the social problem rather than being fully realized characters with their own inner lives.

Since novels of ideas use characters mainly to prove an author's political belief, these characters tend to be flat—they don't change substantially during the course of the novel. Rhoda grew up believing that marriage meant "shame and misery." Women's most important work was helping other women to attain independence from men and marriage. Except during an aborted holiday and a brief flirtation with the idea of marrying Everard, Rhoda continues strong in her beliefs until the end of the book. The second protagonist, Monica, changes more than Rhoda, but ends in a place that her early propensities pointed to from childhood: the prettiest and most vivacious of the six Madden sisters, she was destined to marry. Despite learning the feminist lesson—that she had given up personal fulfillment in return for material comfort—she ends up financially dependent on her husband, wishing for her own demise, and achieving it through that most Victorian of ways—death from complications of childbirth.

In contrast, Hardy's Gabriel Oak and Bathsheba Everdene are rounder; they change substantially from their youthful to their mature personalities. Upon Oak's first proposal, Bathsheba declares, "I hate to be thought men's property in that way" (26). But by the time she has endured the shame and misery of marriage to Troy, learned of his adultery with Fanny, and witnessed his death and Boldwood's insanity, she is able to conceive of salient differences between men's and women's approach to romance. In a statement that shows her dawning awareness that men shape language to fit their needs, she reveals a fundamental aspect of patriarchy. When Boldwood asks whether she loves *or* respects him, she replies, "It is difficult for a woman to define her feelings in language which is chiefly made by men to express theirs" (308). She has understood that male lust is a thing apart from a man's respect for a woman's mind and character. Having experienced her own lust for Troy, she can now appreciate and regret the pain she caused Boldwood. Bathsheba has changed. Courting is no longer a game of power, and she now feels the benefit of having a husband to run her farm. Whether this is a concession to patriarchy or, instead, a wise and practical financial decision, readers will have to decide. Bathsheba has changed and matured in significant ways; Rhoda and Monica do not experience any such transformation. They never grow out of their childhood predilections for independence and dependence, respectively.

Urban living offers more opportunities for a woman to earn her living, and the London setting helps to distinguish Rhoda Nunn from Bathsheba Everdene. During the course of her tenure as farm owner, Bathsheba deals with many catastrophes. The reader may support her decision to marry, or alternately may feel that Bathsheba acquiesces to the patriarchal institution just at a point when she might have conquered her work challenges on her own. In Gissing's London, the odd women prove that marriage is not necessary for their survival, despite earning far less than men for similar work.

Opportunity is not class-blind, however. Gissing makes an interesting distinction between women willing to enter business and those who consider themselves too genteel for "trade." Mary Barfoot's secretarial-school graduates succeed in living independently, while the Madden sisters do not. Mary and Rhoda train women for office work, which gives them more independence than women like Virginia and Alice, who, given their genteel status, dare only to be governesses or lady companions. Office work doesn't require the genteel, "ladylike" social skills that lady-companion does.

Urban living is not all that distinguishes Gissing's women from Bathsheba. Rhoda and Mary's feminism is far more developed than Bathsheba's and is situated within an institutional framework rather than an individual life. Mary Barfoot's speech, "Woman as an Invader," illustrates her knowledge of the extensive history of the woman question. She has given much thought to woman's role in the world, not only to her own individual life circumstances. In the speech, Mary calls for no less than total revolution—not by taking up arms, but by converting every woman to a self-supporting, self-esteeming individual: "There must be a new type of woman, active in every sphere of life: a new worker out in the world, a new ruler of the home" (154). In contrast to Mary, Bathsheba does not think about changing women's role in society, but rather about changing a woman's potential role on a farm. ("Do not think that because I am a woman, I do not know the difference between evil-doings and good," Bathsheba told her workers.) While Bathsheba tends to her own interests and those of her tenant farmers, Mary makes common cause with other women, activating them to change the world by changing themselves: "Because we have to set an example to the sleepy of our sex, we must carry on an active warfare—must be invaders" (154). Her urgent rhetoric resembles the fervent appeals of the militant suffragettes that would be led by Mrs. Emmeline Pankhurst in the next decade. Mary Barfoot demands absolute dedication to the cause of independence: "At any cost—at any cost—we will free ourselves from the heritage of weakness and contempt!" (154)

Each of these novels about female independence has its place in the English literary canon. Although Hardy's is fuller in conception, more imbued with spirit of place, and more realistic about women and men's chances for success when defying convention, Gissing's offers many other pleasures. Gissing's plot is pleasing by its originality. In nineteenth-century novels, it is unusual to see what appears to be a well-matched couple reject marriage, as Rhoda and Everard do. Yet Gissing has carefully established the reasons why Rhoda and Everard are, in fact, not appropriately matched. Each one thinks that their greatest satisfaction would be to enjoy dominance over the other. Each displays a touch of misandry and misogyny, respectively. Even if they were to solve their initial conflict—Everard refusing to disprove the sexual scandal about himself and Monica—other occasions for disagreement would arise. With Rhoda Nunn and Everard Barfoot, Gissing gives powerful examples of what happens when we live single-mindedly by our ideals. As much as *The Odd Women* is a pro-feminist novel, it's also a cautionary tale about ways in which our ideals can damage our relationships.

Works Cited

Franks, Jill. *British and Irish Women Writers and the Women's Movement.* McFarland, 2013.
Gissing, George. *The Odd Women.* Penguin, 1993.
Hardy, Thomas. *Far from the Madding Crowd.* Penguin, 2000.
Steinbach, Susie. *Women in England, 1760–1914: A Social History.* Phoenix, 2005.

28

The Skewed Income Scale: Intersections of Gender and Class

Question:

With his keen interest in socioeconomic conditions and their effects on the quality of people's lives, Gissing provides specific income figures for many of his characters, spanning from £12–4,000 per annum. The author is also concerned about ways in which the Victorian separate-spheres doctrine hampers women's happiness and financial security. In Gissing's novel, how do gender and class identities intersect to impose limitations and create opportunities for working women? What is the economic relationship between class and gender in Gissing's *The Odd Women*?

Analysis:

The Odd Women amply illustrates the thesis that gender and class oppressions are interrelated in determining one's placement on the Victorian socioeconomic scale. A Victorian's maximum attainable income depended not only on their class, but also on their gender: "More than anything else, the Victorian middle class was distinguished by its gender regime and notions of domesticity" (Steinbach 125). Since middle-class women were to play the role of Angel in the House, married women weren't allowed to work; the jungle of commerce was men's exclusive territory. Working outside the home was thought to either risk damage to women's frail constitutions or to coarsen women and decrease their suitability for being caregivers.

For single women in the workplace, the same biased notions of women's fragility applied. Women were assigned to auxiliary and so-called female work, even in jobs that carried the same titles as men's, such as clerking (Steinbach 125). Yet working conditions could be just as rough in women's jobs, and the girls who sickened and died from being store clerks (in *The Odd Women*, Monica's colleague at the drapery shop and her sister, Gertrude) prove the point. Mildred Vesper and Winifred Haven would have earned less at their office jobs than men with equivalent titles, such as Edmund Widdowson. Prior to 1860, respectable middle-class women were not allowed to work in jobs other than governessing or dressmaking, both low-paid. Although the year is 1893, Alice and Virginia Madden are a throwback to this pre–1860 era, thanks to their father's idealism about gentility and gender. After 1860, many options opened for middle-class women's employment, such as shop assistant (Monica Madden's job), clerk (graduates of Miss Barfoot's school), civil servant (often as inspectors), and teacher (a job that could be stultifying and that smart women in *The Odd Women*, from Rhoda Nunn to Alice Madden, wished to avoid).

The class into which one is born is determinative of success in English nineteenth-century society. Aristotle expressed his belief in environmental and/or biological determinism when he said, "Give me a child until he is seven and I'll show you the man." Starting in 1964, directors Michael Apted and Paul Almond made practical application of this thesis in the *Up* film series—each episode spaced seven years apart—that tracks the lives of fourteen people chosen from each level of British class society. The *Up* series continued, with the last installment (2019) based on interviews of the cohort at age 63. Some participants dropped out of the project along the way, angry that their lives were considered so predictable. The films do, however, bear out Apted's predictions about the correlation between English social class and success—he accurately predicted the socioeconomic outcomes of his seven-year-old subjects' lives, based on the class into which they were born.

This notion of the importance of one's social ranking at birth (especially in England) applies to the characters of Gissing's novel. Besides class, the novelist adds another element—an emphasis on gender—as a cofactor in determining outcome. I propose that, in the era of the New Woman, a female worker's class determines her earning potential in a different way than a man's, because of the ways in which gender and class oppressions intersect. Specifically, belonging to the middle class poses obstacles for women trying to obtain higher incomes, whereas the same status assists men to rise up the scale, and working-class women might actually fare better than middle-class. Nineteenth-century notions of respectability for middle-class women severely hampers them economically. Gissing dramatically illustrates this problem when his female victims of gender ideology are scattered along the wayside of the novel's path. All but two of the six Madden sisters die horrible deaths after lifetimes of poverty and disgrace. Of the survivors, one ends in a rehabilitation center for alcoholics, and the other is saved only when named guardian of her sister's child, for whom she receives child support money. As discussed in the lecture "Bathsheba's Feminism," Victorian society created an inverse relationship of gender and class. Late Victorian middle-class women tended to be seen either as marriage bait or good earners, but not both. The higher your class status as a woman, the more likely you would marry instead of work, and most jobs had "marriage bars," the disqualification of married women for the job. Due to patriarchal notions of female gentility, working tended to lower single women's class status. Because she is overtly feminist, Rhoda Nunn is attractive only to men who are progressive iconoclasts such as Everard Barfoot, a rare specimen of his class and gender.

To provide a practical, detailed view of how income relates to class and gender in the time and place of this novel, I constructed a list, in descending order of value, of the characters' incomes that were either stated or suggested. Where incomes are not stated, I use Steinbach's class-income figures as a guide (116–118). These figures are for households, rather than individuals. The purpose is to show that men are on the top, women on the bottom, with the exception of those women who receive money through inheritance. The list also dramatizes what I think is Gissing's main point: not all the ambition and perseverance in the world would provide single women with a good income without assistance from men— usually inheritance—such as that enjoyed by Mary Barfoot and Mrs. Cosgrove. This condition severely limits the opportunity of becoming a full-fledged New Woman living independently. Retaining the genteel status of the middle class without the required income was a constant stress for those on the lower end of the middle class. A minimum income of £300 per annum would technically place you in the lower middle class, yet Steinbach reveals that a majority of middle-class families actually lived on only £100–£300 per annum (124). They lived in constant anxiety of being declassed or dropping down a rung on the social ladder.

The fact that women in this novel consider themselves comfortable when living on about £25–50 per annum—with which they may or may not be helping to support family members—reveals the discrepancy in male and female earning power, the difference in male and female expectations, and the disincentive for women to work instead of marrying. Middle-class born, these women are living on working-class incomes, which Steinbach defines as "usually under £100 per annum" (116). This is exactly the situation that Dr. Madden wanted to avoid for his daughters, but his sexist ideology ensured that they would be poor. In the first pages of the novel, Gissing's thesis becomes clear when he notes that it never occurred to Madden that his daughters should study "with a professional object" (3). The author satirizes the doctor in many ways: "Doctor only by courtesy," he became "nothing more than an empiric," and "should never have entered the medical profession" (2). But the most cutting comment is this one: "Dr Madden's hopes for the race were inseparable from a maintenance of morals and conventions such as the average man assumes in his estimate of women" (3). In this statement, Gissing reveals the misogyny (a low estimate of women) inherent in patriarchal ideologies, such as separate spheres and Angel in the House, that relegated women to the home.

Characters' incomes in descending order of value:*

*"PA" stands for per annum, the yearly income of each character.

Mrs. Luke Widdowson, later Lady Horrocks: £4,000 PA.

This large annuity is her widow's inheritance. Looking for a second marriage, she uses her riches to attract men with aristocratic titles. She succeeds in catching a baronet (the lowest rank of the peerage), but she is unhappy in the marriage. The author's viewpoint, that all marriages are doomed, is expressed by Lady Horrocks when she tries to solace her brother-in-law about his own unhappy marriage: "You oughtn't to have married at all, that's the fact; it would be better for most of us if we kept out of it" (380). The lesson is not simply that money isn't enough to make people happy, but that social climbing is likewise unrewarding, and, implicitly, that men and women have trouble finding harmony in intimate relationships.

The Bressendens: Income so high that the author doesn't mention an amount.

Everard wishes to marry one of the Bressenden daughters because he needs a larger income to "travel in a more satisfactory way than during his late absence" (160). Later, he sees that their culture is an additional asset: "He was making friends in the world with which he had a natural affinity; that of *wealthy and cultured people who seek no prominence,* who shrink from contact with the circles known as smart, who possess their souls in quiet freedom. It is a small class, especially distinguished by the charm of its women" (italics mine, 366). These upper-class women do not need to work, nor do they want to, and they would lose value on the marriage market if they did. Their capital (besides money) is culture, and this bait enables Agnes to catch an intelligent, independent man.

Everard Barfoot, retired engineer: £450 PA as engineer; £1,500 PA inheritance.

Everard is an interesting case of troubled (and troubling) class identity. Initially scornful of his father's class aspirations, he nevertheless selects a marriage partner based on her class status and her family's income. Everard's father was a social climber who would have bought a title, were this permitted in his time. He wanted his son to belong to the gentry and enrolled him in Eton and Oxford for training. Everard rebelled, became a Radical, and rejected learning for learning's sake. He became an engineer for its manly, practical associations, but he hated the profession. He stuck with it until age thirty-three, when he received a large inheritance from his brother. Note that Everard thinks £450 PA would be "grinding poverty" if he married on it, whereas some female characters are surviving on sums as little as £16 PA. Of course, the man's salary is intended to support himself as well as a wife and children, whereas the need to support dependents is not assumed or factored into a working woman's salary. This assumption is at the root of the damaging double standard; if women aren't paid enough to support themselves (and their dependents), then they have to marry. If they don't want to marry, they'll remain poor. Gissing understands that marriage can be in this sense a form of prostitution for women.

Mr. Bevis, wine merchant: income unspecified, but upper-middle or lower-upper class, therefore at least £1,000 PA (Steinbach 118).

We can identify Bevis's class as that of the gentry by certain indices: he maintains the family estate on Guernsey Island and leases two London flats, and he supports himself, his three sisters, and his mother. Mr. Bevis is a successful wine merchant. He is "in trade," which is considered vulgar for gentry, but he has a management position, good income, and a family landed estate, all of which serve to raise his class status to gentry level.

Edmund Widdowson, retired clerk, inheritor of his brother's estate: £600 PA.

Edmund hated being a clerk: "A clerk's life—a life of the office without any hope of rising—that is a hideous fate!" (48). He retired at forty-two due to his inheritance; the shock of this change may contribute to his chronic anxiety and melancholia: "In one day—in one hour—I passed from slavery to freedom, from poverty to more than comfort" (49). Clerks made a lower middle-class income, or upper working-class income—between £50 and £100 PA is an approximation (Steinbach *UtV*, 116). Women clerks earned less than their male counterparts. Also, for men, clerking offered opportunities for advancement which women didn't have (Steinbach, *Women*, 37). Notice that men and women have different attitudes to the clerk's job and salary: Edmund calls it "slavery" and "poverty," whereas Winifred and Mildred are content and comfortable, even on their lower salaries, which are discounted because of their gender. They do equal work for less pay (bearing in mind that men were expected to support a family on their salaries).

Mrs. Cosgrove, widowed, middle-class: income unspecified, but high enough to have disposable income for charitable purposes.

Mrs. Cosgrove is a counterpart to Miss Barfoot insofar as she uses her inheritance to assist young ladies. She "used a good deal of her income for the practical benefit of those who needed assistance" (233). However, her goal was to help women find marriage partners, whereas Mary trained them for employment so that they could avoid marriage. The narrator implies that Cosgrove is more content after her husband dies: "Her views on the matrimonial relation were known to be of singular audacity" (233). In one instance of matchmaking, Cosgrove doesn't believe there's a personal affinity between the partners, "but there's no harm in trying" (234). In contrast to Rhoda, Mrs. Cosgrove seems to think that marriage is the safest way for women to avoid poverty, regardless of the personal costs and disappointment inevitably occasioned, in her view, by marriage.

Elkanah Madden, country doctor: unspecified income, but only enough to meet expenses.

To put it kindly, Dr. Madden was not a saver: "For twenty years he had practiced medicine at Clevedon, but with such trifling emolument that the needs of his large family left him scarce a margin over expenditure" (1). At death, he had accumulated savings of £800 capital for his six daughters' inheritance. He had meant to ensure his life for £1,000, but he died before getting around to it, an example of his negligence and general incompetence as a father. Gissing creates in Dr. Madden an absurd, dreamy figure whose daughters pay drastically for his lack of clear vision and practical planning.

Thomas Micklethwaite: £150 PA
as math lecturer at a London college.

For seventeen years, he worked as a private tutor at £35 PA. After finally obtaining a salaried position, he is able to marry his loyal fiancée, Fanny, who has waited for him all of seventeen years. He feels, however, that £150 PA is not enough to support his wife, her blind sister, and himself, and hopes to supplement his lectureship income with private tutoring and textbook publication to the total amount of £300 PA. Gissing satirizes this aspiration, suggesting that Micklethwaite will be incapable of earning these supplements to his salary (101).

Mary Barfoot: inherits three-fourths
of her uncle's estate, a "lady of private means
sufficient to combine benevolence with business" (24).

In other words, unmarried Mary can afford a London home, has enough money to run a school for ladies in her own home, enough space for Rhoda to live with her, and enough savings to waive tuition for girls in need, to be repaid once they start earning salaries.

Rhoda Nunn, assistant at Mary's secretarial school:
income unspecified, but comfortable.

We know that honest, kindhearted Mary Barfoot would not underpay her assistant. I think we can assume that Rhoda makes more than the graduates placed in offices because Rhoda's duties include teaching and managerial work. Finances are not a problem; Rhoda pays for room and board at Mary Barfoot's home. She can afford holidays, though she's loath to take them due to her strong work ethic.

Mildred Vesper, Winifred Haven:
female clerks or secretaries, unspecified income.

One clue to her income status is that Mildred pays 8 shillings 6 pence rent per week, or £22 PA (before sharing with Monica). Based on this expense, we might estimate that she earns double this amount, or £44.

Monica's colleague at the drapery shop:
£25 PA as lady's maid.

This unfortunate character dies before she can earn this "good salary" that she was offered. Overwork at the drapery shop results in her fatal illness, so she never begins the new job with its higher salary.

Alice Madden, nursery governess:
£16 PA plus room and board.

Monica, shop assistant at Scotcher's Draperies:
£15 PA plus room and board.

Monica's working conditions are unimaginable by today's standards. Store clerks aren't allowed to sit down on the job. They're on their feet for thirteen-and-a-half-hour shifts on weekdays and sixteen hours on Saturdays. They're allowed twenty minutes for meals, subject to interruption if needed on the floor. They have to meet a sales quota in order to receive their full salary. Their dorm room sleeps six; some of the roommates keep the others up with noisy chatter. Some shop assistants get sick and die from the unhealthy work conditions.

Virginia Madden, lady's companion:
£12 PA plus room and board.

Notice that the salary for lady's maid (see Monica's colleague, above) is more than double that for lady's companion. This is a good example of the cost that gentility exacts from middle-class women. To be a lady's companion, you would need an education—preferably literary—in order to be able to entertain your employer with conversation. For this, Virginia is well qualified. To be a maid, no such education is necessary. Maids can start work at an earlier age and continue working to a later one, making their life-long earning capacity far superior to that of lady's companion, though the work is physically more demanding.

Gertrude Madden, 14-year-old shop assistant:
no pay; room, board, and dress provided.

Like Monica's colleague, Gertrude dies from overwork. I think we can assume that her consumption (tuberculosis) was exacerbated by the hard conditions of retail work.

In addition to these characters, there are three females—Amy Drake,

Miss Eade, and Bella Royston—who don't appear on this list because they don't have annual incomes. Due to their sexual transgressions, they represent various degrees of social disgrace. Amy Drake is an orphaned shopgirl who became part of Mrs. Goodall's liberal social experiment. Mrs. Goodall is a well-to-do Oxonian who likes to mix girls of the educated and working classes to see whether the former could "spiritualize" the latter. Amy is considered a failed participant, as she seduces Everard on a train, and then lies to the Goodalls about whose fault it was. Amy chooses a means of income that might not be unusual for one in her situation: she becomes pregnant by a gentleman so that she can receive an income (child support) without marriage. Amy's case demonstrates one kind of danger of being orphaned, female, working class, and willing to seduce a stranger.

Miss Eade, on the other hand, wants to enter into marriage with her lover, Mr. Bullivant, a fellow shop assistant at Scotcher's. Unfortunately, he is interested only in the prettier Monica Madden. When Monica re-encounters her coworker in the street, years after their shop days are over, Miss Eade has descended to prostitution. She still hopes, however, to find Mr. Bullivant and arrange a marriage, possibly through blackmail. Gissing is hesitant to spell out her profession or intentions exactly but suggests that she "fell" (had sex with) with Mr. Bullivant and that she believes this might serve as a bargaining tool if she's able to find him. Miss Eade's descent into prostitution is an object lesson to all the other girls who are struggling to survive in this novel. Her fate reveals the repercussions of women's hard work for unequal pay, the sexual double standard, and the social penalties enforced on unmarried women who are sexually active.

Finally, Bella Royston illustrates the dire circumstances of "good girls" (or, at least, better girls) who, for whatever reason, believe that their married lovers will eternally provide for them. Bella's case also serves to illustrate the unlikable aspect of Rhoda Nunn, which is her intolerance for women who "succumb" to what she calls their "sex instinct." In an argument with Mary over whether to take Bella back under their patronage after she has strayed, Rhoda argues vehemently that she'd be a bad influence on the other girls. The violence of Rhoda's disdain makes one suspect that there is something more at stake—possibly that Bella's choice represents a temptation that Rhoda herself is fighting, which is to succumb to her desire for Everard Barfoot. Rhoda's situation might have been similar to Bella's if she had accepted Everard's offer of free union, which meant sex without the marriage certificate. Since Bella does accept extramarital sex, she operates symbolically as Rhoda's projected shadow.

If Rhoda Nunn's worst fault is her severe judgment of women who aren't as chaste as she is, Mary Barfoot's flaw is related. Even though she dedicates her life to the betterment of women, Mary Barfoot is a class snob: "In the uneducated classes I have no interest whatever" (58). She openly and shamelessly reiterates her position whenever the subject is broached. She will not accept any pupil who is uneducated—which means, of the lower classes. Effectively, her feminism creates a privileged realm, open only to those who start life at a good enough rank to merit her further assistance. Her refusal to admit working-class students only widens the gap between classes and genders, and seems unnecessary, given that a typist doesn't need a liberal arts education in order to do good work. Looking ahead to the second-wave feminism of the 1960s, such a limitation as Mary's would have a splintering effect on the solidarity of the women's movement. Women of color and the working class protested that the movement was geared to white, middle-class women, and failed to address the needs of other women.

Because of her class snobbery, Mary has more sympathy for the genteel Madden sisters than Rhoda does. They are well-educated daughters of a professional man, so Mary is able to excuse their poverty. On the other hand, Rhoda calls the Maddens "that ragged regiment" of declassed females: "The family is branded. They belong to the *class* we know so well—with no social position, and unable to win an individual one" (57, emphasis mine). The use of the word "class" for the Madden sisters is important, for they form a special subset of the lower middle class, which is also known as "odd women." They are unmarried women who have just enough liberal arts education to give them the air of culture, yet not enough practical education to make them employable outside of the genteel occupations of companion or governess.

There are many class gradations within the Victorian working, middle, and upper classes. For example, Everard marries into a subset of the upper class, a small class of wealthy and cultured families who don't want to be "smart" (fashionable) or gain prominence, but whose social cachet is their appreciation of arts and culture. Another example of an English subset class comes from a later period—the Bloomsbury Circle of the 1920s. They were a small, elite group of Cambridge-educated intelligentsia who didn't have much wealth, but who provided critical analysis and social commentary for a country dealing with the cataclysmic changes of modernity and world war. The Madden sisters inhabit a subset of the middle class that is not so small—Rhoda and Mary "know them well," as the students at the secretarial school belong to this class. This is a set of middle-class females whose fathers made insufficient income for their protection, and insufficient plans for their gainful employment, due to the fathers' antiquated and snobbish notions of genteel femininity. Aristotle said to give him the boy and he'd show you the man. Gissing suggests, "Give me the girl and I'll show you the woman." In the first pages of the novel, the narrator proclaims the impending doom of the Madden sisters—and, on the other hand, the escape from doom of the "masculinized" Rhoda. Notions of female gentility make unmarried women's financial and personal prospects much worse than those of men in the same class. Women's gentility declasses them in an economic sense, and such notions of proper femininity and class hierarchy are shared by Victorian men and women alike, creating a trap from which it's difficult to escape.

Works Cited

Gissing, George. *The Odd Women*. Penguin, 1983.
Steinbach, Susie. "Born into the Lower-Upper-Middle." *Understanding the Victorians*. Routledge, 2012. 113–131.
Steinbach Susie. *Women in England, 1760–1914: A Social History*. Phoenix, 2005.
The *Up* Series. Directed by Michael Apted and Paul Almond. First Run Features, 2013.

Appendix A
Discussion Questions

These discussion questions address the social issues enumerated in the book's subtitle: *Race, Class, Gender and the Uses of Genre*. For each of the novels, I provide a question in each of these four categories. The questions are meant to elicit discussion that will build on the material provided in the lectures.

Wuthering Heights

1. **Genre:** Emily Brontë uses a narrative structure favored by eighteenth- and nineteenth-century novelists: the frame narrative, or story within a story. For instance, Mary Shelley's *Frankenstein* uses the double frames of Captain Walton and Victor Frankenstein's narratives around the Creature's story. *Wuthering Heights* also has two frames around the central story of three generations of Earnshaws, Lintons, and Heathcliffs: Lockwood's narrative provides the outer frame; Nelly Dean's provides the inner frame. Why do you think Emily Brontë uses these frames and how do they affect our interpretation of the events?

2. **Gender:** Heathcliff and the first Catherine are immensely popular heroes whose appeal has continued to the present day. Part of this appeal is their problematic romance that lasts beyond the grave. What else accounts for their ongoing popularity? Could it be the fact that they are androgynous? Each of them has traits that make their personalities a blend of male and female characteristics. Discuss these traits and consider why androgyny might appeal to both Brontë's contemporaries and today's readers.

3. **Race:** Mr. Earnshaw, Nelly Dean, and Hindley Earnshaw call Heathcliff a dark-skinned *gipsy*, a word that today is considered a racial or ethnic slur. *Gipsy* (Victorian spelling) or *gypsy* (post–Victorian spelling) is a term for a member of the Roma or Romani people—Indo-Aryan nomads who live throughout the world (see note 4, "Heathcliff's Social Climbing"). It is also a Victorian catchall term that encompasses people of unknown origin, often beggars or urchins. Some commentators have wondered whether Heathcliff might be Black or mixed race. Film director Andrea Arnold takes this speculation seriously in her 2011 adaptation of the novel; she casts a Black man in Heathcliff's role. Discuss how Heathcliff's gypsy identity affects his self-image and influences other people's opinion of him. How much of their discrimination is due to his perceived racial difference and how much to his low-class origins? Can we even untangle the two categories?

4. **Class:** Emily Brontë starkly contrasts the two houses, Wuthering Heights and Thrushcross Grange, making each an emblem of different lifestyles and values. Discuss whether the class status of the inhabitants determines this difference, or whether there are other significant factors in this dichotomy. What do the two estates symbolize?

Jane Eyre

1. **Genre:** *Jane Eyre* contains elements of several genres. Primarily, it is a novel of social realism in which the heroine's quest to survive is firmly grounded in socioeconomic realities. Additionally, it is a Bildungsroman showing the heroine's growth from age ten to her early twenties. The novel also contains aspects of the supernatural and gothic romance. Discuss these elements and compare Charlotte Brontë's use of the gothic to her sister Emily's in *Wuthering Heights*. Why might a mix of genres in one novel be more interesting than a single genre?

2. **Gender:** In the course of the novel, Jane Eyre makes several feminist statements, including the one that declares women need as large a "sphere of action" as men in order to be fulfilled. Yet Jane's ultimate fulfillment turns out to be marrying Rochester and healing his emotional and physical wounds. What happened to Jane's feminism? Did she attain the "sphere of action" that she dreamed of during her days as a governess?

3. **Race:** Bertha and Richard Mason are Creole colonials. Their racial lineage is indeterminable within the racially defined categories of the time, giving Rochester great difficulty in trusting them. Their status as natives of a British colony raises red flags as to their proper placement in

the English social classes. How does Rochester exhibit white, male, imperial privilege in his interactions with Bertha and Richard? What exactly are the assumptions he makes as a bearer of these identities of race, gender, class, and nation?

4. **Class:** By marrying Rochester, Jane Eyre achieves what every hero or heroine of a Victorian novel wants: the raising of their class status. Yet Jane is one of the most independent, unselfish, and virtuous protagonists in the canon, so we might assume that she doesn't care about her class status. How does righteous Jane view class distinctions in the world around her, and to what extent is her class status important for her very survival?

Vanity Fair

1. **Genre:** Thackeray's frame narrative for *Vanity Fair* is a puppet show of which his narrator is the puppeteer. How does this frame function throughout the novel as a position from which the narrator speaks? Does it provide him the emotional distance he seeks from his characters? Does it have any tendency to either flatten or expand his emotional affect? How effective is this frame for conveying the novel's theme of *Vanitas vanitatum*, all is vanity?

2. **Gender:** Thackeray's narrator makes several generalizations about female and male gender roles, such as: women are crueler than men, and men are foolishly driven by lust. As an unusually strong woman, Becky Sharp stands in a category alone in this book. Do you think Thackeray shows a gender preference, or misogyny, or misandry, at any point in the novel? If so, does he remain consistent in his biases about gender or do they change during the course of the story?

3. **Race:** The lecture called "*Vanity Fair*: Race and Empire" discusses racist references to Arabs and Indians and prejudices toward other ethnic groups such as the Irish, French, and Jews. Choose any one of these ethnic targets (Irish, French, Jews), which are white but non–English, and discuss ways in which the narrator and characters stereotype them. Do you think British racism toward different ethnicities (also known as ethnicism) is as problematic as that against people of color? In what ways are these prejudices similar or different?

4. **Class:** Servants form a specific subset of the working class with special rules of behavior and unique ways of social climbing. There are many servant characters in *Vanity Fair*. Discuss the various ways in which they try to raise their status.

North and South

1. **Genre:** *North and South* belongs to the genre called "industrial novel." The purpose of this genre is to expose working conditions during the Industrial Revolution and to engage readers' social conscience around the extreme inequity of the workplace. Gaskell intends to arouse sympathy for the harsh conditions of work in Manchester's cotton mills. Against John Thornton's traditional paternalistic view, she pits the humanitarian view of Margaret Hale. The typical protagonist of an industrial novel is male, a man who inserts himself into the community to improve working conditions. How does Gaskell's innovation—creating a female protagonist—help or hinder the objectives of the industrial novel?

2. **Gender:** The lecture "Roman Daughter and Milquetoast Father" describes a gender-role reversal, a change from the traditional roles prescribed by the separate spheres doctrine. Margaret is strong and capable, while her father is weak and conflict-avoidant. Are there any other characters or pairs who reverse the typical gender roles in the novel? If so, why do you think Gaskell subverts expectations in this way?

3. **Race:** The Irish characters in this novel are strike breakers whom Thornton hires when the English workers go on strike. They are so poor (Margaret calls them "starvelings") that they are ready to work for lower wages than their English counterparts. The Irish suffer the added indignity of the English strikers' scorn, not only for being of a supposedly "inferior race," but for their willingness to undermine the interests of the local workers. Discuss the treatment of the Irish workers in the novel. Do you find evidence of Margaret or John's ethnicism (a prejudice based on ethnic origin) toward them, or do you think they regard the Irish as equal to the English worker?

4. **Class:** As discussed in the lecture "Regional and Class Prejudice," Margaret eventually changes her views about the farmworkers she knew while growing up in Helstone. Before her time in Milton, she believed that the rural lifestyle of the southern farmworker was superior to that of urban millworkers. After getting to know Nicholas and Bessie Higgins, however, she changes her mind and begins to disparage the farming peasant's lifestyle. Do you think Margaret's description of agricultural versus industrial work is accurate? If not, what factors may be skewing her vision?

A Tale of Two Cities

1. **Genre:** In *A Tale of Two Cities*, Dickens blends genres: a romance between Lucie Manette and Charles Darnay, and a gripping historical

fiction of the French Revolution. Do you think that romance and historical fiction blend well in this instance? Does one genre dominate over the other? What do you think are the challenges of mixing history and romance?

2. **Gender:** In *Aspects of the Novel* (1927), E.M. Forster gives us a handy way to analyze fictional characters. Flat characters are stereotypical and don't change. Round characters are complex and capable of growth. Lucie Manette is a flat character, virtuous and self-sacrificing from start to finish. On the other hand, many of the male characters are round, which makes them dynamic and unique. Do you think Dickens could have improved the Lucie character? Do you think he's hampered by Victorian conventions of female domesticity, including separate spheres and Angel in the House? How do experiences in his own life contribute to his ways of constructing female characters?

3. **Race:** "Othering" of French people is a long-standing British tradition. Representations of this British bias can be humorous, because in many ways the two cultures are very similar. British pride and hypocrisy are favorite targets of Dickens's satire. Dickens is both a Francophile and a participant in age-old British condescension to the Gallic race. How does Dickens satirize aspects of British racism or ethnicism toward the French?

4. **Class:** The class of laborers and shopkeepers that foment revolution (the "Jacques" type) has ample reason to revolt against the injustices perpetrated by the aristocratic and clerical classes. At the same time, there is nothing inherently noble about these underlings, and we know from history as well as from the novel that as soon as the *sans-culottes* gained power in numbers, they proceeded to loot, torture, and assassinate their enemies—in other words, to retaliate with a vengeance. Dickens is not a Marxist, but does he give any serious thought to how to effectuate social change—specifically, a fairer distribution of wealth? We know from the violence of his portraits of Madame Defarge and La Vengeance that he is critical of the peasants' revolutionary methods, but does the text imply that there's any alternative to violent overthrow of the oppressor?

Great Expectations

1. **Genre:** In many ways, *Great Expectations* is a typical Bildungsroman. In the end, Pip fully recognizes the error of his ways and corrects them. But Dickens also felt the need to promise an upcoming marriage. (Victorian middle-class men and women were not to touch each other before marriage, so Pip and Estella's handholding is code for courtship

leading to marriage.) Given Estella's previous relationship with Pip, and his inability to establish good psychic boundaries, do you think that a happy marriage is a realistic outcome of this union?

2. **Gender:** Estella is the opposite female stereotype of *Tale of Two Cities'* Lucie Manette: a witch instead of an angel. As in *A Tale of Two Cities*, female characters are also flat stereotypes in *Great Expectations*. Do you think Dickens is particularly unskilled at creating female characters, or do you think he flattens his male characters as well? If he's less able to create realistic women, what might be the reasons for this disparity of treatment?

3. **Race:** In *Jack Maggs*, the neo–Victorian companion novel to *Great Expectations*, the eponymous hero is transported to the antipodes and acquires an Australian identity that he abjures. What are the characteristics associated with this Australian identity, and why do you think he was unable to retain his preferred British identity while working in Australia for several years?

4. **Class:** Dickens's attitude to class is complex because he descended from a lower-middle-class status to the working class during his youth, then raised himself up to become a solid middle-class citizen. Because of his professional success he achieved entrée into social circles much higher than members of his class would normally achieve. Because of their cultural cachet, many writers hovered in the liminal areas between lower-middle, middle of the middle, and upper-middle class in Victorian Britain. Pip's lesson is that class doesn't matter as much as family and friendships. Social climbing is frowned upon in the novel, but economic status remains important. Using examples of other characters, such as Herbert Pocket, Mr. Pumblechook, and Mr. Wemmick, discuss Dickens's complex attitude to class status and social climbing.

Middlemarch

1. **Genre:** Henry James called the serialized nineteenth-century novel a "large, loose, baggy monster with queer elements of the accidental and the arbitrary" (Preface, *The Tragic Muse*, 1889). Typically, such a baggy novel has multiple plots, many characters, historical events, philosophical digressions, and numerous settings. Obviously, James's epithet is pejorative. Do you think *Middlemarch* is a large, loose, baggy monster with queer and arbitrary elements, or would you argue the opposite, that it is a tightly organized whole in which every component has a logical and meaningful place?

2. **Gender:** Dorothea Brooke, Rosamond Vincy, and Mary Garth are

the three leading female characters in *Middlemarch*. Each presents a different type of womanhood and a different way of looking for a marriage partner. The Epilogue shows that, of the three, only Mary Garth is happy. Discuss the different outcomes of the three women's lives. Consider the ways in which the separate spheres doctrine inhibited these women, or ways in which they used it to their advantage.

3. **Race:** As in most Victorian novels, *Middlemarch* contains racist references to Jews and Jewishness. Will Ladislaw's lineage is suspect because it's assumed that at least one of his ancestors is a Jew. George Eliot is arguably the most politically sensitive and socially aware author in this collection of Victorian writers. Can you determine her attitude to these racist references? Discuss also the intersection of race and class attitudes in this case—especially, the issue of whether or not Will should be admitted into the gentry class.

4. **Class:** *Vanity Fair* and *Middlemarch* are the longest of the Victorian "loose, baggy monsters" (see *Middlemarch* Question 1, above). Compared to *Vanity Fair*, *Middlemarch* is a lighter satire of the human desire to climb socially. Eliot shows genuine compassion for characters in financial difficulty. Characters are highly motivated to rise but become anxious about backsliding by doing or saying something that might declass them (demote them from their former class status). Nicholas Bulstrode is the character with the most to lose if his nefarious activities are discovered. How is his dilemma related to class anxiety?

Far from the Madding Crowd

1. **Genre:** Hardy structures the romance plot suspensefully, keeping our attention as suitors number one, two, and three try their luck with Bathsheba. After many years, suitor number one proves ultimately to be the victor. In depicting Bathsheba's love life, Hardy utilizes the number three, which is a popular symbolic concept in fairy tales, myth, and nursery rhymes. Discuss how the use of three suitors—and the return of the first—amplifies the themes of the novel and develops Bathsheba's character.

2. **Gender:** Apart from Rhoda Nunn of *The Odd Women*, Bathsheba Everdene is the only female protagonist in this collection of Victorian novels who steps outside her proper gender sphere and supports herself in a man's field. Just how successful is this move for Bathsheba, and what is the narrator's attitude to her challenge to patriarchy?

3. **Race:** Wessex is an imagined self-contained community based on Dorsetshire, England. In 1874, there was little influx of people of color

to Dorset except in port towns, where colonial servants or slaves passed through. In another of Hardy's Wessex novels, *The Mayor of Casterbridge*, a part–French woman moves to town from the Isle of Jersey, providing a measure of cultural otherness to stir up the townspeople. Generally, in the Wessex novels, all the characters are from Wessex. The isolation of the region, captured in its title, *Far from the Madding Crowd*, is part of its appeal and also part of its limitation. How do you think the novel is affected by the absence of nonwhite characters?

4. **Class:** The rustics belong to the working class. They are tenant farmers in the region's agricultural industry. The lecture "The Role of the Rustics" examines their aesthetic and social roles in the text. They have some of the homogeneity of a Greek chorus but enough heterogeneity to enjoy one another's company in pubs, where they pick on their friends' flaws and idiosyncrasies. The rustics seem more adapted to their lives than the main characters, whose fortunes tend to fluctuate. Do you think the rustics' relative insouciance (vis-à-vis the other characters' seriousness) reflects upon the stress that the middle-class characters feel in regard to maintaining their status? Do you think Hardy longs for the simplicity of a working life?

Dr. Jekyll and Mr. Hyde

1. **Genre:** Psychological horror is different from the psychological realism of George Eliot or Thomas Hardy insofar as the states of mind it explores (terror, disgust, and trauma) are more exaggerated. Psychological realism, on the other hand, investigates all states of mind and everyday emotions, aiming to understand the motivations for characters' actions and seeking to render realistic representations of so-called "normal" thinking processes. If *Dr. Jekyll and Mr. Hyde* had been written in the psychological realist mode, the reader would learn of the childhood events that led to Dr. Jekyll's shameful acts, would learn what these shameful acts were, and would also know what Mr. Hyde does on his nighttime excursions. Stevenson is more interested in the shock value of the characters' insinuated actions than what these actions are and why the characters do them. What do you think are the assets of the psychological horror genre? Can it present some aspects of human experience that psychological realism doesn't address?

2. **Gender:** *Dr. Jekyll and Mr. Hyde* is famously a novella without women. A maid who witnesses Hyde's murder of Sir Carew and a girl with whom Hyde collides are the only females and are mentioned only in passing. Why do you think women characters are absent from this story?

3. **Race:** One possible interpretation of the novel is that Mr. Hyde represents an imagined racial Other whom Dr. Jekyll finds repellant. The psyche has a tendency to distrust and reject anything it finds strange, different, or difficult to understand. What parallels can we find between racism and people's reactions to Hyde? Can we understand racism better by looking at our own psyche's abjection of the things it finds repugnant? See Julia Kristeva's *Powers of Horror: An Essay on Abjection* (Columbia University Press, 1982) for a full discussion of abjection.

4. **Class:** Valerie Martin, author of *Mary Reilly*, returns to the site of Dr. Jekyll's horror from the viewpoint of a maid who has learned his secret. Her lower-class status means that she deals with a similar trauma very differently from the way her master deals with his own. How does Dr. Jekyll's upper-middle-class status both protect him from and expose him to the psychic division in his soul? Did middle-class proprieties harm Victorians' ability to integrate the various components of their psyches?

Tess of the D'Urbervilles

1. **Genre:** Not content with traditional social realism alone, Hardy strives to make a philosophical statement about the corrupting tendencies of Victorian sexual double standards. Despite Hardy's occasional abstraction of the characters' dilemmas into philosophical propositions, this is not a novel of ideas—perhaps because the author doesn't tell the reader what he thinks is right or propose a solution to Tess's problem. Choosing several instances of Hardy's philosophizing, consider the ways in which his philosophical tendency enhances the story, or, alternatively, whether it detracts from the story's power.

2. **Gender:** Victorian working-class women enjoyed certain liberties that middle-class women didn't have—working outside the home, going to pubs, and walking unaccompanied in the countryside. A "fall," or sexual experience, of a working-class woman would cost less socially than that of a middle-class woman. How do Tess's working-class liberties lead to tragedy when they collide with middle-class expectations of women? Describe the intersection of class and gender oppressions in this text.

3. **Race:** As in *Far from the Madding Crowd*, nonwhite people don't visit or live in the villages where *Tess of the D'Urbervilles* takes place. The most significant encounter with otherness is Angel's trip to Brazil, where he hopes to buy a farm and eventually bring Tess to live once he's forgiven her. Rather than develop the setting as a contrast to Wessex, however, Hardy leaves Brazilian characters off the page. Brazil was a Portuguese colony which enticed Europeans to emigrate with advertisements

of "exceptionally advantageous land deals." The emigration experiment is a failure for Angel, due to extreme weather, recurring fever, and sadness about losing Tess. The best thing that happens to Angel in Brazil is meeting a well-traveled Englishman whose experience has given him a cosmopolitan outlook. He assures Angel that he shouldn't fret about Tess's past, for it's only her future behavior that matters. When Angel tells his mother of his intended move to Brazil, she reveals her anti–Catholic bias: "Brazil! Why they are all Roman Catholics there, surely!" (261) Why do you think Hardy uses a remote Catholic colony to alter Angel's categorical religious views about women's sexual purity?

4. **Class:** Finding out that they're related to the medieval D'Urbervilles doesn't result in any economic improvement for the Durbeyfield family, yet it makes a deep impression on John Durbeyfield and Angel Clare. Why do you think aristocratic lineage is so important to British people? Do Americans have any analogous ranking system? Are Americans truly more democratic than British people, or do they substitute other categories of discrimination?

The Odd Women

1. **Genre:** In the lecture "The Challenge of Writing a Novel of Ideas," I describe the tension between polemics and story in *The Odd Women* and suggest that Gissing's characters are hampered by the ideological weight they carry. Choose another novel of ideas that you've read and discuss whether it achieves its purpose without detracting from characterizations, pacing, and settings. Do the ideas and the story blend well? You might try George Orwell's *Animal Farm* and *1984*, Ray Bradbury's *Fahrenheit 451*, Voltaire's *Candide*, David Foster Wallace's *Infinite Jest*, Aldous Huxley's *Brave New World* and *Point Counter Point*, Ayn Rand's *Atlas Shrugged* and *The Fountainhead*, Fyodor Dostoyevsky's *Crime and Punishment*, Franz Kafka's *The Trial* and *The Castle*, Thomas Mann's *The Magic Mountain*, Laurence Sterne's *Tristram Shandy*, and Herman Melville's *Moby Dick*.

2. **Gender:** The novel's many events and characters make Gissing's sympathy for women abundantly clear. Does he also demonstrate sympathy and respect for men? Is the "performance of masculinity" a challenge or burden for any of the male characters in the novel, or does Gissing care only for his female characters?

3. **Race:** In keeping with the novel of ideas, *The Odd Women* focuses on one main topic—women's emancipation—without digression or dilution. Gissing does, however, deeply appreciate the intersection of class- and gender-based oppressions. What would Gissing have done with race

discrimination as a topic if there were any opportunity to address it in the novel? Discuss whether you think Mary Barfoot and Rhoda Nunn would have allowed any applicants of color to enroll in the business school, whether any such applicants were likely to exist, and if not, why?

4. **Class:** Mary Barfoot refuses her school's services to uneducated women, who by definition are lower class. Rhoda is also exclusivist; she wants to refuse fallen women and agrees with Mary about refusing working-class women. Only one minor character, Mrs. Smallbrook, disagrees with Mary's exclusivist position: "I aim at the solidarity of woman.... I grieve that your charity falls so far below the Christian standard" (59). Other than this one small instance, why do you think Gissing neglects to criticize Mary Barfoot's classist attitude?

Appendix B
Glossary of Literary and Historical Terms

The following terms are selected and defined according to their use by Victorians or scholars of Victorian literature and history.

The Abject: That which the psyche rejects as repulsive and having no part in its own identity and no place within its boundaries. The term refers both to material things—such as vomit, feces, and corpses—and to abstract things, such as dirtiness, depravity, and cruelty. We react in horror to such things because they threaten a breakdown in meaning; the distinction between self and other is disturbed by their presence. Closely related to the terms the Other and the Shadow, the abject is a psychological concept about the ways in which the self protects itself from contamination by the Other.

Androgyny: Having both female and male characteristics. In *A Room of One's Own* (1929), Virginia Woolf said that a creative mind must be androgynous in order to fully utilize its faculties, as the male and female parts need to "fertilize" each other. A successful writer needs an androgynous perspective in order to accurately represent both female and male characters.

Angel in the House: Closely related to the separate spheres doctrine, this idealization of woman's capacity for virtue and her duty to nurture others takes its name from Coventry Patmore's 1854 poem of the same name. The role of the woman is to preserve the sanctity of the home, to provide emotional and moral support for her family, and to keep her menfolk sober, hardworking, and faithful. She is self-sacrificing and benevolent. The doctrine applied most strongly to middle-class women.

Bildungsroman: A novel about a character's coming of age through their spiritual and emotional development. Of the selections in this book, *Jane Eyre*, *Great Expectations*, and *North and South* are Bildungsromans.

Chartism: A large movement for workers' rights occurring between the 1830s and 1860s, especially strong in West Yorkshire and south Wales. It presented a threat to established voting laws and the privileges of the aristocracy. Women were active participants in the movement. Its 1838 Charter asked for universal manhood suffrage, secret ballots, and no property qualifications for Members of Parliament. Chartists didn't obtain any of these objectives until the 1867 Reform Act, when urban working men got the vote.

Colonialism: The practice and policy of exerting political control over another nation, occupying it with settlers, and exploiting it economically. According to Edward Said, the difference between imperialism and colonialism is that imperialism involves "the practice, theory, and attitudes of a dominating metropolitan center ruling a distant territory, while colonialism refers to the implanting of settlements on a distant territory" (*Culture and Imperialism*, 1993). Although most former colonies achieved independence between the time of World War II and 1980, the law, economic structures, and cultural basis for colonialism have remained. The term *neocolonialism* refers to an ongoing imbalance of power between colonizing countries and their former dependencies. The legacies of empire continue to affect former colonies' borders, migration, prisons, labor conditions, healthcare, education, and international aid.

Colorism: Discrimination against those with darker skin, typically among people in the same racial or ethnic group. The belief that those with lighter skin color are superior to those with darker. This form of prejudice is a way of attaining increments of status over others of one's group in order to advance oneself within structures of institutional racism as well as in interpersonal relationships.

Cosmic Irony: Irony is the difference between what is expected and what actually happens. Cosmic irony is when these unexpected results are caused by factors outside of human control, such as gods, fate, or nature. Thomas Hardy's fiction is the classic example, especially *Tess of the D'Urbervilles*. Strange and suspenseful contingencies in the plot obstruct the characters' opportunities for happiness. Tess and Angel might have been happy together if Angel had never said, "I can never be with you as long as that other one [Alec] lives," which drove Tess to murder Alec.

Darwinian evolution: Based on his studies of plant and animal adaptations to their environments, Charles Darwin theorized that evolution is a gradual process of natural selection. Only the fittest species survive the competition for resources and pass on their genes; unfit species die out. Therefore, nature "selects" the species that are most adapted to their environments. The idea conflicts with the creationist theory found in the Christian Bible, where God created man and other organisms within a few days. Reading *On the Origin of Species* (1859), Victorians had to come to terms with the clash of religious and scientific theories about the nature of existence.

Dissolution of Parliament, 1830 and 1831: These were political acts necessary for the passing of the First Reform Bill. The death of King George IV on June 26, 1830, dissolved the Parliament by law, and a general election was held. Several political unions canvassed for voting reform. The Tories won a majority of votes, but their party was internally divided, and the Prime Minister (the ultra–Tory Duke of Wellington) was unpopular even in his own party. Parliament was dissolved and a Whig government under Earl Grey appointed on November 30, 1830. He produced the radical Reform Bill on March 22, 1831, which carried by only one vote. Tory leader General Gascoyne moved a wrecking amendment which quashed the Reform Bill. Earl Grey then asked for a Dissolution of Parliament and King William IV agreed. The New Parliament passed the bill, finally, on June 7, 1832. This achievement represented several years of political organizing, canvassing, repeated dissolutions of Parliament, and even some rioting and freeing of prisoners—England's very own Storming of the Bastille.

Domesticity: An idealization of the home as a site of comfort, love, and safety. According to the Victorians, this paradigm works only when women are willing and able to stay at home and take care of children, husband, and house. The New Woman and women's suffrage movements profoundly threatened the Victorian ideal of domesticity.

Double consciousness: The internal conflict experienced by subordinated groups in an oppressive society. W.E.B Du Bois coined the term in *The Souls of Black Folk* (1903) to mean the struggle of African Americans to remain true to Black culture while conforming to the dominant white society: "One ever feels his two-ness—an American, a Negro; two souls, two thoughts, two unreconciled strivings; two warring ideals in one dark body, whose dogged strength alone keeps it from being torn asunder" (2). Feminist critics use *double consciousness* to describe women in patriarchy. In second-wave feminist novels, a character can be said to have a double consciousness when she performs one persona (that of an obedient female) and uses the dominant language in order to escape censure, while at the same time she mounts a private protest in her own language against patriarchal expectations for women.

Education Acts of 1870, 1880, 1891: The 1870 Act set the framework for schooling children aged five to twelve in England and Wales. The 1880 Act made education compulsory for children up to age ten. The 1891 Act made schooling free for residents of England and Wales. Scotland had a different history; its 1696 Education Act provided for a school and schoolmaster in every parish. Scotland's 1872 Education Act made education compulsory as well as universal.

Epigraph: A short poem, or lines from a poem, or passage from another literary or historical source, placed under the title of a novel, story, drama, poem, or book chapter. The purpose of an epigraph is to establish the theme of the novel or chapter in the wider context of the literary canon. An epigraph is intertextual, so it presumes a well-read audience. Each *Middlemarch* chapter begins with an epigraph, showing Eliot's erudition and providing thematic context for the chapter.

Eugenics: Developed by Sir Francis Galton (Charles Darwin's cousin), the theory that humans should practice controlled breeding to ensure the dominance of the optimal human race in the interest of improving civilization. He advocated eradicating the inferior races, specifically those not white or European, to remove inferior genes from the collective gene pool of humanity. Eugenics was "the science of improving stock … to give the more suitable races or strains of blood a better chance of prevailing speedily over the less suitable than they otherwise would have had" (Francis Galton, *Inquiries into Human Faculty and Its Development*, 1883, 24–25).

Fallen women: Euphemism for women who had sex outside of marriage (including prostitutes), thus ruining their reputation and destroying their chances for marriage. In the nineteenth century, preservation of a woman's chastity until marriage was essential. Fallen women were recipients of philanthropy from Christian societies, such as the Women's Christian Temperance Union, and wealthy individuals. Lady Angela Burdett-Coutts helped Charles Dickens found Urania Cottage, a rehabilitation home for fallen women. Mary Barfoot's school for women (*The Odd Women*), on the other hand, refused them admittance.

Feminism: The belief that women are equal to men in every particular, so should be granted equal rights under the law. Feminism is expressed differently by women of different classes, races, sexual orientations, and generations. One question up for debate is whether a feminist has to be an activist who fights for all women's rights or whether a woman (or man, or nonbinary person) is feminist by virtue of her own conduct and personal achievements. My working definition is: A feminist is a person who believes that women and men are equal and who acts in such a manner as to convey this belief to other people. A feminist engages in a fight, however private or public, against the beliefs and practices of patriarchy.

Gender: We now regard gender as a social construct rather than a biological reality, whereas Victorians saw it as a biological category. Men and women were essentially different. Men were intellectually able, physically strong, and emotionally resilient. Women were physically delicate and inclined to hysteria. Women's bodies were made for maternity; too much mental labor or sport would drain energy away from the womb, making it difficult for them to produce and care for children.

Genre: A type or category of literature characterized by a particular style, form, or subject matter. The first genres in literature were epic poetry, comic drama, and tragic drama. The genres discussed in this book are subgenres of the larger genre category—the novel. These include social realism, satire, metafiction, romance, gothic, neo–Victorian, industrial novel, pastoral novel, psychological realism, psychological horror, problem novel, and novel of ideas.

Gentry: In its most general sense, people of a high social class. In the United Kingdom, the term refers to landed gentry, meaning those who own landed estates but don't have the right to bear a coat of arms—in other words, are untitled. In social position, the gentry are just below nobility. The category also expands informally to include upper levels of clergy and "gentle" families of long descent.

Gothic romance: A genre of fiction featuring horror, death, romance, and the sublime, set in an abandoned or haunted castle, especially popular in the late eighteenth and early nineteenth centuries. The Romantic gothic features a delicate, helpless female exposed to the whims of a tyrannical, impulsive man. The Victorian gothic blends horror and romance elements with realism. Edgar Allan Poe's tales, Samuel Taylor Coleridge's poems, Mary Shelley's *Frankenstein*, Ann Radcliff's *The Mysteries of Udolpho*, and Bram Stoker's *Dracula* are examples. The earliest case is Horace Walpole's *The Castle of Otranto* (1764). Jane Austen makes fun of the genre in *Northanger Abbey* (1817).

Hegemony: The dominance of a shared system of values, ideas, and ethics within a community during a particular historical period. A dominant ideology determines the practices and policies of institutions, informs the way that they are structured, and pervades the conscious and unconscious assumptions of the community.

Imperialism: A policy of extending a nation's power by diplomacy or military force. Ideologically, it signifies Britain's belief in her right to conquer other lands and peoples by virtue of her superior morality, intelligence, and military strength. Queen Victoria and her deputies justified the expansion of empire by their belief that they were protecting weaker peoples from harm and improving their level of civilization.

Industrial Revolution: The First Industrial Revolution lasted from approximately 1760 to 1840, a period when manufacturing moved from small shops and homes to large factories, necessitating the migration of a large segment of the population from rural to urban areas. It produced new technologies in transportation and power and engendered new social problems such as abysmal working conditions, crowded slum dwellings, and a rise in prostitution.

Intersectionality: Analytical framework with which to understand how a person's various personal and political identities combine to create discrimination and privilege. Race, class, gender, and sexual orientation are the traditional identity categories, and many other categories are also relevant, such as ability, nationality, ethnicity, region, and religion.

Intertextuality: The shaping of a text's meaning by another text. The practice of alluding to other canonical texts within one's writing, often without attribution. It signals the author's high level of education. Referencing other texts signifies that we are always influenced by the culture around us, sometimes unconsciously. Intertextuality adds depth to interpretation of texts and historizes one's reading of a work.

Jungian Shadow: The Shadow archetype is that unknown or dark part of our personality which our ego (or conscious part of the psyche) cannot accept, usually a perceived personal inferiority. Consequently, we deny this as part of ourselves and project it onto someone else in the quality of a perceived moral deficiency. The Shadow personifies everything that a person refuses to acknowledge about themselves.

Landed estate: A property, usually in the countryside, that generates income for the owner without his having to do the actual work of the estate. Tenant farmworkers pay rent to live and farm on the estate. A leftover from feudal times, it leaves the owner free to pursue other roles—such as positions in government, military, law, or religion.

Madwoman in the Attic: Signaling both women's insanity and their sequestration, the term is derived from Sandra Gilbert and Susan Gubar's *The Madwoman in the Attic: The Woman Writer and the Nineteenth-Century Literary Imagination* (1979). *Jane Eyre's* Bertha Mason is the original madwoman in the attic; she is driven mad by her circumstances. She is married off by her father, then sexually rejected by Edward Rochester, taken to England, and locked up in the attic because she embarrasses her husband. According to Gilbert and Gubar, Bertha's condition speaks for all nineteenth-century women. It is both the way that patriarchy regards women (emotional, hysterical, irrational) and the ways in which men and institutions sequester and demonize women, especially once they have caught them in the trap of marriage. In novels, women's insanity is sometimes a tragic attempt to escape from the desolation caused by oppressive gender roles.

Manliness: Character traits highly valued in a Victorian man included a strong work ethic, ability to provide for his family, independence, integrity, nonviolence, and dedication to the home. John Thornton (*North and South*) defines manliness (as opposed to gentlemanliness) as the appropriate conduct code for middle-class men.

Married Women's Property Acts, 1870 and 1882: Allowed women to legally own the money they earned and the property they inherited or brought to a marriage. Before this legislation, a woman's property automatically transferred to her husband upon marriage. The 1882 Act extended rights so that women could buy and sell property, could divorce and receive alimony or child support, could sue and be sued; in short, a woman was finally recognized as a legal entity in her own right.

Metafiction: Fiction in which the narrator self-consciously refers to their own act of writing. The narrator might comment on the requirements of the genre, make moral judgments on the characters, and directly address the reader. The narrator of Thackeray's *Vanity Fair* enters the action of the story and meets the characters face to face.

Middle class: This class of people earned a salary rather than wages, ranging from £300 to £1,000 per annum, per family. They held non-manual jobs such as retail clerk, office clerk, doctor, lawyer, banker, teacher, professor, nurse, bureaucrat, and others that required at least some education. Middle-class women were expected to stay at home, raise children, support their husbands emotionally and morally, and do charity work for local religious and social institutions and poor neighbors. Until 1860, the only respectable jobs for middle-class women who had to work were governess, teacher, or dressmaker.

Modernity: In its most general usage, any historical period that is described in terms that contrast it to the previous period. Ideologically and aesthetically, it refers to the breaking of traditions and introduction of new social norms. In specifically literary terms, it refers to the period between 1890 and 1930 (or some say 1945) in which writers critiqued social institutions, questioned authority, and adopted radical new beliefs and customs. In place of Victorian prudery came the New Woman and the flapper. In literature, modernists respond to radical social change by experimenting with form. Novelists use new methods, especially stream-of-consciousness, interior monologue, and fragmentation, to represent the destruction of old ways of thinking. A characteristic modernist tone is one of melancholy, anxiety, and dread (as in Thomas Hardy novels). To replace traditional religion, writers seek new, secular sources of meaning and belief.

Neo-Victorianism: An aesthetic movement characterized by nostalgia for Victorian literature and culture. The neo–Victorian novel reinterprets Victorian classics, often to reflect contemporary (twentieth- and twenty-first-century) concerns about race, class, and gender oppression. These novels may retell the original story from the viewpoint of a disadvantaged or minor character, such as a woman, servant, ex-convict, or person of color.

New Woman: In the 1890s, a woman who sought, in varying degrees of seriousness, the independence of women from patriarchal expectations. Popular culture represented her as a woman who wore culottes, rode a bicycle, wrote for publication, and smoked tobacco. She was characterized by her desire to pursue higher education and work for her living. She may or may not have believed in free unions between men and women (as Everard proposed to Rhoda in *The Odd Women*). She believed in women's rights. The New Woman ideal was supported by the suffrage movement. It was a harbinger of the gradual emancipation of women, in the twentieth century, from separate spheres and other discriminatory ideology and practices.

Nobility: People with rank. In the United Kingdom, the ranks in descending order of importance are: duke, marquess, earl, viscount, baron, and baronet. Baronets' titles are hereditary, but baronets are not peers, and thus were not entitled to sit in the House of Lords in the Victorian era. The highest ranked character we encounter in this selection of Victorian novels is the Marquis de Steyne in *Vanity Fair*.

Novel of ideas: A genre of fiction in which the author's ideas, especially regarding political or philosophical problems, are advanced through the characters and plot. In the novel of ideas, the political or philosophical idea of the book is as important as character, plot, and setting.

Orientalism: A set of beliefs and practices that frame the "Orient" and "Orientals" (any non–Western country or people) as exotic and essentially different from their opposite, the West. For example, British explorers stereotyped Middle Easterners as lazy, sensual, indulgent, effeminate, irrational, and superstitious, and

Islam was seen as a religion of barbarity that fosters polygamy and fatalism. At the same time, "Orientals" titillated the Western imagination. The charades chapter in *Vanity Fair* presents Turkish rulers as tyrannical, violent, and sexually powerful, which is believed to excite the ladies in the audience.

The Other: In phenomenology, the Other, or Constitutive Other, is another human being who, in their difference from the Self, is a cumulative and constituting factor in the self-image of a person. In linguistics and social theory, the Other is a psychological category that an individual (or a group) creates in order to maintain its psychic boundaries and differentiate itself from persons and groups whom it fears, or exoticizes, or dislikes. "Othering" is a defense mechanism as well as a strategy to gain or retain power. "Othering" is the verb for the psychic and linguistic activities that label a person as someone who belongs to a socially subordinate category. The basis of ethics is determining our responsible relation to the Other.

Oxbridge: A portmanteau term meaning University of Oxford or University of Cambridge or both. They are the most prestigious universities in England. The term is often used in contrast to the poorer redbrick universities (Oxbridge buildings are made of amber-colored limestone). The term also refers, sometimes disparagingly (denoting elitism), to upper-class intellectual life in the United Kingdom.

Panoramic realism: As John Carey defines it in the introduction to *Vanity Fair*, a form of realism which "surround[s] the main characters with seemingly endless minor ones to create an impression of life proliferating in all directions" (xvii). This genre gives the narrator a quality of omniscience and an air of erudition. A panoramic realist novel has a large geographical range and refers to current and recent political and/or military events.

Patriarchy: A system of government or society in which men hold power and women are excluded from power. A socioeconomic and ideological structure that assumes men are better or more deserving than women and consequently gives to men rights and privileges that are denied to women.

Peerage: The social category of those with hereditary or honorary ranks and titles.

Poetic justice: The freedom of an author to reward virtue and punish vice in their fictional works. Because of the author's "poetic license," a type of justice can be achieved in books that doesn't always occur in real life.

Poor Law of 1834: Nationalized the welfare system of Britain, which formerly had been administered by parish churches. The law required all recipients of welfare to live in workhouses. Most people tried to avoid the workhouse, because the food was bad, the accommodations uncomfortable, and the work extremely hard. The Poor Law was an incentive to find work at all costs and a deterrent from seeking government subsidies.

Primogeniture: The wealth, title, and estate of a gentleman pass to his eldest son. *Jane Eyre*'s Edward Rochester, a second son, suffered because of this legal doctrine, as he had to seek his fortune in Jamaica instead of inheriting Thornfield Hall (though he later inherited it when his brother died).

Psychological realism: The characters' motivations and behaviors are based in well-described backgrounds that make them believable. The characters speak and behave as real people do. Psychological processes are a key focus in the narrative.

Race: In the early nineteenth century, this term could mean many things, and was synonymous with the word "type." It could be as broad as a group of people with similar linguistic and cultural markers (similar to what we now call "ethnicity"), or as narrow as the members of one family. By the 1860s, "race" took on the meaning of skin color, certain distinguishing physical characteristics, and the relative moral and intellectual worth of certain groups. The late Victorian period was characterized by belief in scientific racism—a set of theories that claimed the biological difference of the races. Specifically, Blacks were considered either to be a different species than whites, or to have degenerated over time because of climate and culture, while the white race improved by the struggle for existence in colder northern climes. Jews were also considered biologically different from gentiles, and Asians from whites. In the twentieth century, "race" as a biological category was discredited because of a lack of evidence for familiar racial groupings. In fact, more genetic diversity is found within certain "racial" categories than across them (see *Race in the Making*, by Lawrence Hirschfeld, MIT Press, 1996). Twentieth- and twenty-first-century social scientists developed a theory that race is a social construct, a classification system that is used to oppress certain groups of people and privilege others.

The Raj: Britain's sovereignty over India from 1858 to 1947. Before the Raj, Britain had established its commercial presence in the subcontinent as early as the 1600s, when the East India Company (EIC) was founded. By the 1700s, the EIC dominated the world's textile trade, creating a monopoly and driving the French and Dutch out of India. By the 1800s, the EIC had taken over many important Indian administrative roles such as tax collecting. It formed its own army. The Indian Rebellion of 1857 instigated changes in its structure: the Crown nationalized the EIC and established direct rule over India. To ensure native acquiescence, Queen Victoria promised to refrain from British intervention in Indian social and religious practices, such as suttee, the burning of a widow with her deceased husband. After ninety more years of foreign rule, Indian achieved independence in 1947.

The Reform Act, 1832: Also known as the First Reform Act, the Great Reform Act, and the Representation of the People Act, this legislation made wide-ranging changes to the electoral system. Some historians consider it the launch of modern democracy in the United Kingdom. The Act granted seats to cities that had expanded during the Industrial Revolution and removed seats from rotten boroughs (those with a small electorate, controlled by a wealthy patron). It extended the franchise to male householders living on property worth at least £10 a year—in effect, to middle-class men. The Reform Act spurred the women's suffrage movement because women's requests to be included in the reform were ignored.

The Reform Act, 1867: The Second Reform Act extended the franchise to urban working men with property qualifications—they must either be heads of household or pay £10 in rent. Created new boroughs in Parliament and abolished rotten boroughs.

The Reform Act, 1884: The Third Reform Act extended franchise to rural working men on the same basis as the Second Reform Act (householders or leaseholders paying at least £10).

Repression: An unconscious defense mechanism of the psyche by which unwanted thoughts, unpleasant emotions, painful memories, and socially unacceptable desires are blocked from one's conscious mind and relegated to the unconscious. Sigmund Freud said that we can gain access to the unconscious only in dreams, jokes, and slips of the tongue. Psychoanalysis aims to bring unconscious feelings to awareness so the patient can understand them instead of being led blindly by them.

Respectability: A fundamental requirement for maintaining one's class status, to be respectable meant different things for men and women. A man must be "manly," i.e., support the family, refrain from sexual adventures, and cultivate personal integrity. A woman (especially of the middle class) must refrain from any sign of sexual desire, including with her husband, but must submit to his advances. Cleanliness, neat dress, regular hours, financial solvency, speaking English rather than dialect, and hiding signs of drunkenness, adultery, gambling, or idleness—these were just a few of the requirements of respectability for those trying to maintain middle-class social status. Working-class and middle-class people had different standards of respectability to maintain.

Separate Spheres Doctrine: Reigning Victorian gender ideology, which was strongest from about 1780 to 1880. Women and men have different roles in different spheres. Women belong to the domestic sphere, where they're responsible for the management of household affairs and the moral guidance of their children and husband. Middle-class women should not work outside the home. Men belong to the public sphere, and are subject to its moral contamination, which is a byproduct of economic competition. Manly men (in their performance of masculinity) are also home-loving. Home is a sanctuary from the vices of the outside world.

Serialization: The publication of a novel in magazines and newspapers in weekly, bimonthly, or monthly installments. Although it was used before the nineteenth century, Dickens started the craze for serialization in 1836 with *Pickwick Papers.* Many novels were serialized before they came out as one- to four-volume editions. The advantage of serialization was that it reached a wider readership—poorer people could afford the smaller segments, spread out over time. The advantage to a publisher was that they profited from both the serialized and the later multivolume publication. The demands of serialization resulted in finely honed chapters; each segment had to be entertaining and stand on its own. Serialization also increased censorship of subject matter, since families read aloud together.

Service: Being "in service" was shorthand for being a servant in the household of another. Service was the largest field of work for working-class unmarried women. Servants were required to live at their employer's house and remain single. Standards of conduct were rigid; it was necessary to be as unobtrusive as possible to avoid disturbing one's employer. The job entailed long hours and subservience, but offered room and board, and sometimes the patronage of the employer. For instance, a good employer might pay for unexpected expenses that their servant incurred but was unable to cover.

Sexual double standard: There were different rules for men and women. Men were considered highly sexed and women passionless. If a woman had sexual desire, she was considered aberrant, like a prostitute. Woman's ultimate self-actualization was to bear and raise children; she was seen as inherently maternal. Men were expected to restrain sexual desire except with their wives, but for those unable to refrain, prostitution served their needs and prevented them from committing the worse sins of masturbation and sodomy with men. When divorce was made legal by the 1857 Divorce Act, male plaintiffs could attain divorce by proving just one instance of adultery, whereas women had to prove a pattern of adultery in addition to another aggravating condition, such as cruelty or incest. Also, women made lower wages and salaries than men for the same work (less than half, in many cases).

Social Darwinism: Emerging in the 1870s, various theories that applied Darwin's ideas of "survival of the fittest" and "natural selection" to the realms of politics, sociology, and economics. These ideas are based on the belief that, in the struggle for survival, strong people (whites) survive at a higher level (with more wealth, health, and power) than weak people, due to their genetic superiority. The term was closely associated with racism and eugenics and was used to justify the Armenian Genocide and the Holocaust.

Suffrage: The legal right to vote. Women's suffrage became a national movement in 1872. A militant branch was formed in 1906. In 1918, women over thirty (with property qualifications) gained the vote in Great Britain. In 1928, franchise was extended to all people twenty-one and over.

Tory: A supporter of the Conservative Party in the United Kingdom. One who upholds the supremacy of the social order as it has evolved through English history. Their motto, "God, Queen, and Country," indicates their allegiance to Anglicanism, monarchy, and political conservatism.

The unconscious: The part of the mind which is inaccessible to the conscious mind but which affects behavior and emotions. It is filled with wishes and fears that the conscious mind represses. In Freudian theory, the unconscious has a powerful influence on the ego and superego; it drives our actions and feelings without our awareness.

Upper class: A group whose incomes derive from rents and profit from landed estates and investments. Constituting only five percent of the population, they held the political power of the country from their positions in the House of Lords, the House of Commons, the cabinet, and as Justices of the Peace. Their per annum incomes were at least £1,000.

Voice: The tone or emotional quality of a novel. A narrator's voice can be distant or intimate. The voice of Jane Eyre, narrator of the eponymous novel, is intimate, addressing us as "dear reader."

Whig: A member of the British reforming and constitutional party that sought the supremacy of Parliament at the time of the English Civil War (1642–60). It was succeeded by the Liberal Party in the late nineteenth century. At the time of *Middlemarch*, the Whig platform included Catholic emancipation, the abolition of slavery, and expansion of the franchise. With the help of liberal Tories, this party finally got the First Reform Act passed in 1832.

Working class: Those who earned wages at manual labor in fields such as industry, mining, service, or farming, sometimes as day laborers. Their annual income was usually below £100 per annum but could be as high as £300 at the upper end of the scale.

Acknowledgments

All books are the product of many people. I am thankful to those whose work contributed to mine, starting with the authors of Victorian novels. The world is richer for the presence of characters such as Jane Eyre, Sydney Carton, and Dorothea Brooke, whose challenges and achievements are relevant to today's readers since we inhabit a world that holds many of the same ideals that they cherished. I admire the courage of the indefatigable Dickens, toiling in his Tavistock House study to create *A Tale of Two Cities*, and resolute Charlotte Brontë burning the midnight oil at Haworth Parsonage to pen *Jane Eyre*. They shared the conviction that their stories would not only entertain but also uplift their readers and they were correct in their belief.

I have benefited from the many friends and colleagues who have talked to me, read my chapters, and offered advice, help, and encouragement: Gloria Biamonte, Susan Buechler, Kitty Florey, Jan Franks, Heidi Holder, Melba Jensen, Jane Kristal, Turi MacCombie, David Neelon, Susie Steinbach, and Barbara Yngvesson—whose specialty in social anthropology made her an excellent resource for improving my understanding of race as a social construct. Publishing the lectures as a book was Leslie Lorber's idea. Randall Knoper generously offered a course schedule that supported my research and writing on this topic.

Reading Victorian novels with students over many years has been a joy. I am privileged to acknowledge the huge debt I owe to countless students for their energy and enthusiasm while reading and discussing these novels. The student of Victorian literature is inherently patient and dedicated, for many of the novels are the longest we have in the English language. As this book demonstrates—though it touches only the tip of the iceberg—the amount of background knowledge required to understand the Victorians is vast. To their credit, my students never balked at the implications of a phrase such as "understanding the Victorians" but plowed onward uncomplainingly through the sixty-seven chapters of *Vanity Fair* and eighty-seven of *Middlemarch* in addition to supplemental readings in Susie Steinbach's *Understanding the Victorians* and Gilbert and Gubar's *Madwoman in the Attic*. Although most students don't realize their role in opening their professors' minds, teaching is a symbiotic relationship between students and teacher. Not only do students bring up-to-date perspectives on social issues confronting young people; they also reinforce the ongoing value of teaching non-contemporary literature by demonstrating their enthusiasm for learning about "the olden days."

I want to thank my editor, Gary Mitchem, who saw the value of such a textbook and encouraged me to pursue my objective. The McFarland team, from editors to public relations staff, is efficient and respectful. I thank them for their continued assistance over the years.

My greatest debt is to my family, especially my parents, for instilling a love of the Victorians and their literature in me, starting from the impressionable age of twelve or thirteen. In the 1970s, my father brought us along on his conference and sabbatical trips to England, giving us an introduction to the exciting world of English history, architecture, and culture. Back home, I escaped into the fictional worlds of Dickens, Hardy, Stevenson, and the Brontë sisters with renewed enthusiasm for the landscapes they inhabited. Sharing these worlds with a sister, Jan, who is imaginative and linguistically sophisticated made the subject of Victorian literature much more inviting. With small dolls and tiny houses made of pine needles and cones, we created our own Gondal—an orphanage filled with diverse characters playing out their melodramas. Thank you, Jan, for sharing your imagination, wordplay, and aspirations. Our neo–Victorian imaginary world was a childhood haven of ideas and solidarity.

Index

Numbers in **bold italics** indicate pages with illustrations